Victorian Pastoral

Victorian Pastoral

Tennyson, Hardy,
and the
Subversion
of Forms

OWEN SCHUR

OHIO STATE UNIVERSITY PRESS

Columbus

Library of Congress Cataloging-in-Publication Data

Schur, Owen, 1956–
    Victorian pastoral : Tennyson, Hardy, and the subversion of forms
/ Owen Schur.
        p. cm.
    Bibliography: p.
    Includes index.
    ISBN 0-8142-0483-X (alk. paper)
    1. English poetry–19th century–History and criticism.
2. Pastoral poetry, English–History and criticism. 3. Tennyson,
Alfred Tennyson, Baron, 1809–1892–Criticism and interpretation.
4. Hardy, Thomas, 1840–1928–Poetic works. I. Title.
PR 599.P3S38 1989   88–27130
821'.8'09–dc19   CIP

The paper in this book meets the guidelines for permanence and
durability of the Committee on Production Guidelines for Book
Longevity of the Council on Library Resources.

Printed in the U.S.A.

9 8 7 6 5 4 3 2 1

For Ed and Joan

Contents

	Acknowledgments	ix
	Introduction	1
I.	The Poet's Melancholy: Pastoral and Community in Early Tennyson	21
II.	Myths of Exile: Tennyson's Poetry of Loss	60
III.	Songs from *The Princess*	111
IV.	Victorian Pastoral and the Poetry of Hardy	157
V.	A Dwelling's Character: From Pastoral to the Country House in Hardy	200
	Conclusion	219
	Notes	221
	Index	235

Acknowledgments

THE CRITICS AND SCHOLARS OF TENNYSON AND
Hardy to whom I am indebted are numerous. Many of their names
appear in the following pages. I wish to express my special thanks
to J. Hillis Miller, who read and commented on the manuscript
at various stages. I would also like to thank Martin Price, Louis
Martz, and Alan Liu, whose comments on early parts of the manuscript helped me to rethink a number of points. Studying poetic
influence with Harold Bloom also had a large bearing on the approach I have taken here. Finally, I would like to express my grati-
tude to two undergraduate teachers who many years ago instilled
in me an interest in literary studies: William Buckler first intro-
duced me to the greatness of Hardy's poetry, and Perry Meisel
helped me begin to think seriously about literary theory.

Introduction

THE BASIC ARGUMENT SET FORTH IN THIS BOOK
is a fairly straightforward one. We usually perceive Tennyson and
Hardy as poets shaped by tradition, conservers of the past. Yet we
also acknowledge that Tennyson and Hardy contribute to a transition in English literary history from nineteenth-century poetics to
modernism. This sense of both tradition and modernity in the two
poets suggests a value in reading Tennyson and Hardy side-by-side,
not to measure the degree of influence the former exerted on the
latter, but to explore the ways both poets perceived literary tradition as a problem, a problem out of which emerges their particular
contribution to modernity.

For all their differences, Tennyson and Hardy are similar in their
sense of partial exclusion from the traditions they draw upon. One
of these areas of literary tradition is pastoral. There has been a fair
amount of discussion of Tennyson and pastoral, much less so in
the case of Hardy. The following chapters read Tennyson and Hardy
in the light of pastoral, suggesting the specific ways each poet confronts pastoral as a problem, the larger issues being the rhetoric of
tradition and literary history itself. As we read Tennyson and Hardy
from this perspective, certain connections become clear. Pastoral
as a set of forms provides a model for Tennyson and Hardy to follow, yet the genre limits and constrains their poetic work, especially at the primary levels of figuration and rhetoric. Poetic voices
in Tennyson and Hardy are repeatedly lured into the figurative
strategies of pastoral, only to be stifled by the duplicity of their
own rhetoric. On the one hand, pastoral rhetoric in Tennyson and
Hardy exerts inhibitive pressure on their poems. Pastoral forms
assume a formulaic or programmatic character in the narrowest
sense. What is equally interesting, however, is the way the symp-
toms of this inhibition, so to speak, emerge to lay bare these figura-

tive strategies and in so doing make available power for the poetic voice.

Tennyson and Hardy deliberately subvert the forms of pastoral by means of the genre's traditional rhetoric. Out of this subversion, the two poets create a renewal of forms, new kinds of pastoral poetry.

The readings in the following chapters demonstrate the fascination Tennyson and Hardy have for the figurative strategies of traditional pastoral and the specific ways they foreground and thus subvert these strategies. These readings also demonstrate the new kinds of pastoral which the two poets create through these experiments in form. Before we can see how Tennyson and Hardy respond to the pastoral tradition, however, we have to get a sense of what that tradition is. We need to determine the principal figurative strategies of pastoral as a genre. We need, in other words, a working definition of pastoral.

There are many definitions of pastoral, but few of them are entirely satisfactory.[1] Pastoral may be understood as poetry about shepherds or goatherds and their flocks in the countryside. But Theocritus, who is often considered the principal creator of pastoral, wrote poems with a different cast of characters and settings from this. Some of his idylls take as their settings urban centers and take as their characters sophisticated cosmopolitans. A strict literary historian and classicist might place these poems under another category. Such a historian might also exclude several of the mythological poems in Virgil's *Eclogues*. And yet these poems participate in the values we have come to associate with pastoral. It is not simply country life and shepherds that define the pastoral impulse. Even if we were to limit ourselves to this setting and this group of characters, there would still exist a crucial division between the poet/speaker and his subject. As students of pastoral have observed, much of the genre's power derives from the tension between the sophisticated (in Theocritus, Alexandrian) speaker and the "naive" subjects whom he describes within the pastoral world.[2]

Pastoral in its very beginnings moves beyond the bucolic world. In fact the bucolic acquires its definition by interacting with its opposite: the bucolic world cannot exist without its urban counterpart. But to say that pastoral involves a contrast between country and city, naive and sophisticated, does not take us all that far in our search for an adequate definition of pastoral. After all, parts of the *Iliad*, *Odyssey*, and *Aeneid* explore these contrasts, as do Virgil's *Georgics* and Horace's *Odes*. Yet we do not call these works in their entirety pastoral. All of these texts do, however, explore in part an idea closely associated with pastoral: the retirement theme.[3] Granted that the epic, georgic, and ode share with the pastoral the retirement theme, what then distinguishes pastoral from these other genres? Characters and setting, goatherds and shepherds, flock and countryside–these provide helpful signals but are not definitive. Between pastoral and epic, there are distinctions of length, contrasts between narrative and primarily lyric forms, and the difference between heroic action and acts without heroes (if we omit Renaissance pastoral drama, there are no heroes in pastoral). Despite contiguities of mode in epic and pastoral, few readers have difficulty telling them apart.

The case is more complicated as to the distinctions between georgic and pastoral. If we begin with Hesiod, the georgic is about work within nature, and such is also the case in Virgil's *Georgics*, which like its predecessor is a type of farming manual. The setting is the country. But the characters are farmers who transform nature through productive labor throughout the seasons. Virgil extols the farm worker as hero, and we are just a step or two away from the epic heroism of Aeneas and the creation of a new world in the *Aeneid*. Yet in the other direction, we can observe the differences between the georgic and pastoral. The former is about work and the latter about play. Does this mean that pastoral poems are humorous? Sometimes they are: sometimes pastoral play makes the characters appear to be children of the world, simultaneously naive and calculating. But the play of pastoral has a serious side to it. Play becomes the means through which the characters master a wide range of problems associated with day-to-day life. If pastoral poems differ from the georgic to the extent that they depict a world of childlike leisure and a world of play, pastoral also involves the serious value of play in friendship and in language. This value inheres in the ability to work through differences in emotional life just as the georgic farmer works through the land to produce the crops that sustain his existence.

We can better understand the nature of pastoral, then, through the concept of play. However, viewing pastoral in this way should not lead us to understand pastoral as an exclusively happy genre. One need only think of Theocritus's *Idylls* I and VII, the songs of Thyrsis and Lycidas, or Virgil's first *Eclogue* (Meliboeus's lament of exile) to realize that happiness is by no means an uninterrupted presence in the pastoral world. The play in pastoral often draws its material from events that are sad (the obvious and important variant of the genre relevant here is the pastoral elegy). Yet even when the speakers describe events that are sad, the pastoral impulse remains a playful one.

Pastoral tends to be constructed along formal lines, like a game the rules to which are known in advance. Students of the genre often describe this quality as its artificiality. The goatherd or the shepherd, the flock, the country landscape setting, the song contest—these are some of the rules. Part of the play of pastoral stems from departures from the expected pattern. There are rules in pastoral, but they are not rigid and exacting. They are nonrestrictive. The georgic describes rules for the work involved in the maintenance and production of the land; the epic describes rules for the moral conduct of men acting within the dynamics of historical change. Pastoral holds out certain rules for playing games, but serious games whose consequences have bearing on the emotional life of the individual within the social community. Yet paradoxically one of the aspects of pastoral and one of the qualities of its play that remains decisive must be the genre's willingness to entertain, indeed to encourage, respite from rules. Pastoral play opens up imaginative space. And it is the connection with imaginative process that distinguishes play in pastoral from the physical play we find in the classical epic. Games in the classical epic are physical: contestants compete in games of physical strength. Pastoral games, on the other hand, involve imaginative strength. They are contests in language that take, as their material, emotions such as joy and sorrow, and, especially in Theocritus, lust and remorse. Pastoral involves play through and about language, and the genre takes form around language games, often song contests. Parts of the classical heroic epic may be narrated by singers as a type of framing device. And these epic narratives or songs do have some of the qualities of song contests; but their scope is so broad and the singer's role so subtle that this element of language play as itself a subject of the discourse is not highlighted. All poetry is about language, obviously, but in pastoral, language assumes a special importance. Within the enclosed pastoral world of imaginative space, the various protagonists explore emotional and erotic attachments, social issues, the question of community, and types of emotional loss. And they explore these problems through the highly self-conscious play of language. In that sense, pastoral's principal mode of understanding and, in fact, its principal subject is language itself.

We are moving closer to a provisional definition of pastoral. Pastoral is less about work (georgic) or heroism (epic) than about play. Language is the principal mode of play in pastoral. This play can be humorous and light-hearted, but it can also be serious and sad, confronting such problems as unrequited love or the death of a friend. Pastoral is a genre that explores rules and boundaries and the ways the individual transgresses them. Pastoral creates a self-contained world, normally composed of a country setting, with rural simple folk as the principal characters. But it ventures into the city at times, and the tone and style hold in a state of tension rural simplicity and cosmopolitan sophistication. Pastoral makes little effort to disguise or dissimulate the urbane and witty poet who creates the poem.

Pastoral is an eminently dialectical genre. The genre functions in terms of a constant tension between thesis and antithesis, opposites working toward an unfolding synthesis; this is the modality of the form's progression. Pastoral's dialectical play takes as its ground the idea of song. In fact, one of the key aspects that distinguishes the genre is the stress on the dynamics of vocal response.[4]

Pastoral, perhaps more than any other poetic form, is about voices: giving voice to something, hearing voices, responding. This quality is particularly salient in such pastoral devices as the

refrain and the call-and-response structure. If we turn back to
pastoral beginnings in Theocritus, we note various qualities in the
refrain. Refrain creates continuity; it binds sections of the poem
together. Conversely, refrain also separates or articulates the sections. Refrain signals voice; it insists on the poetic fact of human,
oral production. Refrain tells the reader this is a spoken as well as
written artifact. Like the oral-formulaic phrase of the classical epic,
refrain creates the sense of a human voice, a speaking voice reciting
the poem. As a written text, the pastoral poem explores this dialectic between voice and written word, between what is on the page
and what is not. The refrain's insistence on voice sets up a tension
between text and performance and between silence and sound.
This tension prevails in all written texts, but pastoral's self-contained
dynamics of song foregrounds the tension.

Call-and-response also gives central importance to human voice.
In pastoral song contests, one singer often responds in emulation
and departure from the pattern set up by the other speaker. Often
the response is given an epistemological turn. The response pat-
terned on the echo is both natural and poetic. The poet structures
a play between not only silent text and vocal reading, but between
different voices of different origins: human voice and nature's
voice. Call-and-response recapitulates the very dynamics of voice
posited by the text's relation to the reader; that is, it creates silence
as well as sound in that pause or break between the two voices.
The pause or break again differentiates pastoral from any other genre.

As both visual and spoken text, the division of voice, the articulation of the text into the voices of different speakers, dramatizes
the play of language against the silence and blank space which surround it. From this perspective, we see the affinities of pastoral
with drama. Yet the pastoral lyric, because of its self-contained
brevity and because of the tension between the poet and the speakers in the poem, focuses not on the narrative action of drama but
on linguistic action. The drama of the pastoral lyric explores the
responsive dynamics of poetic language in ways that drama is less
well-equipped to handle. Unlike the divisions of voice in drama,
in pastoral the refrain and the call-and-response work through repetition. Word choice, metrical choice, and patterns of language key

the nature of linguistic play rather than the nature of the subject matter the speakers may be exploring. These choices create and constitute the subject matter.

Pastoral is about song and voice. It is also about society. Pastoral explores the nature of social groups. But, paradoxically, pastoral poems often involve just one or two speakers. This paradox reveals another aspect of the dialectics of pastoral: it is social but also solitary. The norms and expectations of the social group—household, community, state—are never far away from the pastoral world. Yet the pastoral world is itself a device if not to escape at least to humanize these expectations. And if the expectations of the larger community bear upon the behavior of the inhabitants of the pastoral world, those same inhabitants through imaginative play create other expectations, other values, and other communities.

Pastoral calls into question the very idea of community itself because it can be the most solitary of modes. One has only to think of Polyphemus's lament to Galatea in Theocritus to realize how much of both the pathos and comedy of pastoral grows out of the solitary individual; indeed, *Idyll* XI is paradigmatic of the close relation between pastoral play and pathos. Often, the playfulness of the genre stems from the characters' attempts to moderate feelings of loneliness, expatriation, and loss. Playfulness and pathos are never far apart in pastoral. And this range of emotion is itself never far from the dialectic of solitude and community, individual and society.

The aspect of pastoral concerned with society and community develops a subgenre in English literary history: the country-house poem. While pastoral and country-house poetry are not identical, they share certain themes and concerns. The country-house poem draws upon the ethos of retirement and leisure found in classical writers such as Homer, Theocritus, and Virgil.[5] Country-house poems are pastoral poems in the broad sense that the setting is in nature. The city is never far away, and that is true for pastoral also. Like pastoral, the country-house poem explores the tensions between country and city and between nature and artifice. But these explorations assume an entirely different cast in the country-house poem. While the economic man is part of the pastoral heritage, it is in the country-house poem that economics come to the fore. Pastoral downplays economics through the ideal space it creates and through the imaginative play enacted within this space. The country-house poem often takes as its principal theme the proper building of a stately retreat for the wealthy landowner: the country house imposes the reality of capital and labor on the pleasure principle of idyllic play.

Paradoxically, despite pastoral's insistence on the values of the imagination and leisure, the genre takes into account the realities of work in a way that the best-known country-house poems do not. As one commentator has pointed out, there is a tendency in the country-house poem to ignore the actual labor that creates the leisure of the country retreat.[6] While pastoral explores leisure, it does so within the dialectics of labor and leisure: the inhabitants of the pastoral world are country workers. On the other hand, the figures within the country-house poem are usually upper-class gentry reaping the profits of the men and women who labor on the land. Despite these differences, in terms of poetry the two genres are closely related. And as one moves into the modern, post-enlightenment period, we find country-house conventions side by side with pastoral conventions, but with the latter shorn of many of the ideas about labor and the dynamics of class out of which the country-house poem originated. In part, this suppression of the economic "ground" of the country house is the result of Romantic ideology and the rise of individualism. In part, it is the result of the increasingly self-referential nature of poetry and poetics in the modern period. In any event, in nineteenth-century England we are less likely to find poems that are, in a strict sense, country-house poems. We are less likely to find poems about the gentry and palatial retreats. We are more likely to find poems that draw upon the conventions of the country house but transform them to a point at which the term itself may no longer seem applicable.

In terms of nineteenth-century literary history and poetics, it may not make sense to follow too closely the distinctions between pastoral and country-house poetry. In fact, one of the most critical developments in nineteenth-century poetics is the breaking down of rigid genre conventions. Following Fowler's distinction, one might argue that poems experimenting with mode or modality of poetic discourse begin to displace poems that follow strictly the traditional boundaries of poetic genre.[7] Many of the poems that we will discuss draw upon country-house conventions while exploring the vagaries of the pastoral ideal.

Perhaps the major exception to nineteenth-century experimentation with genre boundaries is the elegy.[8] Major poets produced elegies in nineteenth-century England, elegies which follow quite closely the strictures and norms of the traditional genre. Most of the poems to be examined here are not elegies in a strict sense, but many of them incorporate selected conventions and concerns of the elegy within their experiments with pastoral poetics. If we understand elegy to be formal mourning at the death of someone loved by the singer and the community the singer represents, most of the poems we will discuss cannot be called elegies. Yet most of these poems involve the "work of mourning" that Sacks has described as a central dynamic within the elegy. Before we look at melancholy as psychological affect and as literary idea, before we discuss its relation to pastoral, we need to examine perhaps the most typical aspect of pastoral.

We have mentioned the country setting and the goatherds and shepherds. But what marks out the difference between a pastoral poem and a mere nature poem? Part of the dialectics of pastoral involves the artifice of situation and setting. In Theocritus and Virgil, we are never far away from the consciousness that the pastoral retreat is a constructed fiction. Unlike the conventional nature poem, where the poet presents nature deceptively, as unmediated experience, the true pastoral song insists on the experience as a mediated one: it insists on the reality of boundaries which limit and define natural space. If pastoral song is about the play of language, pastoral nature is about the play between nature as a real experience common to all people, and nature as rhetorical trope, an experience mediated and in fact created by the play of language.

The principal rhetorical trope of pastoral is the *locus amoenus*.

The *locus amoenus*, or "lovely place," is not exclusive to pastoral. There are pastoral oases in Homer's *Iliad* and *Odyssey*, contained natural retreats from the demands imposed on epic heroism. The epic *locus amoenus* is especially interesting in that it highlights the ambivalent value of the retreat. Some of these retreats, such as Circe's island, are deceptive and dangerous to those who enter. This type of epic *locus amoenus* develops in English literary tradition into the dangerous bowers in Spenser. The true pastoral *locus amoenus* does not contain such powers of ethical reduction. It is simply a place secluded from the demands of the larger society. The true pastoral *locus amoenus* is a good place, drawing upon the simplicity of its natural setting and on the simplicity of the people and animals who live within it. In pastoral song, the *locus amoenus* is more a part of the forest of Arden than of the Bower of Bliss.

The distinctive difference between the conventional nature poem and the pastoral poem consists in the artifice and boundaries of natural space in the latter. Since language play is at the heart of pastoral, nature and the natural setting play a secondary role. Nature is not the subject or the main action of pastoral; it is the ground or setting. In fact, when we think of nature in Theocritus, we realize how sparse it is: Theocritus merely sketches in a setting. The pastoral *locus amoenus* is more an idea than a place. Nature becomes fuller and lusher in Virgil's *Eclogues*, yet nature remains mediated and demystified because it is so often described and recounted at second hand by one of the singers within the poem. The *locus amoenus* is a linguistic vision; it is imaginary to the second power by virtue of its creation in the language of the inhabitants within the poem. The poet imagines them, and they imagine the space within which they dwell.

The *locus amoenus* is a rhetorical trope. The history of Western poetics attests to its rhetorical status. Its language derives, we are told, from the tropes of forensic rhetoric in classical theory.[9] Unlike the continuous and apparently unmediated representation of nature in the straightforward nature poem, the *locus amoenus* defines a nature that is discontinuous, fragmented from its surroundings, inherently artificial because it is openly language-constructed. All of these qualities prevail in nature poetry in general, certainly in the work of the romantics, but only after the critical reader has worked through the poet's claims to unmediated representation. The difference rests in that the pastoral poet and the pastoral singers within the poem openly explore the mediated and artificial status of this nature they represent. The *locus amoenus* constitutes the ground for the full range of rhetorical play that occurs in the pastoral poem. Pastoral singers insist that the trees, brooks, and shady bowers they sing about are not simply created by words; the substance of these natural objects is neither more nor less than words themselves.

One could say the pastoral *locus amoenus* is the paradigmatic example of the arbitrariness of the signifier/signified relation: the play of naming, in pastoral, acts within a poetic language that insists on its own unreality. Pastoral takes life in a language of the signifier without the signified. If the signified were to arrive, we would no longer be within the world of play, the acts of the imagination that define the pastoral experience. The signified is reality's intervention. And pastoral always tries to displace reality with another world.

One would imagine that the characters who dwell within the *locus amoenus* are happy, but more often than not, the *locus amoenus* serves as a foil to their unhappiness. If we think of Theocritean pastoral, we know that the playfulness of the genre is the dialectical antithesis of the melancholy that the characters feel. We now confront the second half of our subject: the confluence of the idea of melancholy with the pastoral genre. Since pastoral is especially about language, it is also about the maker of language – the poet. And the poet or artist figure in Western tradition has often been associated with the idea of melancholy. The connection between melancholy and genius may have originated in the work of Aristotle.[10] But it is in the Renaissance that the idea began to exert a strong fascination among scientists, scholars, and artists of all sorts. Melancholy was thought to be the product of biological and chemical imbalance in the body. According to Renaissance medical and psychological knowledge based on classical sources, the body contained four humors, and a preponderance of one of these was a key factor in the physical and psychological makeup of the individual. But at the same time, melancholy seemed most prevalent among those who possessed a certain type of sensibility: artists and thinkers.

In Dürer's *Melencolia* I, the tools and instruments of scientific

knowledge and discovery surround the bowed and sorrowful figure of Melancholy. She is a solitary figure. She is as much concerned with the heavens above as with the earthly things around
her. Dürer's engraving is *the* emblematic representation of the solitary and melancholy thinker. We find a more earthly depiction of
the melancholy man on the frontispiece of Burton's *Anatomy*. A
man is standing or rather slouching with arms folded; a broad-
brimmed hat overshadows his downturned head. Unlike Dürer's
Melancholy, the figure looks down at the ground rather than up
toward the heavens.

Part of the irony of melancholy would seem to be that it encompasses both heaven and hell. In the melancholy tradition, we find
people concerned with the sublimities of imaginative vision, but
we also find people caught in webs of anger, deceit, and violence.
In English literary history, the second type of melancholic abounds
in drama.[11] In Shakespeare, Marlowe, and the Jacobeans, the melancholic is one whose brooding often turns to violence (less evident
in these writers is the melancholic as thinker). On the other hand,
in Shakespeare's pastoral comedies and romances, the melancholy
figure is often comic: he is less a thinker than a jester or clown.
Jaques may be the best example of this type. Here we find a figure
related to the world of pastoral play. We do not associate this figure
with the darker melancholy of mourning in the elegy, yet a figure
such as Jaques is a maker of language, one whose ethical commentary on the state of things achieves its force and resonance through
the play of language.

It is in lyrical poetry and shorter narrative poetry, however, that
we find the idea of melancholy itself becoming both a figure within
the poem and its principal idea or theme as well. The touchstones
of this tradition are "L'Allegro" and "Il Penseroso." While not strictly
pastoral poems, they contain the dialectic of play and melancholy
that will define all pastoral thenceforth. They define the outer
limits of conventionalization in both nature and human psychology.
That is to say, here the abstract conceptualization of nature as a
setting within which the poet explores the psychology of human
emotions achieves a synthesis that Theocritus had only begun to
sketch out centuries before. Nature is not a fully detailed field.
This will come later in the latter half of the eighteenth century,

and it will achieve full realization in the British romantics. Instead of the fullness and "reality" of nature, we have a group of almost abstract forms, a grid or symbolic field within which the personified figures move. This abstraction of nature in "L'Allegro" and "Il Penseroso," combined with the personified figures or abstract psychological ideas, constitutes a crucial tradition in pastoral, one explored throughout the eighteenth and nineteenth centuries.

Milton interrogates, among other things, the relation between figural language and the representation of literal states of mind. This dialectic is central to pastoral song, and it remains central in the confluence of pastoral and melancholy. Symbolic landscapes and iconographic figures within them stake out a space more imaginary than real. Henceforth, in English literary history we find a type of poem which explores psychic states through personified figures. These personified figures move within a landscape that, despite its claims to naturalness, is in fact a symbolic grid or pattern through which the poet presents fluctuating psychic states. We associate many of these poems with the melancholy tradition.

Perhaps the largest concentration of this type of symbolic landscape poem occurs in post-Augustan eighteenth-century poetry. But melancholy and religious meditations set within a natural landscape were a major presence throughout the seventeenth century.[12] Poets who wrote poems of this type often structured them along the lines of "L'Allegro" and "Il Penseroso." Even in the lesser versifiers, the melancholy poem is still important and revealing. Such poems juxtapose the physical body, descriptions of the inner emotional life, iconographic objects—nightingale, owl, graveyard, and so forth—with personified figures such as Melancholy. These poems develop out of the epistemological dialogue between melancholy and mirthful play in "L'Allegro" and "Il Penseroso." The poem that takes as its subject "melancholy," or addresses Melancholy, or personifies Melancholy, involves an exploration of figural and literal representation, an exploration of whether, in fact, that distinction holds good. It involves this exploration because the idea of melancholy as it attains conventional status in history and poetics is that of an allegorical figure, but one situated within a personal mode. The melancholy poem is usually a fairly short lyric or, if long, an autobiographical narrative (an example of the latter is James Beattie's *The Minstrel*). Paradoxically, melancholy as a literary idea is at once one of the most abstract, external ideas, and one of the most psychologically embodied and internal. Thus, it is fitting that poets experimenting with the pastoral tradition would adopt the idea of melancholy.

The iconographic personification of melancholy becomes one of the main strategies of figural language in this tradition. In addition to the silent and sad figure in "Il Penseroso," one thinks of the "goddess of a tearful eye" in Joseph Warton's "Ode to Fancy," and the personified female form in Thomas Warton's "The Pleasures of Melancholy." In these representations of Melancholy, the poet depicts the idea as a female goddess: quiet, bowed in sadness, often tearful. The allegorical dimension of the figure means also that the figure is "sketched in," a composite of symbolic traits rather than a detailed realistic image. In visual terms, these representations of melancholy have a Byzantine quality. They sketch a geometry of forms that stand for the state of melancholy; they do not involve, to any great extent, representations of emotional or psychological realism. The poet represents the emotion through idea more than through psychology and visual portrayal of affect. Something similar is at work in James Thomson's invocation to Melancholy in *Autumn*. At this point in the tradition, Melancholy only partially describes the speaker's state of mind. Melancholy is at the same time a philosophical abstraction, yet none of these figures is entirely disembodied nor entirely abstracted from the real world. Like the bowed figure of Burton's frontispiece, these figures look to the grounds of reality as well as to the ideals of heaven. And the grounds of reality to which they look are the grounds of nature turning from abstraction toward representational realism.

Poets usually set poems of melancholy within a natural landscape. In fact, while seventeenth-century poems of melancholy concentrate on religious and philosophical issues, eighteenth-century melancholy poetry tends more and more toward descriptive nature poetry. This combination affords the poet an opportunity to explore the dialectic of figural and literal language. The language represents melancholy as both an external allegorical figure and an internal psychological state. An area within which these two levels meet is nature – the pastoral landscape scene. The eighteenth-century landscape poets constitute a curious turning point in terms of both melancholy and pastoral traditions. From the perspective of the poetry of melancholy which precedes it, the later eighteenth-century poem of melancholy—Thomson and the Warton brothers, for example—appears a radical "naturalization." Natural description acquires greater detail. The descriptive poem truly is descriptive and not simply an excuse for philosophical or religious musings. From the perspective of English Romanticism, the poems of Thomson and the Warton brothers appear, on the other hand, abstract and nonrepresentational in terms of description and psychology.

Personified figures of Melancholy are rare by the early nineteenth century. Keats's great ode on the subject is really a farewell to the tradition. The tension within the two traditions between two modes of representation, one figural and allegorical and one psychologically and descriptively realistic, is an important feature of the confluence of pastoral and melancholy. The Victorian poets who inherited these traditions also inherited this dialectic: Tennyson and Hardy exploit this dialectic of representation, pursuing its disjunctions in order to create a singular Victorian pastoral.

The task that yet remains is to describe what exactly melancholy was to these poets, what sort of permutations the idea undergoes as we move toward the Victorian period, and what the idea of melancholy means to us today, since we unavoidably read the past in the light of the present. In the seventeenth and eighteenth centuries, poets understood melancholy to mean more than just sadness. It was a part of the chemistry of the body. Melancholics were not merely sad; they were physically sick. Burton's *Anatomy* provides a compendious account of the remedies used to alleviate this illness. Distinctions between body and psyche were much less sharply drawn in the Renaissance and seventeenth century than would come to be the case in the modern period. Thus, people who ate certain foods, who lived in certain climates, who possessed a certain physical type were diagnosed as potential melancholics.

Melancholy was also the focal point for many of the intellectual anxieties of the times, and this became increasingly the case in the later seventeenth century and during the eighteenth century. Death, for example, was one of the great melancholy subjects in these two centuries. Despite the power of religious faith—in certain ways because of it–death remained a frightening mystery; even with the promise of an afterlife, the prospect of death was a cause for melancholy and pensive thought. Poets were moved to address personified Death. Melancholy was the emotional response to the end of life and also to the absence, the unrepresentable blank, that lay beyond. From earlier religious-oriented melancholy, this strand of the tradition eventually led to the so-called graveyard school. And thence it developed into such key transformations and modernizations of the death theme as Gray's *Elegy*.

The melancholy response to death occurs obviously in the traditional elegy, but the elegy is a different part of this tradition. The elegy is a poem of mourning. The "death theme" poem is not so much about mourning as about fear for one's own spiritual fate. In Gray's *Elegy*, the poet conflates the two traditions: it is a traditional elegy, a poem of mourning, but it is a poem of mourning for the fate of the self. As in the traditional elegy, the melancholy death poem becomes a way of mastering, through representation in language, problems that are frightening by virtue of their unrepresentability. The melancholy death poem attempts to represent and thus domesticate this blankness.

Another strand of the melancholy tradition involves not terror before death but the ennui, the tedium, of life. Here melancholy turns from sublime terror before death to the more subdued tones of lamentation at the daily struggles of life. In its very broadest sense, this tradition in Western poetry goes back to Job and the Psalms. In a narrower sense, *taedium vitae* is a standard theme in the minor versifiers of the seventeenth and eighteenth centuries. In the dynamics of its psychology, the poem of ennui and lamentation assumes in those years an artificial quality. This quality leads into a structure of feeling that one associates with the later eighteenth century: the age of sentiment or pre-Romanticism.

At that turning point, the poem of melancholy assumes a programmatic structure or deliberate cultivation of feeling that may have no actual bearing on the mind of the speaker. The sense of artifice relates very much to the dialectic in pastoral whereby the characters appear simple people in a natural setting. But pastoral insists that this world is artfully constructed and much more complex than initially appears. The death theme or life's ennui as a set stance enables the poet to explore the dynamics of literary artifice: how can one be sincere within a language characterized by deception and artifice? This theme enables the poet to explore whether sincerity is desirable in poetic language. It enables the poet to ask whether dissimulation may in fact be the poetic mode par excellence.

Keats's "Ode on Melancholy" is a farewell to this tradition. What could follow it? The dismissal of the melancholy tradition, even if only in its exclusively conventionalized forms, is perhaps a bit premature in the nineteenth century. English poets still drew upon the melancholy tradition, but usually in self-conscious ways. The concerns which motivated the poem on death, *taedium vitae*, and the retirement theme had not disappeared: they are concerns that all human beings have faced at all times. The very notion of convention itself marks off the nineteenth-century adoption of the melancholy poem. By the latter half of the eighteenth century, melancholy conventions had become routinized. The poem of melancholy had become a predictable configuration of figurative strategies, and it was this predictability to which Keats was responding. But rejection is only one strategy of response. One could instead use this configuration of conventions as a starting point for a renewal of the genre. This renewal would incorporate contemporary concerns, as well as the concerns that the melancholy poem had traditionally addressed.

With the vast increase of scientific knowledge in the nineteenth century and with the crisis in religious faith, the traditional melancholy poem assumed new force and new forms.[13] In conjunction with the Victorian intellectual crisis of belief came a poetic crisis of belief. The Victorians experienced a crisis of belief about the nature of poetic tradition and the nature of language itself. Thus, the Victorian poets who drew upon the melancholy tradition also subverted it through a conscious, insistent interrogation of language's relation to meaning. Given its extreme conventionalization, the melancholy poem is one through which the Victorian poet could explore the problems of figural language. The Victorian poets found a similar situation prevailed in their relation to the other genre under discussion; the Victorian pastoral poem became a vehicle for exploring the problematic nature of poetic language.

The best example of this confluence of tradition and crisis is a poem not discussed here in detail – *In Memoriam*. Tennyson is indeed the "master of melancholia," and his long poem in memory of Hallam is one of the subtlest and most complex explorations of the psychology of mourning in the language. It is also one of the most profound explorations of the Victorian intellectual crisis of faith that we have. This crisis is, not coincidentally, a crisis of language and poetics as well. The combination of narrative long poem and short lyric is a part of this crisis and part of the poem's experimental greatness. It is both a spiritual narrative in the tradition of *The Prelude* (or, on a lesser level, of Beattie's *The Minstrel*), and an elegy structured through series and repetition. *In Memoriam* looks back to the great elegies in the English tradition but also looks ahead to the fragmented, disjunctive experiments in the modern long poem.[14] Interwoven through the lyrics of mourning are lyrics in which Tennyson meditates on modern science and its impact on religious belief in his day. Tennyson also interweaves his narrative with self-referential explorations of language and the nature of poetry. The poet conducts many of these explorations by means of the pastoral idea: the metacommentary on language involves frequent allusions to pastoral conventions. Far from being sentimental and emotionally self-indulgent, Tennyson's major elegy is ironic and acutely self-critical. The melancholia of the poet's work of mourning is both strengthened and offset by the pastoral allusion. The pastoral themes and conventions represent the poet's melancholia through the employment of elegiac conventions, and also through the poet's self-conscious alienation from those conventions. Tennyson himself was aware of the irony in presenting himself as a poet/shepherd in mid-nineteenth-century England, and he was aware of the pathos of exile in such invocations. Tennyson's melancholy pastoral is invariably ironic.

One of the great Victorian poets of melancholy is excluded from this general discussion: Arnold must be set apart from Tennyson and Hardy in terms of the pastoral and melancholy traditions. Arnold is one of the great poets of Victorian melancholy, but his concern is with the intellectual crisis of the times more than with the poetic crisis. The idea of melancholy in his poems is one that reflects Victorian spiritual anxiety, not anxiety in the face of poetic tradition. Arnold seems undaunted by tradition. Indeed, he sees himself as the great inheritor of the classical tradition, and thus, "Thyrsis" belongs with the best pastoral elegies in English. But it is an outright imitation of a classical elegy rather than an exploration of the differences between the tradition and the poetry of his time. None of this is to say that Arnoldian melancholy does not merit extensive research and discussion beyond that which it has so far received. But that is a different subject from the one to be explored here.

If Arnold's "Thyrsis" remains squarely within the traditional genre of pastoral, Tennyson and Hardy wander outside of the genre's conventions. In the texture of their language, Tennyson's and Hardy's poems are very much concerned with figural and generic error; their figurative language turns from the expected norms. In terms of broader formal categories, Tennysonian and Hardian pastoral and melancholy poetry involves departures from the norms as well. One could argue that pastoral and melancholy as discussed here are too broad to serve any useful purpose. This view involves an implicit assumption that genre is only functional when its categories strictly delineate the differences between generic types, and when specific works fit easily within one of these categories. It is a highly problematic view. However much one may admire, for example, Frye's system-building, or Hirsch's idea of "intrinsic genres," recent work in genre theory suggests the arbitrariness of such categories.[15] Students of genre are now more likely to perceive the fluidity and transformativeness of any specific text in its relation to genre categories, no matter how those categories may be defined.

The Victorian poets, and Tennyson and Hardy in particular, provide especially persuasive evidence of the transformativeness of a literary text in regard to generic rules. It is not sufficient to speak of "elegy" or "pastoral" or "melancholy" in Tennyson's work. In Tennyson these categories become areas of experimentation, for Tennyson is always crossing boundaries of genre. When he writes pastoral, he writes ironic pastoral: his pastoral poems question their own status in terms of the demands of the genre. This generic self-questioning prevails in his elegies and also in his poems that draw upon the melancholy tradition. In this light, the medley form of *The Princess* no longer appears an aberration but a logical step in Tennyson's ongoing experiment with the boundaries of traditional forms. In terms of social, political, and religious themes, Tennyson is a conservative poet. In terms of poetics and the transformation of tradition, he is arguably one of the most daring poets of the century.

Daring is not a word that we readily associate with Hardy. But Hardy was an experimentalist. His adaptations of traditional poetic forms, and what has been called his "arbitrary metrical choice," type him not as a traditionalist but as a modernist.[16] He is one of the late-nineteenth-century poets who transformed tradition by subverting it from within. In even more subtle and decisive ways than Tennyson, Hardy exploits the prescriptive limits of traditional generic categories and turns from those limits. His pastoral poems draw heavily upon traditional pastoral conventions, but they are not limited to those conventions. Like Tennyson's works, Hardy's poems are "medleys," experiments in language and form. The idea of genre retains its defining power but becomes a starting point for a poetic process of natural selection between generic types. Hardy's poems often depict struggle and transformation within nature. But the deeper struggles, the more crucial transformations, occur in the very language of his text. Tennyson and Hardy cross the boundaries of traditional form.

I

The Poet's Melancholy:
Pastoral and Community
in Early Tennyson

THE WORD "MELANCHOLY" HAS OFTEN BEEN
associated with the poetry of Tennyson. Eliot, in his essay on *In
Memoriam,* says, "Tennyson is the great master of metric, as well
as of melancholia; I do not think that any poet in English has ever
had a finer ear for vowel sound, as well as a subtler feeling for some
moods of anguish."[1] Auden makes a similar though less flattering
observation: Tennyson, he says, "had the finest ear perhaps, of any
English poet." But Auden adds, "he was undoubtedly the stupid-
est; there was little about melancholia that he didn't know; there
was little else that he did."[2] The general tendency in Tennyson criticism, when speaking of melancholy and Tennyson, is to ascribe the
emotional state to the poet and then praise the poet for his ability
to represent in his verse the psychology of this state. Critics tend
to view melancholy as a personal attribute of the poet rather than
as an idea or a problem the poet chose to explore. The critical approach to melancholy in Tennyson's poetry has largely been biographical, or medical and psychological. The two best recent bi-
ographies, those of Ricks and Martin, stress the history of medical
and pyschological problems in the Tennyson family—the notorious
"black blood" of the Tennysons—and point out how these prob-

lems shaped the sensibility of the young poet and the central concerns of his poetry.[3] Another recent critical work, *Tennyson and Madness* by Ann Colley, approaches the problem of melancholy in Tennyson's poetry by way of Victorian medical, psychological, and philosophical theories and attitudes about madness.[4] This type of critical perspective provides a needed corrective to the misconceived and oversimplified view of Tennyson as the comfortable and complacent poet laureate of Victorian England. The critical revision began with Harold Nicolson's biography in the twenties: he suggested that the view of Tennyson as the public poet of Victorian pieties needed to be qualified by renewed attention to Tennyson as a subjective poet of dark and brooding vision.[5] E. D. H. Johnson later developed this view in his study of the ambivalent nature of the Victorian poetic imagination, *The Alien Vision of Victorian Poetry*. In his view, Tennyson is a divided poet: he is both a public poet of Victorian optimism and a solitary and melancholy poet of vision.[6] Johnson's study is especially valuable in the way it relates melancholy to the poet's exploration of the nature of his art; there is the suggestion in Johnson's study that melancholy constitutes in Tennyson's work a kind of poetics. The idea of melancholy will be pursued here less in its biographical and psychological dimensions than in its triple role as, first, an idea and form within literary tradition; second, an idea and form in Tennyson's developments and transformations of this tradition; and third, a concept that plays a part in Tennyson's theory of poetry itself. Our concern is Tennyson's pastoral art and the poetics of melancholy.

In "Mariana," Tennyson deals with both the psychological economy and the poetic dynamics of melancholy. A number of critics have discussed the psychological dimensions of the poem. Jerome Buckley calls it a "study in frustration."[7] John Stuart Mill, in his essay on Tennyson for the *London Review* in 1835, said of "Mariana":

> Words surely never excited a more vivid feeling of physical and spiritual dreariness: and not dreariness alone—for that might be felt under many other circumstances of solitude—but the dreariness which speaks not merely of being far from human converse and sympathy, but of being *deserted* by it.[8]

W. David Shaw looks at "Mariana" from a somewhat different slant when he says that Mariana is "actively engaged in imagining her annihilation, defying the nothingness by filling it with images she knows."[9] "Mariana" is, however, more than simply a study of personality. James Kincaid provides a useful hint of how Mariana's psychology ties in with several other concerns of Tennyson: he suggests that the irony of the poem is brought about by the images of Mariana's "youth and hope" being connected with pastoral conventions that are "distorted."[10] This point deserves to be pursued.

"Mariana" is a character study, certainly. But it is also an early example of Tennyson's self-conscious treatment of certain genre conventions (types of imagery and figurative language) associated with pastoral melancholy. The poem suggests some of the ways Tennyson works with traditional conventions and also goes beyond them. "Mariana" examines the idea of the poet's task, and the melancholy of the solitary artist confronting the aesthetic "community" created by the poetic texts from the pastoral tradition that lies behind these texts.

In order to understand the nature of the "textual community" that lies behind "Mariana," we need to turn to the poem's sources. In his edition of *The Poems of Tennyson*, Christopher Ricks lists numerous sources for the poem, preeminent among them Shakespeare's *Measure for Measure* and Keats's "Isabella." The poem's epigraph, "Mariana in the moated grange," is not a direct quotation, but Tennyson does draw on a passage from Shakespeare's play. Ricks sees the function of the allusion to Shakespeare as being that of contrast. In the play, Angelo does finally wed Mariana, whereas in the poem we sense that there will be no such happy outcome. In terms of style, Ricks points to Keats's "Isabella" for its quality of melancholy pensiveness: "She weeps alone for pleasure not to be; / Sadly she wept until the night came on. . . . / And so she pined and so she died forlorn."[11] Robert Pattison, in *Tennyson and Tradition*, also stresses Shakespeare as a source: he notes that Tennyson chose to pair "Mariana" with "Isabel" in his editions of the poems. According to Pattison, "Isabel is a model of chastity in contrast to Mariana's withering sexuality."[12] In addition to these important sources, there are, on the level of form and style, other textual debts in "Mariana." Paul Turner observes the similarity between "He cometh not" and a line from "Leonine Elegiacs": "she cometh not morning or even." Turner then suggests that the basic structure of the poem is like that of Ovid's *Heroides*, his verse epistles from abandoned women of renown. Finally, Turner says that the refrain may also have been suggested to Tennyson by the refrain in Theocritus's *Idyll* II (where the sorceress uses a refrain as a part of a spell in the hopes of calling back the lover who has abandoned her).[13] We begin to observe the mixture of genres, styles, and forms that shape "Mariana." Pattison describes this quality thus:

> Part of the fascination of "Mariana" is its playful distinction of form. Somewhat like a ballad, it is not a ballad; somewhat lyrical, it is too detached in its narrative to be truly a lyric. We can recognize "Mariana" for what it really is, of course, from Tennyson's later work. It is an idyll.[14]

Behind Keats and Shakespeare in "Mariana" lies Theocritus, the inventor of pastoral. Some of the more subtle literary debts in "Mariana" come from much later examples of the pastoral tradition in English literature that combine descriptions of nature with moods of melancholy, but they all stem, to a certain degree, from Theocritus. Traces of these influences will help make clear the path that Tennyson follows from the pastoral melancholy of the classical idyll of Theocritus and Virgil up to Keats and then beyond.

The subtle melancholy of the classical pastoral idyll is bound up with the description of nature, as it is in "Mariana." As many critics have observed, Tennyson's poem is more a description of a place than of a person. In his article for the *London Review*, Mill remarks on Tennyson's skill with "scene-painting":

> not the mere power of producing those rather vapid species of composition usually termed descriptive poetry—for there is not in these volumes one passage of pure description; but the power of *creating* scenery, in keeping with some state of human feeling; so fitted to it as to be the embodied symbol of it, and to summon up the state of feeling itself, with a force not to be surpassed by anything but reality.[15]

We can add to Mill's comments, those of Jerome Buckley on the representation of nature in "Mariana": "the mode of rendering the emotion in lyric form through the expressionist description of setting is characteristically the poet's own."[16] One final critical observation on the quality of nature in "Mariana" that will be of use in this analysis comes from Tennyson's recent biographer, Robert Bernard Martin: "It is nature unnaturally constrained and distorted by man."[17] One can take this point even further. The "constraints" and "distortions" in the representation of nature are not only bound up with the melancholy of the figure within the poem but with the melancholy inherent in Tennyson's relation as a poet to the forms, images, and figurative strategies of the pastoral tradition.

The first stanza of "Mariana" provides an example of the quality and structure of feeling produced by Tennyson's representation of nature:

> With blackest moss the flower-plots
>   Were thickly crusted, one and all:
> The rusted nails fell from the knots
>   That held the pear to the gable-wall.
> The broken sheds looked sad and strange:
>   Unlifted was the clinking latch;
>   Weeded and worn the ancient thatch
> Upon the lonely moated grange.
>   She only said, 'My life is dreary,
>   He cometh not,' she said;
>   She said, 'I am aweary, aweary,
>   I would that I were dead!'[18]

As Mill points out, the purpose and effect of the scene are different from what we find in much descriptive poetry. It is worth looking carefully at the nature of these differences, because they are very much related to the pastoral tradition. We can compare this stanza with a passage from an eighteenth-century poem that belongs in the tradition of both descriptive poetry and pastoral melancholy:

> Haste, Fancy, from the scenes of folly,
> To meet the matron Melancholy,
> Goddess of the tearful eye,
> That loves to fold her arms, and sigh;
> Let us with silent footsteps go
> To charnels and the house of woe,
> To Gothic churches, vaults, and tombs,
> Where each sad night some virgin comes.[19]

This is from Joseph Warton's "Ode to Fancy," an example of the graveyard school of poetry in the eighteenth century. As with other poems of this type, there is the obligatory invocation to the personification of melancholy, and a solitary human figure within a dark and forbidding landscape. Most of these poems, as Amy Reed has shown in her study of Gray's *Elegy*, associate the landscape with melancholy. The typical themes explored in this genre are the death theme, the retirement theme, and the complaint of life.[20]

At first glance, the comparison of Tennyson's "Mariana" with this type of poetry may seem invidious. Tennyson's poem does not contain a church or a graveyard, nor does it contain any personified figures such as Fancy or Melancholy. Yet the mood is as somber and pensive as anything one finds in the Warton brothers, or in Edward Young, Dyer, Thomson, and Gray. Death, the retirement from the world, and the complaint of life are all central to the way Tennyson represents nature and presents Mariana's emotional state. Warton is useful to us here because he is a transitional figure who stands between mid-eighteenth-century neoclassicism and late-eighteenth-to-early-nineteenth-century Romanticism. Tennyson's pastoral melancholy has affinities with both schools. There are certain similarities, certain continuities, in feeling and structure between Warton's "Ode" and "Mariana," but the differences are even more suggestive. In terms of figurative language, Warton freely uses apostrophe and personification. Warton follows, without self-consciousness or uneasiness, the rhetorical traditions for representing melancholy. Melancholy here is not so much a person or a place as it is an idea. The "Goddess of the tearful eye" is not a realistic figure; she is an iconographic symbol. Warton is saying something here about the relationship between fancy and melancholy. What is crucial, however, in terms of this discussion, is that he is saying it by means of an allegory that is constituted by a whole set of poetic conventions. The apostrophe to the female figure is conventional: both Reed and Sickels give numerous examples of the image of the "tearful eye" in the poetry of melancholy.[21] In addition, most readers acquainted with British literary tradition will recognize the significance of the image of the folded arms: it is one of the principal figurative gestures that signify the melancholic. We find it in the frontispiece of Burton's *Anatomy*. The following description of the Renaissance playwright John Ford provides another witty example of this convention: "Deep in a dump John Ford was got / With folded arms and melancholy hat."[22] We can see, then, the extent to which Warton's "Ode" is indebted to the whole tradition of melancholy poetry in English (and, in its description of and retirement to nature, to the pastoral tradition also). What does the poem tell us, by comparison, about Tennyson's departures from these traditions? Do the conventions in "Mariana" constitute a different type altogether of figurative representation?

Unlike Warton's "Ode," "Mariana" is extremely specific and contains detailed natural description. In the first stanza, Tennyson takes great care to choose the word that evokes the anxiousness and desolation of the woman. The moss is not simply "black" but "blackest." The superlative conveys the color but also emphasizes the tangible existence of the moss. The flower-plots are not covered or overgrown but "thickly crusted." This first image is detailed and precise: with an almost microscopic scrutiny, it brings the reader within the world of the landscape. Tennyson apparently dispenses here with formalities of apostrophe and personification in order to decrease the psychological distance between reader/subject/poet.

It is significant as well that Tennyson opens the poem with a startling abruptness. "Mariana" begins as if in mid-sentence with a preposition. Without setting the scene in any conventional sense, Tennyson begins with the details. In this, he draws away from eighteenth-century descriptive poetry, which tends to order the descriptive structure so that it moves from the larger, generalized representation, to the smaller perspective, with its closer details. The poet also departs here from even as important an influence as Keats. Keats, too, moves away from the representation of nature through personification. Moreover, along with Wordsworth, Keats places a new emphasis on a realistic representation of nature in language that conveys sensuous, concrete detail. Indeed, as George H. Ford has demonstrated, this emphasis is one of the main qualities that Tennyson learned from Keats.[23] In a significant way, however, Tennyson diverges from both the eighteenth-century poets and Keats. Keats tends to use a kind of "camera eye," moving from the larger scene to its component parts. Along with the eighteenth-

century poets, Keats represents nature and landscape as essentially
a continuity of images. In "Mariana," Tennyson disrupts or distorts
this sense of spatial continuity.

The first images in "Mariana" are discrete. They stand apart
from a larger context. They are disorienting.

> With blackest moss the flower-plots
> Were thickly crusted. . . .

This type of natural description, with its fragmented, disconnected
quality, is a crucial aspect of the Tennysonian landscape of melancholy; furthermore, it constitutes a symbol of the poet's melancholy sense that he is an exile from the very traditions he draws
upon. To adopt Martin's words about the quality of nature in this
poem, the poet feels "constrained" by the conventions of tradition, and in the process of re-representing them, he "distorts"
them. The melancholia of the poetic voice in "Mariana" is the result of the poet's sense that he is apart from the community of tradition. This, in turn, results in the disfigurations and distortions of
the conventions of pastoral melancholy itself. He can refer to these
conventions and echo them, but the re-creation of the concerns
of traditional pastoral and melancholy poetry will be imbued with
artifice. We can observe, then, that in the association of melancholy and nature, there is a curious circularity of structure and feeling when we proceed from the eighteenth-century descriptive poets
to Keats and then to Tennyson. The eighteenth-century poetry of
melancholy (and, tangentially, of pastoral) tends to invest the natural
scene with allegorical significance, using iconographic elements
long associated with the idea of melancholy. Their landscapes are
symbolic of concepts drawn from the philosophy and psychology
of melancholy in its various forms: the retirement theme, the death
theme, the complaint of life, the love lament. In Keats, the relation of melancholy and description changes in part because of the
richness of detail and the objectively concrete realism of his representations of nature, and because his descriptions work more to
evoke moods and feelings than to symbolize certain set ideas, philosophical or otherwise. This is to say that Keats uses natural description to create not so much a philosophical or moral allegory, as
a faithful depiction of man, nature, and process that is less sym-

bolic than realistic. We can concede an allegorical aspect, certainly, to the Keatsian description of nature, but it remains a highly personal allegory of nature and artist, mind and world, subject and object (his images of nature turn back upon themselves, are both sign and signified).

Keats's transformation of pastoral melancholy involves an internalization within the solitary poet of the problems that in eighteenth-century melancholy poetry were external abstractions. This internalization also records a shift from the classic pastoral idyll, which explored similar problems but through a community of human figures and a community of tradition within which the poet felt at home. In addition, Keatsian melancholy is the result of both this internalization and the poet's troubling sense of alienation from this community of texts. Paradoxically, the intensity of his literal representation of the pastoral landscape becomes the figuration of an allegory about the poet's sense of apartness from the very texts that help produce that literal representation. One of the conclusions to be drawn from these observations is that in Keats, pastoral melancholy is both literal and figurative, realistic and allegorical. Tennyson goes even further in the exploration of this dichotomy. In Tennysonian natural description the realism, by virtue of its fragmentation and its discrete positioning, is also figurative, but not in the way that Warton's poem is figurative. Warton draws upon the iconography of tradition to convey abstract ideas (in this case about the nature of fancy and melancholy). His method is in line with the tradition going back to Renaissance allegory. Tennyson, following Keats, further pursues personal lyric, the exploration of the individual state of mind. Moreover, as we have observed in the first stanza of "Mariana," his natural descriptions are, like those of Keats, realistic.

In a curious way, however, Tennyson also turns toward the allegorical mode. The types of fragmentation, framing, and distancing that we observe in the first stanza of "Mariana" are adapted, in part, from the Theocritean idyll, and they play a crucial role in the transformation of the romantic and Victorian lyric of personal utterance and natural description, into the poetry of symbolism of Mallarmé and Eliot. Tennyson was highly conscious of the tensions involved in the development and transformation of these genre conventions, and thus, his poetry assumed an allegorical cast. Keats's allegory of melancholy centers on process. In Tennyson's allegory of melancholy, the focus is on the discontinuity of process.

Tennyson not only feels a sense of alienation from the community of tradition, but he questions the coherence and even the existence of this textual community. The literary conventions of tradition, which ought to work as responsive and reciprocal supports for the present work of the poet, become instead discontinuous fragments that are the allegorical signs of the apartness of the poet. These fragmented images also suggest the poet's fear that the textual community itself may be an illusion. Tennyson's representation of nature confronts this problem. It is through the fragmentation of the pastoral world that Tennyson realizes the fragmentation of tradition. For example, the first two lines of "Mariana" image a natural process that has outgrown its use: moss has overtaken the flower-plots. It is an image of nature and pastoral that comes after the Keatsian abundance and sensuousness. It is the plenitude of nature and poetry crossing over to impoverishment. The fragmented images of impoverishment continue in the next lines:

> The rusted nails fell from the knots
> That held the pear to the gable-wall.

Tennyson originally used the word "peach" rather than "pear," and Ricks quotes the poet's explanation: "'peach' spoils the desolation of the picture. It is not characteristic of the scenery I had in mind."[24] The comment reveals how carefully Tennyson chose his words in order to produce this effect of "desolation." We note, in addition, how the desolation of the scene is further effected by the disconnectedness of lines 3 and 4 from lines 1 and 2. What is the connection between the gable-wall and the flower-plots? At the outset the answer is none: the reader has little sense of how these fragmented images fit together. The natural scene does not cohere, and this lack of coherence contributes to the mood of barrenness. The rhyme scheme ABAB provides a certain binding element, as does the use of internal rhyme: we note the use of "crusted" and "rusted" to bind the first four lines together. But it is significant that this binding is brought about by images of decay. Despite these formal elements of coherence and despite the precision of detail, the description is still primarily one of disparate images that create a subtle emotional symbolism. It is the symbolic landscape of melancholy.

Tennyson uses the symbolic landscape of melancholy effectively elsewhere in the poem. Here follows the example of stanza four:

> About a stone-cast from the wall
>   A sluice with blackened waters slept,
> And o'er it many, round and small,
>   The clustered marish-mosses crept.
> Hard by a poplar shook alway,
>   All silver-green with gnarlèd bark:
>   For leagues no other tree did mark
> The level waste, the rounding gray.

Like stanza one, stanza four contains extremely precise details, such as the "sluice with blackened waters" and the "clustered marish-mosses," or the poplar which is "silver-green" and "gnarlèd." The description of the wasteland as "the rounding gray" is especially fine in the way it conveys the overwhelming bleakness of the scene, and in the way it encompasses all the figures and objects contained within it. It is important to observe, however, that Tennyson's description is so concrete, so intense in its focus, that the details become animated. The waters "slept" and the mosses "crept." There is a progressive animation, a progressive anthropomorphism, of the landscape in "Mariana," as if the absence of anything human is ultimately replaced by the nonhuman objects acquiring human form. This is a strange effect and highly characteristic of Tennysonian natural description, with its strong reliance on pathetic fallacy. The effect is very different from the personification of nature in eighteenth-century pastoral melancholy, and also from the movement toward an increasing realism in such English Romantics as Wordsworth and Keats. Tennyson's landscape is real and symbolic. It is literal and figurative. It is mimetic and allegorical at the same time. In Tennyson's early poems, the pastoral landscape (and its constraints and distortions) is finally the visual figure for his troubled poetics. Having drawn upon the concretely realized pastoral world of the Romantics, Tennyson felt uneasy with the abstract personifications and allegorical moralizing of the eighteenth-century melancholy poets. However, as a latecomer to the tradition (like the Alex-

andrian poets themselves who invented the pastoral idyll), Tennyson
possessed a critical consciousness of the limitations of all genre conventions. This consciousness makes it difficult for him to produce
a landscape that is entirely at ease with its own status as realistic
representation. For Tennyson, "realism" itself is a figure, and that
is a subtle but crucial difference from Keats. Tennyson is both inside and outside the boundaries of natural description as defined
by his predecessors; therefore, he feels a sense of aesthetic estrangement that gets translated into the description itself. Robert Bernard
Martin speaks of the scene in this poem as the image of Mariana's
"deserted state."[25] The scene also images Tennyson's "deserted state,"
his sense of exile from the very traditions he wishes to return to.
The form of the landscape becomes the form of the poet's
melancholia.

In Tennyson's ironic transformation of pastoral melancholy in
"Mariana," the *locus amoenus* (here, the farm) fails to provide the
respite from everyday suffering that Rosenmeyer and Poggioli describe as characteristic of the genre.[26] Instead, retirement to the
pleasance is both the embodiment and the cause of Mariana's suffering. In a sense, "Mariana" is about the retirement theme gone
bad. Tennyson here reverses the laments of displacement and disinheritance from the land found, for example, in Virgil's *Eclogues*.
The Virgilian singer often laments exile from home (as Meliboeus
does in the first *Eclogue*). Paradoxically, Mariana laments not this
type of exile, but the fact that she is bound to home. The *locus
amoenus* has turned into a place of entrapment. The difference is
one of community. The Virgilian singer laments not simply the
loss of the farm but the loss of the family and friends associated
with it, as he goes into exile. Mariana, too, laments the loss of a
loved one, but his refusal to return transforms the pastoral retreat
into Mariana's place of exile. Moreover, she becomes a type for the
poet who also feels no longer at home in tradition. In turning the
pastoral retreat into the place of exile, Tennyson is acknowledging
the extent to which he is an exile from the poetic traditions that
the pastoral retreat embodies.

The use of the refrain in "Mariana" produces a similar effect.
Ricks says the "refrains tell of the passing of time – they kill time."[27]
He goes on to quote from an article written in 1831 by W. J. Fox:

The poem takes us through the circuit of four-and-twenty hours of this dreary life. Through all the changes of the night and day she has but one feeling, the variation of which is only by different degrees of acuteness and intensity in the misery it produces; and again and again we feel, before its repetition, the coming of the melancholy burthen.[28]

The refrain is integral to the evocation of Mariana's state of mind. As Martin Dodsworth has argued, repetition in Tennyson's poetry, including refrains such as this one, emphasizes the human figure's isolation from the surrounding scene and also the poet's distance from that human figure.[29] The present discussion of refrain will start from a different perspective. Theocritus frequently uses the refrain as a poetic device in the *Idylls*, and Virgil uses refrain in the eighth *Eclogue*. Paul Turner suggests that the refrain in "Mariana" stems from Tennyson's "Leonine Elegiacs" but also from Theocritus's *Idyll* II.[30] If Tennyson is drawing upon the classic pastoral idyll in his use of the refrain, then the device becomes yet another key to the poet's relation to the pastoral melancholy tradition.

In a later chapter, we will see that Tennyson's use of the Theocritean idyll in one of the songs from *The Princess* is related to Tennyson's exploration of contemporary feminist themes and the female rejection of domesticity. Something like this is at work in "Mariana," as well. The transformation of the pastoral retreat into the decaying farm is a sign not only of Mariana's despair and sense of desertion but of her active rejection of traditional ideas of home. The quality of active protest inheres also in her refrain. This in turn has bearing on Tennyson's poetics of melancholy; just as Mariana transforms home in the traditional sense, Tennyson transforms the poetic conventions of the traditional pastoral idyll. Mariana is unwilling to accept the bucolic retreat without protest. She is suffering from love-melancholy, but there is an element of parody in it.

> She only said, 'My life is dreary,
> He cometh not,' she said;
> She said, 'I am aweary, aweary,
> I would that I were dead!'

The refrain goes beyond the pastoral love lament or pastoral elegy in its exaggerated longing for death, a longing for death that is the result not simply of her abandonment but of her rejection of tradition in the form of the retreat or "home." This leads to her sense of exile within tradition, and to her awareness that she has no alternative tradition to look toward. Of course, Tennyson here, as in *The Princess*, has mixed feelings about the feminist wish to break with tradition. The refrain also works as a criticism of Mariana, in that it suggests her unwillingness to pursue actively other possibilities, to move away from the dependence on the lover who will never return. The refrain is the figural representation in language of her idée fixe. What is ironic about Mariana's relation to pastoral melancholy as a tradition is her sense of being outside the conventions and yet trapped by them all the same. She does not believe in them, but she is doomed to repeat them.

Such is also Tennyson's situation as a poet. Tennyson has always been viewed as a poet drawn to the major traditions of Western literature. But the fact that he is a very traditional poet in many ways, should not blind us to the tensions within his relation to tradition, nor to how those tensions lead to poetic innovation. His development and transformation of pastoral melancholy (as here in "Mariana") offer a paradigm for his troubled sense that the great traditions are in the past, and while he can look back to them with longing and nostalgia, just as Mariana looks back to her lover, they will never return. In this sense, despite his traditionalism, Tennyson is not a part of the textual community to which he alludes, and his poetry becomes a melancholy commentary on his very sense of exile from the literature out of which his own poetry originates. Repetition and refrain in "Mariana" have to do with Tennyson's compulsion to act out again and again the scenes of the poet's suffering. One one level, these scenes are the poetic texts that lie like a palimpsest beneath his own text. The pastoral landscape is many-layered. There is the realism of description, the concreteness of detail, that we find in Keats. Beneath this there is the allegorization of melancholy that goes back to eighteenth-century poetic practice, and even earlier to Renaissance allegory: Mariana as the displaced figure of personified Melancholy, Warton's "goddess of the tearful eye." But behind the "literal" representation of the landscape that owes its debts to the English Romantics, and behind the forced rhetorical allegory of the earlier melancholy tradition, there is a kind of poetic thought that is different from both of these modes. Mariana's landscape of melancholy and Mariana's refrain are types for Tennyson's highly self-conscious poetic practice.

Mariana's inability to stem the transformation of the landscape from one of abundance to desolation is the very problem Tennyson faces in his use of pastoral melancholy itself. In addition, Mariana's refrain suggests the stifling repetition that the poet fears. Her inability to break free of her obsession with the lover who will never return (in other words, to break free of the past) is analogous to the poet's concern about this danger in his relation to the poetic texts of the past that have shaped his own voice. Mariana's obsessional repetition constitutes her denial that she is the creator of her own suffering. She displaces her responsibility onto her absent lover. Unwilling to acknowledge this responsibility, her voice says the same words over and over: she cannot say anything new. This is what Tennyson fears as he uses the conventions of the pastoral and melancholy traditions. The return to the past is a source of power, a landscape of poetic abundance, but it is a past of which the poet can never be a part; instead, he is apart from it. The isolation from the past and the return to it can become mere repetition which is desolating. In this sense, Mariana has fallen prey to the pattern of desolation that Tennyson fears for his own poetry. Mariana has created her landscape of melancholy but now it entraps her. The pastoral love lament, which in its classical guise was meant to ease the singer's suffering, is now the very form in language of her entrapment.

If, however, Mariana is, in one sense, an image of what Tennyson fears in using the conventions of poetic tradition, in another sense, she is an image of how he may free himself from potential entrapment in worn-out literary forms. Mariana is defined by certain conventions of pastoral such as the landscape and the refrain, but she also actively works to redefine those same conventions; thus, Mariana is a type for the work of the poet. As the farm decays around her, we realize this occurs because she refuses to maintain it. Yet her refusal in itself is a form of creation. She is the creator of her pastoral landscape because her vision of it is highly self-conscious and highly selective (just as Tennyson's vision of tradition is):

> She could not look on the sweet heaven,
>   Either at morn or eventide.
> After the flitting of the bats,
>   When thickest dark did trance the sky,
>   She drew her casement-curtain by,
> And glanced athwart the glooming flats.

We observe that the landscape can offer the sight of the "sweet heaven," but she is unable or unwilling to see it. There is a large element of volition in the way she perceives the landscape. In this stanza, there is a traditional landscape of melancholy, but it is "framed" (a very common device in Tennyson's poetry, and, logically enough, in the Theocritean idyll). The emphasis is on her creation of the scene through her selective vision, through her active disruption of the continuity of the landscape: "She drew her casement curtain by / And glanced athwart the glooming flats." Critics often speak of Mariana's passivity, but the verbs here are active; furthermore, by placing her beside the casement and by having her view the landscape through the window, Tennyson is emphasizing the ideas of perspective and framing, with all the choices and limitations these ideas imply. Mariana consciously limits herself. There is the implication here that her melancholy is self-created, is perhaps the conscious acting out of a conventional attitude. If Mariana is a substitute figure for the poet, it is possible that Tennyson sees himself as acting out a conventional attitude also. He is consciously choosing to echo the conventions of the poetry of melancholy and wondering about the extent to which these conventions undermine the authenticity of his poetic voice. The sense that the poetic voice in "Mariana" may only be adopting a self-conscious pose, as Mariana herself does, is one of the secondary subjects pursued by the poem.

The early poem "Mariana" affords a paradigm for certain transformations of pastoral and melancholy poetry that look ahead to new directions that English poetry will take after Tennyson. One passage from "Mariana" is exemplary of two of these directions:

> All day within the dreamy house,
>   The doors upon their hinges creaked;
> The blue fly sung in the pane; the mouse

> Behind the mouldering wainscot shrieked,
> Or from the crevice peered about.
> Old faces glimmered through the doors,
> Old footsteps trod the upper floors,
> Old voices called her from without.

The passage is a proleptic model for two directions that the modern poet will take to represent his estrangement from society and from the community of texts that constitute poetic tradition. As Wimsatt and several other critics have pointed out, certain types of poetic structures and imagery in Tennyson look ahead to the symbolic method of Eliot.[31] This passage is a good example. The poet uses words and images to evoke moods that are, paradoxically, beyond language; moreover, the surreal juxtaposition of incongruous and jarring images – the "blue fly"; the mouse; the spectral figures and voices – will be developed by Eliot in such poems as *The Waste Land*. Hardy is the other direction toward which the passage points. Like this passage from "Mariana," much of Hardy's poetry involves the representation of landscape and external world as the forms that both contain and signify the past. Many of his poems describe objects that have been worn down through human use and through the passing of time itself. One other observation is worth noting: this moment in "Mariana" is one in which the country house (a topos related to the pastoral idyll and the georgic) begins to fall apart. Many of Hardy's poems, and even some of Eliot's, have roots in the pastoral conventions that Tennyson is exploring here.

The passage from "Mariana" serves as a fitting conclusion to our discussion of the poem because it looks ahead to new traditions and also back to old ones. The decaying house, with its strange juxtaposition of animals, objects, and sounds, reveals the types of discontinuity and fragmentation of conventions that are a sign of the poet's estrangement from the community of texts that embody those conventions in the poetry of the past. The old sounds here are sounds of the past, but they are now the cause of Mariana's (and the poet's) estrangement, rather than a source of assurance. What the passage figures is the profound separation between Mariana and the house, and between Tennyson and the "old voices" of the poetry of the past. The "old voices" are the source of the poet's creativity but also of his melancholy. These are the voices of pastoral melancholy that ultimately go back to Virgil and Theocritus.

One of the principal thematic sources of melancholy in Tennyson's poetry is love. Important criticism has been written on the social and biographical roots of Tennyson's fascination with the difficulties of love; the unhappy affair with Rosa Baring has been seen as the impetus for some of Tennyson's best work on the aberrations of personality in the throes of love.[32] In such poems as "Locksley Hall" and *Maud*, Tennyson represents love-melancholy in distinctly Victorian terms: here the poet emphasizes the social impediments to love and marriage in Victorian society, and he explores the abnormal states of mind (including melancholia) that thwarted love can produce. Tennyson views the latter concern in these poems in the light of Victorian society's renewed interest in the medical and psychological explanations for such states. However, there is another type of poem in Tennyson that deals with love-melancholy in ways that are more closely associated with poetic traditions of the past. Love-melancholy has always been a major theme in the melancholy tradition in English literature: Burton devotes an entire book in the *Anatomy* to it, and throughout the seventeenth and eighteenth centuries, the love-lament was one strand in the large tradition of melancholy poetry. The pastoral love-lament can be traced to such classical writers as Ovid, Virgil, and Theocritus.

In a number of Tennyson's poems, the poet brings together the tradition of pastoral love poetry in English with classical themes, and the pastoral love-lament of the Greek and Latin idyll. The poem "Œnone" is one example of Tennyson's use of a classical story involving the theme of love and of the classical pastoral love-lament. "Œnone" is marred by Tennyson's lapses into didactic moralizing in several passages, passages where the poet's sophisticated distance from his materials collapses. The poem has also been derided as being overly Keatsian in its sensuousness. In his critical review of the 1833 *Poems*, Bulwer-Lytton spoke of "Œnone" and

"The Hesperides" as "of the best Cockney classic and Keatsian to the marrow."[33] Even as sympathetic a student of Keats's influence on Tennyson as George H. Ford remarks on the "diffuseness" of the poem as being comparable to early Keats: "We find the same difficulty in tracing out Endymion's feelings for Diana amidst the luxuriant settings of Keats's poem as we do in following Œnone's lament against the background of the vale of Ida. Both are suffused in the pictorial, 'like bees in their own sweetness drown'd.'"[34] The influence of Keats in 'Œnone' is undeniable, but a number of Tennyson's literary debts in the poem lie elsewhere.

Over twenty years ago, Paul Turner in "Some Ancient Light on Tennyson's 'Œnone'" showed the extent to which the poem is modeled on classical sources and pointed out Tennyson's specific echoes and allusions to these sources. The poem is a pastoral love-lament based primarily on Œnone's epistle in Ovid's *Heroides*. Tennyson also drew upon passages from Theocritus's *Idylls* and Virgil's *Eclogues*. However, the poem is not simply an idyllic medley or pastiche of classical forms and imagery.[35] It is an investigation of the modern poet's ("modern" here means Victorian) relation to those forms and images. The poem is highly relevant to this general argument about Tennyson and the poetics of melancholy, not simply because it contains a depiction of love-melancholy, but because Tennyson here explores the nature of the Ovidian epistle, the Theocritean idyll, and the pastoral tradition from the vantage point of the Romantic and post-Romantic poetic tradition in England: he explores how these forms constitute models for the modern poet and are simultaneously forms of limitation to the modern imagination. Such forms exact demands on the poet's desire for original creation. Paul Turner suggests this critical perspective when he says "Œnone" "is a distillation not of life but of literature. . . . Tennyson's reactions to poetry were unusually intense, and such reactions form the chief subject matter of 'Œnone.'"[36]

Tennyson bases "Œnone" on the classic story of the Judgment of Paris. Having to choose between Here, Athene, and Aphrodite, Paris gives the golden apple to the fairest. He chooses Aphrodite and wins Helen. Tennyson, like Ovid, decides to present the story from the perspective of Œnone, the nymph whom Paris abandons for Helen. In Ovid's *Heroides*, Œnone's epistle is a love-lament that gives her response to the loss of Paris and to the fatal choice that he makes. It is, therefore, fitting that Tennyson opens his poem with the traditional setting of the pastoral love-lament:

> There lies a vale in Ida, lovelier
> Than all the valleys of Ionian hills.
> The swimming vapour slopes athwart the glen,
> Puts forth an arm, and creeps from pine to pine,
> And loiters, slowly drawn. On either hand
> The lawns and meadow-ledges midway down
> Hang rich in flowers, and far below them roars
> The long brook falling through the cloven ravine
> In cataract after cataract to the sea.
> Behind the valley topmost Gargarus
> Stands up and takes the morning: but in front
> The gorges, opening wide apart, reveal
> Troas and Ilion's columned citadel,
> The crown of Troas.

Tennyson bases his scene here on Paris's description of the setting of the judgment in his letter to Helen in the *Heroides*:

> There is a place in the woody vales of midmost Ida, far from
> trodden paths and covered over with pine and ilex. . . . From here,
> reclining against a tree, I was looking forth upon the walls and lofty
> roofs of the Dardanian city, and upon the sea. . . . [37]

Ovid begins the description with the valley and closes it with the view of Troy (in between are two lines describing flocks of animals grazing on the grass). This compression of description gives way in Tennyson's "Œnone" to a more elaborately detailed picture. Turner ascribes the additions to Tennyson's wish to make the setting even "lovelier."[38] Turner's use of quotation marks here suggests that this is simply word-painting, perhaps the indulgence in Keatsian sensuousness.

If we look closely at Tennyson's additions, however, we observe that he is doing something different and more interesting than mere word-painting. We observed how, in "Mariana," Tennyson "defamiliarizes" the landscape. Tennyson creates a similar sense of estrangement in the first verse paragraph of "Œnone." He effects this estrangement of the landscape in part by his use of pathetic fallacy—a type of figurative language used with great frequency by Tennyson. There is nothing in Ovid's description like the "swimming vapour." Tennyson describes the mists in human terms: he emphasizes the eerily human aspect of the natural scene through words like "loiters," "creeps," "puts forth." The mists are alive with activity: the vapor is "swimming" and "slopes athwart the glen." The Victorian poet replaces the clarity and economy of Ovid's description of the scene (an example of the Ovidian *locus amoenus*) with a more lushly descriptive style that fuses precision of detail with what can best be described as a kind of visionary strangeness. At least one aspect of this style is the result of the influence of Keats. The richness is Keatsian, but the strangeness is not.

Douglas Bush says the difference between Tennyson and Keats is one of style and feeling:

> If we turn to "Œnone" after "Endymion," we are aware at once of Tennyson's cool and conscious artistic detachment; even where Keats is writing badly, the intensity may be mawkish and uncontrolled, but it is intensity, and he seldom fails to apprehend myth with warm human sympathy. Tennyson's sympathy partly evaporates in a concern for style.[39]

Another way of looking at this distinction, however, is to see Tennyson's concern here as that of a poet with the idea of genre conventions—myth, allegory, pastoral melancholy—rather than with the emotions and feelings usually associated with these conventions. Tennyson is interested in the idea of the pastoral love-lament as a set of poetic conventions (forms and tropes). Thus, his concern for style has less to do with an absence of feeling than with an active interrogation of the poet's relation to tradition. Tennyson's "artistic detachment" can be interpreted, from another perspective, as his sense of estrangement from tradition. The visionary strangeness of nature in this opening scene of "Œnone" is the result of Tennyson's use of the pastoral idyll as a group of conventions with which he can no longer have complete emotional affinity. The language of artifice, the heavy reliance on pathetic fallacy, is the figurative expression for the poet's sense of the artifice that inheres in his relation to the past texts upon which he draws. Tennyson elaborates on Ovid's scene of the Judgment of Paris not simply to make a lovelier picture, but to emphasize the scene as a picture, to emphasize the scene as a framing device. In describing the setting of the judgment, Tennyson takes fourteen lines, Ovid six. The circumlocution is intentional on Tennyson's part. Tennyson opens up a space through language between the intitial naming of the landscape—"There lies a vale in Ida"—and the closing perspective on Troy—"the gorges, opening wide apart, reveal / Troas and Ilion's columned citadel, / The crown of Troas." The framing device serves to distance both poet and reader from the emotional utterance of Œnone that follows. It is an example of what Martin Dodsworth calls Tennyson's distancing "himself from the morbidity of his subject." As Dodsworth says, "The excellence of 'Œnone' lies in the internal consistency that enables us . . . to stand outside it and see the heroine for what she is."[40]

In the first stanza of "Œnone," then, Tennyson is opening up a space through language, framing the story, emphasizing the poet's distance from Œnone's emotion. The frame is a standard device of the Theocritean idyll, one that Tennyson uses frequently. The device suggests detachment from the subject matter, but in Tennyson's case it reveals something else as well. When Tennyson uses the frame at the beginning of "Œnone," it indicates not simply the creation of distance from Œnone through language, but a distance from language itself. Conventional types of language and imagery become the subject that Tennyson examines in a detached way through the space of the frame; furthermore, this framing and detachment suggests a certain lack of ease on the poet's part before the conventional language and imagery he is using in the passage. In a number of ways, the representations of nature in "Œnone" have much to tell us about Tennyson's complex relation to the traditions of pastoral and melancholy poetry. Indeed, in this opening description in "Œnone," we can observe types of language and imagery that have affinities with eighteenth- and early nineteenth-century pastoral melancholy as well as with Ovid and Theocritus. The richly detailed description goes back to Keats, but also further back to the lesser poets of the eighteenth century:

> . . . . here vine-clad hills
> Lay forth their purple store, and sunny vales

In prospect vast their level laps expand,
Amid whose beauties glistering Athens tow'rs.
Tho' thro' the blissful scenes Ilissus roll
His rage-inspiring flood, whose winding marge
The thick-wove laurel shades; tho' roseate Morn
Pour all her splendours on th' empurpled scene;
. . . .
He views the piles of fall'n Persepolis
In deep arrangement hide the darksome plain.[41]

(251–62)

This is from Thomas Warton's "The Pleasures of Melancholy" (1745). In the ornate blank verse, the richly adjectival descriptions, and the imagery of sublime, distant perspectives, we see the connection with the opening of "Œnone." When we also acknowledge Warton's great debt to Milton here, we can then note that Tennyson is not only drawing upon Theocritus, Ovid, and the classical idyll, but upon the line of English pastoral melancholy that goes from Keats, to the eighteenth-century descriptive poets, back to Milton. The development of pastoral melancholy from Milton to Warton and then to Keats is a complex one involving many important changes. Behind Milton's ornate style and landscape descriptions lies the rigorous moral vision of his Christianity. In Warton (midway into the eighteenth century) the moral and religious context of natural description begins to recede, as Eleanor Sickels points out, to be replaced by an artificial and abstract representation of nature that indulges in sentimentalism.[42] Warton is part of a shift from seventeenth- and eighteenth-century neoclassicism to late eighteenth- and early nineteenth-century Romanticism, a shift that has been described as a period of sentiment and sensibility. This is classicism in its decadent stage, or Romanticism in its infancy. Warton's representation of landscape and its concomitant melancholy has neither the simple economy of the Theocritean or Ovidian landscape, nor the grandeur of the sublime in Milton or the Romantic poets; here the descriptions of nature are merely the form of an attenuated cultivation of sentiment. This type of description has implications for Tennyson's detachment from the conventions of pastoral melancholy. But another example, from James Thomson's *The Seasons* (1730), will make the contrast even clearer:

> Still let me pierce into the midnight Depth
> Of yonder Grove, of wildest largest Growth:
> That, forming high in Air a woodland Quire,
> Nods o'er the Mount beneath. At every Step,
> Solemn, and slow, the Shadows blacker fall,
> And all is awful listening Gloom around.
> These are the haunts of Meditation. . . . [43]
>   (*Summer*, 11.516–22)

The pastoral melancholy of Thomson and Warton signals the new emphasis on the solitary figure in a desolate scene that is a departure from seventeenth-century English pastoral, but it also suggests the increasing artificiality of the form. The conventions are beginning to rigidify into didactic abstractions. While the Romantics drew upon this growing sense of withdrawal and solitude in mid- and late-eighteenth-century pastoral, they struggled against artifice and false sentiment. Tennyson, however, as different as he is from Thomson or Warton, is interested in what happens to the conventions of pastoral melancholy when the artifice of those conventions has become patent. Thomson and Warton represent the beginnings of that problem in the history of pastoral melancholy. The point is not that Tennyson, in his setting the scene for Œnone's love-lament, drew directly upon these poets, but that he was highly conscious of the extent to which the writing of nature had become artificial in such poets (and even, in certain ways, in the romantics), and that his retreat into a perspective of detachment (as through the device of the frame) is both the outcome of and the response to his awareness of this development.

The difference between Tennyson's association of landscape and melancholy in "Œnone," and their association in Thomson and Warton rests in the following: in Thomson and Warton, there is no critical distance between the poetic voice, the scene, and the melancholy mood; in Tennyson the distance among these three elements is enormous. We can see the distinction by noting how, in "Œnone," Tennyson subtly modulates from the poet's opening frame description to Œnone's melancholy lament:

>   Hither came at noon
> Mournful Œnone, wandering forlorn
> Of Paris, once her playmate on the hills.

Her cheek had lost the rose, and round her neck
Floated her hair or seemed to float in rest.
She, leaning on a fragment twined with vine,
Sang to the stillness, till the mountain-shade
Sloped downward to her seat from the upper cliff.

   'O mother Ida, many-fountained Ida,
Dear mother Ida, harken ere I die.
For now the noonday quiet holds the hill:
The grasshopper is silent in the grass:
The lizard, with his shadow on the stone,
Rests like a shadow, and the winds are dead.
The purple flower droops: the golden bee
Is lily-cradled: I alone awake.
My eyes are full of tears, my heart of love,
My heart is breaking, and my eyes are dim,
And I am all aweary of my life.'

W. David Shaw says, "The impersonal descriptive poet of the
proem does not know how the more personal sequel will develop."[44]
This is the measure of his distance from his subject. But the interesting thing about "Œnone" is the way the language of Œnone's
monologue also negates the possibility of mere sentimentality, the
bane of eighteenth-century pastoral melancholy. In the two stanzas quoted above, there are aspects to the language which distance
Œnone both from the landscape she describes and from her own
emotion. Paul Turner has shown that this passage is densely packed
with classical echoes and allusions: Tennyson uses phrases and images from Ovid, Virgil, Bion, and Theocritus in the passage. Turner
suggests that the description of her face combines Bion's description of the dying Adonis, "the rose leaves his lips," with Virgil's
description of Aeneas's glimpse of Dido in Hell, "aut videt aut
vidisse putat" (he sees or fancies he has seen), and with Ovid's
description of Cassandra in the *Heroides* as "diffusis comis" ("with
her hair all over the place"). Turner says, "All three expressions are
combined to describe Œnone."[45]

Her cheek had lost the rose, and round her neck
Floated her hair or seemed to float in rest.

              (11.17–18)

The allusions make Œnone a figure constituted by poetic convention instead of a "real person." This ironically qualifies any potential indulgence, on the part of the reader, in sentimental emotionalism about her plight. In addition, the sense of artifice that inheres in the manner in which her identity is constituted produces a distance between Œnone as a figure and the emotion she expresses. Another example of this can be found in the refrain—"O mother Ida, many-fountained Ida, / Dear mother Ida, harken ere I die"—that Turner suggests is derived from Theocritus's *Idyll* II. Dodsworth says, "The monotony of the often-heard refrain is an equivalent for the excessive feelings to which Œnone gives expression."[46] There is much sense in this idea, but one can argue, as Dodsworth does elsewhere in the same essay, that the monotony of the refrain is not the equivalent for the feelings, but is a way of ironically qualifying them, by virtue of the artifice and distance produced by the device of the refrain itself. In this light, the refrain is yet another example of how Tennyson undercuts emotion by means of the highly conscious use of poetic conventions.

There is one more classical allusion in the above-quoted passage from "Œnone" that we should look at. Tennyson closes Œnone's introduction in the second stanza with the following image: "till the mountain-shade / Sloped downward to her seat from the upper cliff." Turner points to the final line of Virgil, *Eclogue* I: "maioresque cadunt altis de montibus umbrae" (longer shadows fall from the mountain heights).[47] In Virgil's first *Eclogue*, Meliboeus has been evicted from his farm. Tityrus offers him lodging for the night, but the image of the "taller shadows" suggests the somber future that Meliboeus will face as an exile from his home. The image from Virgil is an apt one for Œnone's sense of abandonment and also for the impending troubles that will fall on the classical world as a result of Paris's choice. However, Tennyson's use of the image functions in another way, as well. As a "quoted" image from the classical tradition, the falling shadows create a sense of distance between Œnone and the landscape, just as the Theocritean refrain creates a sense of distance between her and her emotions. Like Meliboeus, Œnone has become an exile in the landscape that had been home:

> ". . . I will rise and go
> Down into Troy, and ere the stars come forth

> Talk with the wild Cassandra, for she says
> A fire dances before her, and a sound
> Rings ever in her ears of armed men.
> What this may be I know not, but I know
> That, wheresoe'er I am by night and day,
> All earth and air seem only burning fire."

The austere dignity of these lines takes the reader far away from the effusive emotion that mars earlier passages in her monologue, and from the potential sentimentality in the opening descriptive frame. It is a measure of the poem's irony that it is Œnone herself and the language she speaks that create the necessary distance. Œnone's sense of distance from both her emotions and the landscape is analogous to Tennyson's sense of detachment from the materials of the poem. But rather than seeing this as simply a withdrawal into a preoccupation with style, as Bush does, we may view this distance as the very form that his relation to traditions of pastoral melancholy takes. "Œnone" is one early example of Tennyson's creation of a new language of pastoral idyll. The poet brings about this achievement, in part, by "quoting" or manipulating classical sources and examples of the tradition of the romantic picturesque. As with the Theocritean idyll, which is the primary model for this form, Tennyson's new language of pastoral always contains within it a subtle but abiding sense of melancholy.

"The Lotos-Eaters" is pastoral melancholy in the state of decadence. It contains many of the conventional topoi of melancholy and pastoral poetry: the retirement theme; the death theme; the complaint of life; the pastoral retreat; the opposition between reality and pleasure, work and play; the freedom of the retreat; the sense of nostalgia. Unlike "Mariana" and "Œnone," however, this poem does not directly draw upon the classical idyll as a source. The poem takes its start from the *Odyssey*, Book IX:

> ". . . on the tenth day we landed
> in the country of the Lotus-Eaters, who live on a flowering

food, and there we set foot on the mainland, and fetched water
and my companions soon took their supper there by the fast
    ships.
But after we had tasted of food and drink, then I sent
some of my companions ahead, telling them to find out
what men, eaters of bread, might live here in this country.
I chose two men, and sent a third with them, as a herald.
My men went on and presently met the Lotus-Eaters,
nor did these Lotus-Eaters have any thought of destroying
our companions, but they only gave them lotus to taste of.
But any of them who ate the honey-sweet fruit of lotus
was unwilling to take any message back, or to go
away, but they wanted to stay there with the lotus-eating
people, feeding on lotus, and forget the way home. I myself
took these men back weeping, by force, to where the ships
    were. . . . "[48]

(11.83–98)

Out of this material, Tennyson created his exploration of the
pleasurable melancholy of complete isolation and withdrawal from
the world, and of the undeniable attractions (as well as the dangers) that such withdrawal entails for the poet. Critics have interpreted the poem's significance in a variety of ways. Arthur J. Carr
says, "Exactly because it is managed as an episode in the return of
Ulysses to the responsibilities of Ithaca, Tennyson could follow
very far the impulses to 'slothful ease' and vague erotic happiness."[49]
On the other hand, Bush has little good to say of it: "'The Lotos-
Eaters' in its total effect is an incomparably pretty account of spiritual
disintegration."[50] W. David Shaw notes the mariners' awareness of
"the essential anguish of being in time," and says the poem is about
the "failure to take the lessons of the wavering world outside, the
world of quick decay and change, back into the timeless land of
the Lotos."[51] Finally, Tennyson's biographer, Robert Bernard Martin, views the poem as one that belongs with a group of early
poems in which there is a conflict between the "external world"
and the "world of the imagination." In Martin's view, in the early
poems the world of pleasure and imagination wins out against Tennyson's moral stance.[52] This reading is borne out by Alan Grob's
analysis of the revisions Tennyson made from the 1832 edition to
the 1842 edition. Grob suggests that in the early version of the

poem, Lotos-Land is presented as the place of isolation necessary for poetic creation, but Tennyson adds two passages in the later version that serve as moral criticism of this view of art.[53] What makes "The Lotos-Eaters" such an interesting poem is Tennyson's ability to refrain from making distinct moral judgments, and his willingness to explore the legitimate value of Lotos-Land as well as its dangers.

In addition to its exploration of the possibilities and failures inherent in certain types of moral and aesthetic values, "The Lotos-Eaters" is about pastoral melancholy as a group of literary conventions. At the outset, we can observe that the land of the lotos-eaters is a variant of the traditional pastoral retreat:

> 'Courage!' he said, and pointed toward the land,
> 'This mounting wave will roll us shoreward soon.'
> In the afternoon they came unto a land
> In which it seeméd always afternoon.
> All round the coast the languid air did swoon,
> Breathing like one that hath a weary dream.
> Full-faced above the valley stood the moon;
> And like a downward smoke, the slender stream
> Along the cliff to fall and pause and fall did seem.

The poet creates his landscape through repetition. One observes the near chiasmus in lines 3 and 4: the mariners reach the shore in the afternoon, but the land is a place "in which it seemed always afternoon." The rhetorical structure as well as the temporal structure is tautological; it turns back upon itself. The syntactical organization here does not develop or grow, but simply represents at its end its own beginning. There is a pleasing sense of symmetry about such rhetorical structures, initially; but, as the poem progresses, this sense gives way to one of stagnation, not unlike that found in the repetitive structure of "Mariana." In addition, there is a quality of deceptiveness, of falsity, about the landscape. Tennyson's use of the word "seeméd" is a sign of that illusiveness. It is a very Spenserian word, which is appropriate because, as a number of critics have pointed out, the poem as a whole is very Spenserian (by way of Keats). Spenser frequently uses the word "seemed" and its variants in connection with the type of "good place" that masks its opposite. In such episodes, the word serves as a warning that the benign appearance of the natural scene contains within or behind it potentially evil and dangerous forces. Tennyson's use of the word in the opening description of this poem suggests that the land of the lotos-eaters may contain equally dangerous powers. At the very opening of "The Lotos-Eaters," then, nature is structured through language to be deceptive as well as tautological.

Spenser points toward a related aspect of the landscape of the lotos-eaters. *The Faerie Queene* contains numerous examples of the type of pastoral retreat that is negative in its easefulness and luxuriance, questionable in its morality. In "The Lotos-Eaters," Tennyson's language stresses this side of pastoral. The air is "languid" and "swoons" (examples, yet again, of the poet's heavy reliance on pathetic fallacy). The air is "breathing like one that hath a weary dream," a simile that emphasizes the anthropomorphism of nature. These images and figures of rhetoric help create the proper atmosphere, but their significance goes beyond mere atmospheric word-painting. The poet represents the ambivalent moral value that inheres in this type of pastoral scene and in this type of melancholy. Poggioli says the traditional pleasance of pastoral is a place of refreshment, replenishment, and renewal.[54] The pleasance of Lotos-Land is not one of renewal but of stifling repetition. In classical pastoral, the human figure goes to the retreat to feel the bond between man and nature, and also the difference between them. He goes to renew his sense of humanity. But the pastoral of the Lotos-Land is structured by tautological sameness, not difference. Time never changes; it is always the same. And man is not distinct from but the same as the organic life of the earth. This is not the way Theocritus structures the relation between man and landscape:

> Over our heads many poplars and loftily towering elm trees
> Soughed as they stirred in the breezes, while nearby the numinous water
> Laughed as it flowed from the cave of the nymphs with a metrical chatter,
> Whilst all about in the shadowy branches the smoky cicadas
> Worked at their chirruping—they had their labour cut out for them!
> Far off
> Out of the thick-set brambles the tree frog croaked in a whisper;

Linnets and larks were intoning their tunes, and the wooddove made
  moan.
Busy and buzzing, the bees hovered over the musical waters.
Everything exhaled an odour of bounteous summer and harvest.
Pears at our feet, also apples on every side in abundance
Rolled, and the branches were bowed to the earth with their burden
  of damsons.[55]

(11.134–44)

This is from *Idyll* VII. Rosenmeyer says the passage is atypical of
the economy and concision of the Theocritean *locus amoenus*, and
he types this a *locus uberrimus*. But the very abundance and lush-
ness of the scene bring it closer to what Tennyson is getting at in
"The Lotos-Eaters." For our purposes this can serve as a Theocritean
pleasance.[56] But ultimately how different it is from Lotos-Land.
The Theocritean breeze cools the forehead and stirs the trees to
life. Theocritus does use pathetic fallacy, sparingly, but only to convey the quickness and activity of the natural world, as in "the
numinous water / Laughed as it flowed." In Tennyson's poem, the
poet uses pathetic fallacy to express the passivity and languor of
nature, its decay and ultimate terminus in death. In "The Lotos-
Eaters," the human figures are submerged within and become identical with this languorous nature. In *Idyll* VII, the human figures
afford us the perspective on nature: there is a separation between
the human figures and the landscape that signifies the proper separation between human life and the organic life of nature – the two
are not identical. The people in the Theocritean landscape enjoy
an ease that is a respite from work but not an eternal escape from
it. As Rosenmeyer points out, there is a straightforwardness, a
kind of naiveté and innocence about the Theocritean landscape.[57]
This is rather different from the slightly insidious lure of desire and
pleasure in the land of the lotos.

Tennyson's rhetoric and syntax represent desire and pleasure in
"The Lotos-Eaters" as duplicitous. The pastoral retreat is tautological. It has no purpose outside of itself. The first stanza ends
as follows:

the slender stream
Along the cliff to fall and pause and fall did seem.

The stanza ends with the word "seem," emphasizing, as it did in line 4, that the appearance of the natural scene is deceptive. In the stanza's closure, the rhetorical structure and syntactic organization are, as with lines 3 and 4, that of repetition. In lines 3 and 4, there is the repetition of "afternoon" broken in the middle by "seemed." In line 9, there is the repetition of the word "fall" broken in the middle by "pause." The rhetorical elegance in conveying the sense of carefully interrupted movement, and the repetitions of line 9, contribute to the formal power of the verse but also to the troubling sense of artifice. The whole picture is too highly wrought. It creates a tension in the language that works against the mellifluous ease that supposedly characterizes the poem. "The Lotos-Eaters" is, as James Kincaid says, "a poem about release, the effect of which is to increase tension. . . . We are unable to resist the appeal of the mariners and equally unable to yield to it."[58]

There has always been a sense of artifice, of self-consciousness, in the pastoral idyll, as Rosenmeyer suggests in his study of Theocritus.[59] In Theocritus and Virgil, however, this artifice defuses tension. Contradictions tend to be worked out through patterns of nostalgia and desire, in ways that are poignantly human. In "The Lotos-Eaters," the poet does not work out contradictions this way, despite the heavily laden nostalgia and desire within the poem. The latter emotions here assume an inhuman form. Tennyson takes the sense of artifice to an extreme point that calls into question the values of pastoral itself. Another example of this language of artifice in the poem is Tennyson's use of the simile word "like." (The repetition of the phrase "like a downward smoke" in lines 8 and 10 is an instance of this.) To be "like" something is, obviously, not to be the thing itself. The poet's use of simile contributes to the sense of illusiveness about this landscape. At the same time, for one term in the comparison of a simile to be too much "like" the other term is equally delusive, since the two terms of comparison in a simile are not identical. The nature of simile in the poem leads to the even more troubling anthropomorphism and pathetic fallacy in the figuration of the scene, the ultimate implication of which is that man and nature are the same: "A land where all things always seemed the same!" The word "seemed" appears again, and in conjunction with "same." Turner suggests an echo of Lucretius here: "eadem sunt omnia semper" (all are always the same).[60] The phrase occurs in Book III of *De Rerum Natura* in the passage where Nature argues that life is not worth living and that death is the acceptable alternative. Likewise, pastoral nature in the land of the lotos-eaters does not renew the mariners' sense of humanity; it takes it away from them and puts them on the level of the non-conscious organic life that does not have to think or act or suffer, as men do. The desire expressed in the Choric Song is in its primary sense the desire to be like the natural scene itself.

> Lo! in the middle of the wood,
> The folded leaf is wooed from out the bud
> With winds upon the branch, and there
> Grows green and broad, and takes no care,
> Sun-steeped at noon, and in the moon
> Nightly dew-fed; and turning yellow
> Falls, and floats adown the air.
> Lo! sweetened with the summer light,
> The full-juiced apple, waxing over-mellow,
> Drops in a silent autumn night.
> All its allotted length of days,
> The flower ripens in its place,
> Ripens and fades, and falls, and hath no toil,
> Fast-rooted in the fruitful soil.

The leaf "takes no care" and the flower "hath no toil." In section 2 of the Choric Song, the singers ask, "All things else have rest: why should we toil alone?" The singers are either unaware or choose to ignore the implications of the comparison. Human beings, the comparison suggests, should be as inanimate, as passive, as lacking in consciousness, as the natural world. Further, the natural world is ultimately here an emblem for death itself. This view is a complete reversal of pastoral values. As Panofsky has shown in his discussion of the phrase "et in arcadia ego," death is a part of the pastoral world.[61] It is not, however, a wished-for end or a means of escape from responsibility. We recall the singer in Virgil *Eclogue* III: "o pueri (fugite hinc!), latet anguis in herba" (boys, flee from here; a snake lies in the grass). In the pastoral tradition, one cannot escape death, and while the retreat to the pleasance is where one mitigates sorrow and loss, the singers in Theocritus and Virgil never escape the human duties implied by these emotions. They may feel love-melancholy, nostalgia, or the pain of loss, but these emotions are not ends in themselves: their value lies in how they lead the singer back into the social community where humanity is fully realized. In "The Lotos-Eaters," the pleasance serves another purpose. Here the natural world itself causes melancholy, and it is melancholy of an alluring and destructive sort.

The melancholy in "The Lotos-Eaters" is related more to certain kinds of pastoral retreats found in Spenser than to those of Theocritus and Virgil. A number of critics have pointed out the strong echoes of Spenser in Tennyson's poem.[62] One echo is of Phaedria's floating island in Book II, Canto 6. The floating island is a false retreat of idleness and barren sensuality: here everything is "framed fit, / for to allure fraile mind to carelesse ease." Phaedria argues that the plants and flowers of nature do not struggle or work, so why should man? Spenser's counterargument here and throughout suggests that to give in to easy pleasure – and to abandon the heroic quest for the virtues which, ideally, make man God's representative on earth – implies a debasement of what it means to be human, and constitutes moral and imaginative death. This idea is made clear in one of the other key passages in Spenser to which Tennyson is indebted for his representation of Lotos-Land: Redcrosse's confrontation with Despair in Book I. Despair tries to persuade Redcrosse that suicide is not only acceptable but is part of God's plan, since "did not he all create / To die againe?" Despair's argument continues:

> Then do no further goe, no further stray,
>   But here lie downe, and to thy rest betake,
>   Th'ill to prevent, that life ensewen may.
>   For what hath life, that may it loved make,
>   And gives not rather cause it to forsake?
>   Fear, sicknesse, age, losse, labour, sorrow, strife,
>   Paine, hunger, cold, that makes the hart to quake;
>   And ever fickle fortune rageth rife,
> All which, and thousands mo do make a loathsome life.
>   (*The Faerie Queene*, I. 9. 44)

The ultimate significance of the Choric Song parallels the fallacious argument of Despair. Life is full of unhappiness and suffering, but nature in its passivity and acceptance of death shows man the way to escape. Furthermore, because decay and death in nature are part of God's plan, nature's end (that is, death) is, so the argument goes, therefore man's aim. It is both morally acceptable and wise to cultivate a death-like state.

"The Lotos-Eaters" is an ambivalent poem because the truth of the pastoral landscape is not disassociated from the allure of Spenserian despair. As James Kincaid remarks, "Despite all the negative indications, it is, at the same time, difficult to resist an appeal which is so shrewdly grounded in a comic impulse: the desire for peace and order."[63] The poem is both a condemnation of "mild-minded melancholy" and a qualified validation of it through pastoral song. The Choric Song is, in certain ways, analogous to the songs the shepherds sing in classical pastoral. One of Tennyson's concerns in "The Lotos-Eaters" is with what has happened to the pastoral idea in the language of modern poetry, and the melancholy in the poem is as much the result of his awareness of the limiting power of poetic conventions as it is a type of moral thematics (in this sense the poem is closely related to the aesthetic struggle in "The Palace of Art"). Part of this poem's ambivalence lies in the way Tennyson uses such conventions as the idea of pastoral song itself. We can observe that the impetus to pastoral song is quite different from early examples of the form. Here is how Virgil leads the singer into his song in *Eclogue* III:

> (Sing then, because we sit together on soft grass,
> and every field now, every tree is burgeoning;
> now woods are leafing, now the year is loveliest.)[64]

Here the natural world blooms with healthy growth, and the poet's song is the direct result of his pleasure in nature and friendship. In contrast, the Choric Song in Tennyson is a dark parody of pastoral inspiration. In Virgil, the pastoral song often celebrates nature as home – the natural scene and the singer's home are one and the same. Conversely, pastoral lament explores the loss of this home. In "The Lotos-Eaters," however, the pastoral celebration is not about home but about the impossibility of ever returning home. The song begins with the singers contemplating their "escape" within a pastoral scene that is not home but exile:

And all at once they sang, 'Our island home
Is far beyond the wave; we will no longer roam.'

The song aspires to the passive acceptance of melancholy nostalgia
of exile, a state of mind actively mourned in Virgil. In "The Lotos-
Eaters," Tennyson transforms the pastoral song that should celebrate
man's place in nature, into the celebration of his placelessness, of
nature as the place of exile. Virgilian melancholy involves deep feeling for home, community, loved ones (as in Aeneas's tears before
the pictures of the Trojan War on the walls of Carthage), but the
mild-eyed melancholy of the lotos-eaters is so indulgent in its feeling that one fears there really is no feeling there at all–emotion
is a narcotic like the lotos itself. Furthermore, the nature that gives
rise to pastoral song in Tennyson's poem is not a nature of burgeon-
ing growth and refreshing ease like that found in *Eclogue* III. Rather,
the poet represents nature in a language of beautiful but tired
decadence:

> There is sweet music here that softer falls
> Than petals from blown roses on the grass,
> Or night-dews on still waters between walls
> Of shadowy granite, in a gleaming pass;
> Music that gentlier on the spirit lies,
> Than tired eyelids upon tired eyes;
> Music that brings sweet sleep down from the blissful
>   skies.
> Here are cool mosses deep,
> And through the moss the ivies creep,
> And in the stream the long-leaved flowers weep,
> And from the craggy ledge the poppy hangs in sleep.

The metrical finesse, the skillful repetition of images and rhyme-
words, the gentle lyricism of sound should not deter us from confronting the song's sense. "Sweet sleep" means death, and this is
death's lullaby. Like Despair in Spenser, the singers of the Choric
Song present the passage from life to death as an attractive one.
However, the repetition and mellifluousness of the vowel sounds
and alliteration produce a cloying effect. As with the opening
description of Lotos-Land, the emphasis here is on the persistent
sameness of nature, in which life and death become identical.

Despite its surface attractions, the lyricism of this song is ultimately unappealing. The repetition of sounds in this pastoral song constitutes yet another example of how this is "A land where all things always seemed the same." The repetition of sounds does not, however, strengthen the argument of the Choric Song; rather, it serves to attenuate it. Tennyson's transformation of the traditional pastoral song is another example of how he uses poetic conventions to distance himself from the subject of his poems. His highly self-conscious use of traditional pastoral strategies and the changes he effects in these strategies contain a large degree of irony. In "The Lotos-Eaters," this irony distances and qualifies the melancholy nostalgia of the inhabitants of Lotos-Land. As elsewhere in his poetry, Tennyson here addresses the nature of melancholy nostalgia by means of poetic nostalgia that mocks itself (mocks in the sense that it is a double or imitation of nostalgia, and in the sense of its being Tennyson's ironic and darkly comedic knowledge of the limitations of melancholy both as emotion and as poetic strategy).

In terms of the Choric Song, part of the poetics of melancholy nostalgia in "The Lotos-Eaters" involves the very idea of sound itself. The attenuation of sound in the Choric Song weakens, as it were, the argument that the chorus sings. Here are the sounds Odysseus's sailors hear after they eat the enchanted fruit proffered by the lotos-eaters:

> to him the gushing of the wave
> Far far away did seem to mourn and rave
> On alien shores; and if his fellow spake,
> His voice was thin, as voices from the grave;
> And deep-asleep he seemed yet all awake,
> And music in his ears his beating heart did make.

The sounds of nature become distant and "alien," and the sounds of one's companions are "like voices from the grave." These sounds are "far far away." The phrase occurs often in Tennyson's poetry; it is the refrain of a late poem of the same title:

> What charm in words, a charm no words could give?
> O dying words, can Music make you live
> Far–far–away?

The phrase also occurs in the poet's description of the "passion of
the past" in "The Ancient Sage":

> 'Lost and gone and lost and gone!'
> A breath, a whisper–some divine farewell–
> Desolate sweetness–far and far away–

In Hallam Tennyson's *A Memoir* (I, 11), Tennyson is quoted as saying, "Before I could read I was in the habit on a stormy day of
spreading my arms to the wind and the words 'far far away' had
always a strange charm for me." Critics have devoted much attention to this important phrase. A. Dwight Culler discusses it in
terms of Tennyson's fascination for the significance of sounds and
his ideas about mystic unity. Culler remarks:

> Both by their form and by their meaning they suggest a world
> beyond life and death where the antinomies of this world will be
> reconciled. There, birth and death, joy and pain, the human and
> the divine, will be one, but how this will happen is as mysterious as
> the phrase itself. . . .[65]

The phrase "far far away" signifies a mystical state of mind the
poet was always striving for. In the context of "The Lotos-Eaters,"
however, the phrase bears looking at from a slightly different perspective. Indeed, it has something to tell us about the nature of
pastoral melancholy in Tennyson's early poetry. On the one hand,
the words "far far away" represent the aspect of pastoral that leads
to renewal. It is the aspect that one student of pastoral has traced
to the nostalgia for childhood, with its innocence and imagination.[66]
When Tennyson uses the words "far far away," he is always looking
back to childhood. However, these words also can suggest the
"desolate sweetness" not only of the loss of childhood, but of life
itself. This is the significance of the words in "The Lotos-Eaters."
The world becomes "far far away" to those who eat the lotos, because they have acquiesced to death itself:

> To muse and brood and live again in memory,
> With those old faces of our infancy
> Heaped over with a mound of grass,
> Two handfuls of white dust, shut in an urn of brass!

Memory broods over the dead, over the past that is "far far away," but not in the strains of elegy. The gentle sounds of their song indicate the singers' yielding to the pleasures of death:

> Death is the end of life; ah, why
> Should life all labour be?
> . . . .
> All things have rest, and ripen toward the grave
> In silence; ripen, fall and cease:
> Give us long rest or death, dark death, or dreamful ease.

The Choric Song fuses the pleasure principle and the death principle. The two become one and the same. In "The Lotos-Eaters," the phrase "far far away" signifies the longing for death, but to the extent that it represents and comments on the actual attenuation of sound and voice in this new "pastoral song," it also represents Tennyson's distance from the traditional elements of pastoral. Tennyson's dark irony here works through his bringing together elements of pastoral melancholy that go back through Keats, Spenser, Virgil, and Theocritus. But he embodies these elements in a language and style that, in a highly self-conscious way, are decadent. Behind the "mild-eyed melancholy" of the lotos-eaters lies Tennyson's melancholy recognition that the pastoral pleasance, if merely repeated as a trope, is a type of repetition that leads to poetic death. As Tennyson, in later poems, continued to explore the pastoral idyll form and melancholy as a mood and as a poetics, he would reject the dark and dreamful ease of poetic repetition and move further past conventions toward his own type of pastoral melancholy.

II

Myths of Exile: Tennyson's Poetry of Loss

PASTORAL MELANCHOLY TAKES MANY FORMS in Tennyson. One of the most interesting and successful forms occurs when he incorporates elements of pastoral within the recreation of a story from classical legend and myth. "Œnone" and "The Lotos-Eaters" are early examples of this confluence of forms and traditions. In these poems, Tennyson is less interested in exploring the uses of mythology as it relates to his poetics of melancholy than in exploring specific transformations of pastoral conventions, especially those conventions that deal with the attractions of the pastoral retreat and those that link the description of landscape to the psychology of the love-lament and the elegy. In later poems in which Tennyson draws upon mythology for his story, the poet becomes increasingly interested in how the idea of myth itself, and the modern artist's relation to myth, contribute to the representation of his melancholy disinheritance from tradition. The return to myth constitutes, in Tennyson's view, one type of exile from the poetry of the past.

Richard Jenkyns has described the peculiar sense of the "death of poetry" that had been felt by the Romantics but emerged most powerfully after the English Romantic poets had either died or withdrawn from the poetic fray. Referring to Victorian writers like Ten-

nyson, Ruskin, and Dickens, Jenkyns observes: "The distinctive
tone in English life which we call Victorian was set by men whose
characters were formed at a time when it seemed that English poetry had sunk into insignificance. This feeling, or the memory of
it, persisted a long time."[1] He goes on to observe Tennyson's acute
consciousness of the lackluster present and its meager literary achieve-
ments in the face of literature of the classical age. Jenkyns points,
as an example, to the frame of "Morte d'Arthur."[2] The poet, Everard
Hall, has decided to abandon his plan to write an epic on King
Arthur:

> Why take the style of those heroic times?
> For nature brings not back the Mastodon,
> Nor we those times; and why should any man
> Remodel models?

But this is precisely what Tennyson does again and again – he re-
models models; moreover, many of his finest poems are the result
of this process. As Douglas Bush observes:

> When Tennyson treats much the same subject in an ancient and in
> a modern setting he is almost invariably superior, greatly superior, in
> the former. The antique fable taps that authentic vein of his poetic
> inspiration, his classical memories; it limits the range of thought and
> allusion, forbids anything in the nature of modern realism, and
> compels concentration on the universal and more or less symbolic
> aspects of the theme.[3]

This is true of his use of classical subjects and classical poetic forms
in general, and is especially pertinent to his use of particular myths.
But it is not exactly the exclusion of the modern element, as Bush
appears to suggest, that makes for the success of his mythological
poems; rather it is the play or tension between realism and myth,
between modernity and tradition, that defines the unique power
of his achievement. Tennyson's treatment of mythology is sophisticated because he uses it to explore the relation of his modernity
to literary history, and his use of myth is melancholy because he
bears a profound awareness of what the modern poet qua modern
has lost and can never recover.

This sense of loss, of disinheritance, that underlies his treatment
of mythology is analogous to the melancholy nostalgia found in

his use of pastoral conventions, and not surprisingly, he often combines the two modes. Tennyson's awareness that his poetry of melancholy was closely related to the modern (i.e., Victorian) perspective on mythology was, however, not shared by all students of
mythology in the Victorian period; indeed, much of the Victorian
interest in classical mythology worked with a different set of as-
sumptions. There was a great renewal of interest in myth, but the
work being done on myth was often of a scientific or historicist
nature. Myths were understood to represent the childhood of man
or the origin of human history. In 1822, Hartley Coleridge would
speak of myths as follows: "That youth is flown for ever. We are
grown up to serious manhood, and are wedded to reality."[4] While
there was a renewal of interest in mythology during the period, the
myths themselves as presented to the Victorian reading public were
often bowdlerized, deprived of their power to represent ideas of
a violent or sexual nature. In his discussion of Victorian attitudes
toward Greek mythology, Frank Turner quotes two twentieth-
century students of the history of mythology who perceive a significant shift from the romantic period:

> If the Romantic reappraisal of myth included an affirmation of the
> Dionysian, the violent, the sexual, and the darkly fatalistic elements
> of myth, it therefore included within its appraisal the whole irra-
> tional side of myth. . . . But the Victorian revaluation of myth
> largely ignored or rejected this entire side of myth, and in filtering
> myth through a mesh of decorous and sunny gentility, robbed the
> subject of much of its seriousness, much of its dignity, much of its
> capacity to nourish tragedy. . . .[5]

The Victorians were rewriting myth and to do so involved choices
that reflected on their understanding of what it meant to be modern. We can cite a revealing comment by A. C. Bradley: "The problem is to reshape the material they give us, that it may express
ideas, feelings, experiences, interesting to us, in a form natural and
poetically attractive to us."[6] Bradley sees the problem as being suc-
cessfully dealt with by Tennyson in his poem "Ulysses," a poem,
in Bradley's view, both mythic and intensely modern. The reshap-
ing of myth, therefore, did not have to lapse into gentility; indeed,
there was another side to the Victorian attitude toward mythology, one which freed the imagination rather than limited it.

As James Kissane shows in his essay "Victorian Mythology," there was a struggle in the Victorian period between the scientific and historicist study of myth in terms of origins, on the one hand, and on the other, an aesthetic view in which myth is a highly organized and structured form that embodies the artistic imagination. In the latter view, one does not perceive myths as representing history or moral allegories.[7] Kissane points to the first two volumes of the *History of Greece* by George Grote as an example of the new attitude whereby myths are seen as "a special product of the imagination and feelings, radically distinct from history and philosophy."[8] In fact, much of the historical work devoted to myth at this time did not so much lessen the value of myth as shift that value from myth as a source for discovering the origins of human history to myth as an artistic form of great imaginative force that was, in a sense, ahistorical. Grote countered the scientific interest in origins with his emphasis on mythopoeia and the life of the mind. For Kissane the three great exemplars of the aesthetic approach to myth in the Victorian period are John Ruskin, John Addington Symonds, and Walter Pater. In *Studies of the Greek Poets* (1873), Symonds remarks, "The truth to be looked for in myths is psychological, not historical, aesthetic rather than positive."[9] Kissane points out that Symonds is intrigued by "the mingling of the natural and moral worlds" in mythology.[10] Myth, in Symonds words, is "Humanity defined upon the borderland of nature."[11] Kissane goes on to observe that, in *The Queen of Air* (1869), Ruskin argued for the universal spiritual value of classical myth as the expression of a good and noble people. But the most important discussion of the aesthetic value of myth for our purposes is that of Pater in *Greek Studies*.

Pater sees three aesthetic and spiritual stages within classical myth. The myth of Demeter and Persephone, he suggests, exemplifies these phases:

> There is first its half-conscious, instinctive or mystical, phase, in which, under the form of an unwritten legend, living from mouth to mouth, and with details changing as it passes from place to place, there lie certain primitive impressions of the phenomena of the natural world. We may trace it next in its conscious, poetical or literary, phase, in which the poets become the depositaries of the

vague instinctive product of the popular imagination, and handle it with a purely literary interest, fixing its outlines, and simplifying or developing its situations. Thirdly, the myth passes into the ethical phase, in which the persons and the incidents of the poetical narrative are realised as abstract symbols, because intensely characteristic examples, of moral and spiritual conditions.[12]

We find even more important analogues for Tennyson's use of mythology in two other areas of concern in Pater's essay on "Demeter and Persephone." The first is his emphasis on myth as a special kind of thinking in language, a type of language that bears comparison with the language Tennyson uses in his re-creation of myth. This bears as well on the language of Tennysonian pastoral. It has to do with an intensely close relation between meaning and image:

> The personification of abstract ideas by modern painters or sculptors, of wealth, of commerce, of health, for instance, shocks, in most cases, the aesthetic sense, as something conventional or rhetorical, as a mere transparent allegory, or figure of speech, which could please almost no one. On the other hand, such symbolical representations under the form of human persons, as Giotto's *Virtues* and *Vices* at Padua, or his *Saint Poverty* at Assisi, or the series of the planets in certain early Italian engravings, are profoundly poetical and impressive. They seem to be something more than mere symbolism and to be connected with some peculiarly sympathetic penetration on the part of the artist into the subjects he intended to depict. Symbolism intense as this, is the creation of a special temper, in which a certain simplicity, taking all things literally, *au pied de la lettre*, is united to a vivid pre-occupation with the aesthetic beauty of the image itself, the *figured* side of figurative expression, the *form* of the metaphor.[13]

Pater's comments get to the heart of Tennyson's interest in mythology (and his concern with the question of modernity in its relation to literary history). The aesthetic stance that is intensely literal and yet drawn back to a larger consideration of the form, the figurative nature of his language, the "penetration" of the artist into his subjects and yet the detachment too (as he sees his subjects also as symbols of abstract ideas), define not only the age of Giotto and the mythic imagination of the Greeks, but also the sensibility of Tennyson himself.

There is one more passage from Pater's essay that has relevance to our discussion of Tennyson's mythological poems. It deals specifically with the myth of Demeter and Persephone as it relates to the "romantic" side of the Greek mind. The passage is long but its pertinence to Tennyson's use of mythology justifies quotation in full:

> The "worship of sorrow," as Goethe called it, is sometimes supposed to have almost no place in the religion of the Greeks. Their religion has been represented as a religion of mere cheerfulness, the worship by an untroubled, unreflecting humanity, conscious of no deeper needs, of the embodiments of its own joyous activity. It helped to hide out of their sight those traces of decay and weariness of which the Greeks were constitutionally shy, to keep them from peeping too curiously into certain shadowy places, appropriate enough to the gloomy imagination of the middle age; and it hardly proposed to itself to give consolation to people who, in truth, were never "sick or sorry." But this familiar view of Greek religion is based on a consideration of a part only of what is known concerning it, and really involves a misconception, akin to that which underestimates the influence of the romantic spirit generally, in Greek poetry and art; as if Greek art had dealt exclusively with human nature in its sanity, suppressing all motives of strangeness, all the beauty which is born of difficulty, permitting nothing but an Olympian, though perhaps, somewhat wearisome calm. . . . [T]he legend of Demeter and Persephone, perhaps the most popular of all Greek legends, is sufficient to show that the "worship of sorrow" was not without its function in Greek religion; their legend is a legend made by and for sorrowful, wistful, anxious people; while the most important artistic monuments of that legend sufficiently prove that the Romantic spirit was really at work in the minds of the Greek artists, extracting by a kind of subtle alchemy, a beauty, not without the elements of tranquility, of dignity and order, out of a matter, at first sight painful and strange.[14]

The sorrow that Pater sees in the myth of Demeter and Persephone is one that Tennyson felt. Pater's analysis of the myth's blend of abstraction and realism, of figurative and literal language, defines an analogue for the form of language taken by Tennyson's poetics of melancholy. Classical mythology contained themes that held a perennial fascination for Tennyson: loss, religious doubt, the question of immortality. Classical myth contained an aesthetic characterized by penetration and detachment. This aesthetic suited Tennyson's troubled sense of disinheritance from tradition, and it contributed to his poetics of melancholy.

"Ulysses" is a turning point in Tennyson's development of a new idyll. It is also central to an understanding of Tennyson's treatment of mythological subjects. In his essay "Old Mythology in Modern Poetry," A. C. Bradley speaks of "Ulysses" as follows: "How can the heart that beats in our time find expression in the legend, as the spirit of the old Greek was mirrored in it years ago? . . . [T]his is the question Mr. Tennyson has answered for us, not in an exposition or an allegory, but by recreating; so that he gives us a poem on an 'ancient subject' as we roughly say, yet modern to the core."[15] Tennyson's "Ulysses" is not only a poem that takes myth as a source, it is a poem about myth. It is also a poem very much related to Tennyson's overall transformation of the pastoral idyll. A dramatic monologue, like "Œnone," "Tithonus," and "Demeter and Persephone," its origins go back to certain classical forms. In his article "Monodrama and the Dramatic Monologue," A. Dwight Culler has argued that the monodrama derives from the classical rhetorical exercise of prosopopoeia, examples of which in classical literature are Ovid's *Heroides* and before that the Alexandrian idyll.[16] A Tennyson poem such as "Ulysses" combines mythology with the classical pastoral idyll one associates with Theocritus. As Culler notes, the idyll as a literary form was especially amenable to Tennyson because of his modern sense that the great poetry had already been written, a view that parallels the Alexandrian perspective on the classical epic.[17] Furthermore, as Richard Jenkyns observes, in much of his poetry, Tennyson deliberately contrasts his efforts with the greater models of the classic age; thus, in *In Memoriam*, says Jenkyns, "He stresses the contrast between the vitality of the early poets and his own frailty in order to bring out the pathos of the human condition, in his own time of doubts and uncertainties."[18] But what is involved here is not simply a contrast between past and present; rather, it is Tennyson's recognition of affinity with a specific classical form: the idyll. As Culler points out, in the 1830s Tennyson was already thinking about writing poems in the form of brief epics: "I felt certain of one point then; if I meant to make any mark at all, it must be by shortness, for the men before me had been so diffuse, and most of the big things except 'King Arthur' had been done."[19] Culler argues that this attitude types Tennyson as a "Victorian Alexandrian."[20] Poems such as "Ulysses" and "Tithonus" are modelled on the idylls or "little epics" of Callimachus and Theocritus. Such a line of poetic descent also has ramifications for Tennyson's treatment of myth. The Alexandrians, Culler observes, "took a new approach to myth":

> Writing for a highly cultivated audience in the great research center of Alexandria, they were little inclined simply to tell over again the stories that had already been told by Homer and the Greek dramatists. If they could not find new stories, they would at least seek out little known aspects of the old stories and would tell them from a novel point of view. . . . In this focusing upon one little portion of the story with the rest sketched in briefly or by cryptic allusion, they naturally produced what, from a traditional point of view, was a one-sided or asymmetrical treatment of the myth. This they often intensified by odd forms, by the digression or the poem-within-the-poem, with the result that what was formally a subordinate part of the story became thematically the most important. For they were primarily interested in using old myths as the materials of art—in creating out of narratives that a previous generation had taken rather seriously something that would be shapely, intense, learned, and graceful. This was the "serious" modern poetry of the Alexandrian age.[21]

Combine the detached artistic perspective of the Theocritean idyll with the sorrow and melancholy that Pater rightly perceives within the Greek mythic imagination, and we begin to get a sense of the mixture of generic forms and the singular and complex emotional effects that Tennyson was striving to produce in such poems based on myth as "Ulysses."

One cannot ignore the biographical side to "Ulysses." Tennyson wrote the poem after the death of Hallam, and he made two important comments about the poem:

> "Ulysses" . . . gave my feeling about the need of going forward, and braving the struggle of life perhaps more simply than anything in *In Memoriam*.[22]

> There is more about myself in "Ulysses" which was written under the sense of loss and that all had gone by, but that still life must be fought out to the end. It was more written with the feeling of loss upon me than many poems in *In Memoriam*.[23]

The note of heroism in these comments suggests the Homeric Ulysses. Yet, in Alexandrian style, Tennyson has chosen a more unusual recounting of the myth. In the eleventh book of *The Odyssey*, Tiresias tells Ulysses that after returning to Ithaca and slaying the suitors, he will take one more voyage and die peacefully at sea. The idea of Ulysses's last journey had great currency during the classical age and was also dealt with by writers in the Medieval and Renaissance periods. Dante pursued this aspect of the myth in the *Inferno* when the poet encounters Ulysses in the eighth circle; this is Tennyson's principal source, and he probably relied on the Cary translation. In Dante, Ulysses describes his final journey beyond the pillars of Hercules, the *ne plus ultra* of the Medieval world, and then tells of his ship's sinking at the limits of the world.

Few Tennyson poems have elicited more diversity of critical opinion than "Ulysses." Many of the differences of interpretation center on the moral nature of Ulysses and on Tennyson's attitude toward his speaker. W. W. Robson, in "The Dilemma of Tennyson," argues that the poem exemplifies the tension in Tennyson's poetry between the socially responsible public poet and the private poet during a period of sorrow and loss; in his view, the style and form, the technique, is at odds with the ethos of heroism and struggle. As Robson puts it, "There is a radical discrepancy between the strenuousness aspired to, and the medium in which the aspiration is expressed."[24] E. J. Chiasson, on the other hand, sees Tennyson as critical of his speaker. Chiasson finds fault not with the poem but with Ulysses: in his view, the poem is "a dramatic portrayal of a type of human being who held a set of ideas which Tennyson regarded as destructive of the whole fabric of society."[25] For Chiasson, Ulysses does not represent the heroic struggle Tennyson felt the need for after the death of Hallam, but represents instead the antithesis of that struggle through his moral and social irresponsibility. E. D. H. Johnson is less harsh but basically concurs with this view. Ulysses pursues, says Johnson, "a line of conduct which cannot be justified in any but the most individualistic terms."[26] On the other hand, Douglas Bush emphasizes the heroism of Ulysses: in "Ulysses" says Bush, "the forces of order and courage win a hard victory over the dark mood of chaos and defeat."[27] Bush also hints at Ulysses as a poet figure, "endowed with a nineteenth-century elegiac sensibility and magnanimous reflectiveness, a capacity for not only seeking experience but interpreting it."[28] Some critics have been more interested in the psychology of the speaker and the relation of this psychology to Tennyson's aesthetic, rather than in the poem's moral stance. Langbaum, for example, sees the poem as typical of a large group of poems in Tennyson involving the idea of "weariness" and a "longing for rest."[29] Langbaum observes that Tennyson places great emphasis on Ulysses' age and his "yearning toward disappearance, extinction," and that "Tennyson's Ulysses holds out death in one form or another as the inevitable goal of the journey."[30] Along similar lines is a passage by Goldwin Smith written in 1855:

> You may trace the hues of this character tinging everything in the poems. Even the Homeric Ulysses, the man of purpose and action, seeking with most definite aim to regain his own home and that of his companions, becomes a "hungry heart," roaming aimlessly to "lands beyond the sunset" in the vain hope of being "washed down by the gulf to the Happy Isles," merely to relieve his *ennui* and dragging his companions with him. We say he roams aimlessly—we should rather say, he intends to roam, but stands for ever a listless and melancholy figure on the shore.[31]

The dialectic between heroic struggle and melancholy passivity will be the focus of this discussion:

> It little profits that an idle king,
> By this still hearth, among these barren crags,
> Matched with an agèd wife, I mete and dole

Unequal laws unto a savage race,
That hoard, and sleep, and feed, and know not me.

Our first response is to read these lines as indicating Ulysses's arrogance and social irresponsibility. But while these elements are there, they do not predominate in the way some critics have argued. We need to keep in mind Tennyson's treatment of Ulysses as a mythic figure here. "Ulysses" is a meditation on the three levels of classical myth outlined by Pater, and as a mythical figure, Ulysses himself contains both literal and figurative meaning. The myth of Ulysses is a myth of heroism, but Tennyson's interest lies in the end of heroism, the waning of Ulysses's power and the waning of the power of myth itself. In subtle ways, this aspect of the poem looks ahead to Arthur in the *Idylls of the King*. In Tennyson's epic, Arthur represents a king's declining power and also the way the savage, bestial wasteland begins to return as the Round Table falls apart. In certain ways, Ulysses confronts similar problems: his attitude could be viewed as arrogance toward his people and his wife, but it is better understood as his recognition of the powerlessness of old age. Ulysses's descriptive language, then, is not so much a comment on Ithaca as on his own waning strength and influence. He is "idle," and he resides by a "still hearth" and "barren crags." The images of powerlessness, stasis, and desolation reflect on his own state. Ulysses is not arrogant in this passage, but expresses an acute consciousness of his own losses. When he refers to Penelope, "Matched with an agèd wife," he is not so much critical of her as of his own condition: they are "matched" because he too is "agèd."

When critics speak of Ulysses's haughty condescension, they forget the way Tennyson is dealing with a mythic figure and the life of a myth. The opening lines of the poem are not heroic and grand but prosaic and mundane; they tell us something about the course the myth has run. Ulysses as a figure of power is demystified. Myth is brought down to the level of domestic details and the drudgery of governorship. This language constitutes not simply Ulysses's attitude toward life on Ithaca but toward the life of his own myth. The language also embodies Tennyson's attitude toward myth: he calls the value of myth into question through a diminution to a language of domestic realism. Ulysses's sense of failing power works on the secondary level as a comment on the failing power of myth itself; thus, the poem is both more symbolic and more literal than it is often made out to be, and therein lies the relevance of Pater's discussion of the allegorical figures of Giotto. In representing Ulysses's life on his return to Ithaca, Tennyson uses a language of extreme literalness, or as Pater puts it language *au pied de la lettre*.[32] We get a Ulysses who speaks at the level of any man about his wife and daily work. But because Ulysses is a mythic figure, situated in the context of the heroic voyage just completed and the final voyage on which he is about to embark, there is a strangeness to this type of literal representation. As a mythic hero, Ulysses is not simply a literal figure but an allegorical abstraction for heroic power. He is an example of the "intense" symbolism that Pater sees in Giotto and Greek myth.[33] The literalness of Tennyson's representation of the Ulysses myth is the symbolic embodiment of the myth's failing power. When Ulysses speaks of ruling the people of Ithaca– "I mete and dole / Unequal laws unto a savage race / That hoard, and sleep, and feed, and know not me"– the tone is not one of superciliousness but of exasperation at his own ineffectualness, a powerlessness conveyed by a startlingly literal type of language. There is a prosaic quality about "mete" and "dole," uncharacteristic of a mythical hero and suggestive of Ulysses's diminution. The language of drab realism mocks the mythical hero and, conversely, his old age and dwindling power mock the language of myth. Moreover, when he admits that the Ithacans "know not" him, he is, in part, commenting on their uncivilized state, certainly, but also on his inability to gain their recognition. They do not know him because he now lacks the authority to make himself known.

Ulysses as a symbol of power and authority is closely related to Tennyson's finest poem of mourning, "Tears, Idle Tears." The tears are idle because they cannot signify, cannot embody in language, the meaning of the speaker's grief. Their "idleness" connotes an absence of meaning and power. Ulysses is an idle king not because he feels superior to the Ithacans, but because he feels his own insignificance. He has become a cipher. His age and his weakness drain him of meaning as a mythical figure, and he becomes idle because his function as a figure within myth no longer has much weight. Ulysses is a sign of empty meaning just as the idle tears are a sign of the absent meaning of that speaker's grief. In "Tears, Idle Tears," the speaker attempts to give meaning to the absence of meaning emblematized by the tears themselves. In "Ulysses," the speaker attempts to give new meaning to himself as a figure of myth. At the outset of the poem, he has lost his heroism and power, and the diminished language of the first verse paragraph is the representation of this loss. The first verse paragraph of the poem is not about Ulysses's haughty disregard for the Ithacans and for the social responsibilities of leadership. It is about Ulysses's awareness of his own failing power as a hero and as a figure in mythical language: his idleness or absence of meaning.

The poem describes not simply a quest for adventure stemming from intellectual curiosity or boredom with life on Ithaca, but a quest to recover the power of myth itself, a quest to regain the language of symbolic heroism. Ulysses's monologue constitutes both an elegy on the loss of mythical language and an attempt to recover it. Through the journey, Ulysses hopes to recover the power of his figure within the realm of myth, and the power of the language of myth itself.

> I cannot rest from travel: I will drink
> Life to the lees: all times I have enjoyed
> Greatly, have suffered greatly, both with those
> That loved me, and alone; on shore and when
> Through scudding drifts the rainy Hyades
> Vext the dim sea: I am become a name;
> For always roaming with a hungry heart
> Much have I seen and known; cities of men
> And manners, climates, councils, governments,
> Myself not least, but honoured of them all;
> And drunk delight of battle with my peers,
> Far on the ringing plains of windy Troy.

The elegiac sense derives from Ulysses's contrast of the great heroism of the past with the diminished values of his present life on Ithaca. But Tennyson conveys the plenitude of life in the second verse paragraph not solely through contrasting the fullness of the external world (i.e., the distant regions he has travelled) with the "barren crags" of Ithaca; rather, he contrasts the plenitude of Ulysses's meaning and significance, as figure of myth and emblem of mythic language, with his emptiness or idleness as literal king and husband amid the drab realism of Ithaca. They key moment in the second verse paragraph, and it constitutes an important realization on Ulysses's part, occurs when he says, "I am become a name." For Ulysses, to be a "name" is to recognize the self as mythic figure but at a stage when the myth of the self is in decline. He begins to view himself as a myth. But in so doing, he is no longer fully within the world of myth but outside of it. We repeatedly find this pattern in Tennyson's poems. The speaker begins to look at him- or herself as if from the outside, viewing the self as a convention and often, in fact, as a literary convention. The speaker's division within the self is, in turn, figured forth through the self's sense of exile from its surrounding world, from the external landscape of home. This division within the speaker's self, and the speaker's sense of exile from the native landscape, both become figures for the poet's sense of exile and disinheritance from his home in poetic tradition. Ulysses is a figure for the poet who wishes to recover the power of literary tradition in his own work, but fears that his attempts to do so will end in failure.

Ithaca is not simply a place of "limitation," to use Culler's word. It is an emblem for the pastoral retreat that has failed and from which Ulysses feels psychologically banished.[34] His place within this tradition has become idle or empty. The people do not know him there. But on his earlier travels, when he was within his own myth, he was "honoured of them all." The language changes between the two worlds of paragraphs one and two: it takes on power as Ulysses moves away from the domestic and civil scene of Ithaca to the places of mythical adventure. There is a world of difference between the prose-like literalness of the first verse paragraph and this line from verse paragraph two: "Far on the ringing plains of windy Troy." This line both carries him back through memory to youthful heroism and also prefigures the projected heroism he wishes to recover in his future journey. The language of this line is meant to recover the power of myth, and the language is both literal and figurative in its intense penetration into Ulysses's longing for his lost place within the conventions of myth. To reside before the "still hearth" at Ithaca is to live no longer inside the conventions of myth and to possess no longer the power those conventions bestow upon the inhabitants of the world of myth. In Tennyson's "Ulysses," Ithaca is a place of powerlessness, a place of realism that diminishes the life of the imagination. Indeed, Tennyson's great ironic contribution to the Ulysses story is that the return to Ithaca is actually a psychic banishment and exile. Ulysses has been banished from the myth of his own heroism.

In Tennyson's poem, Ithaca is a place of limitation, and Ulysses symbolizes the need to go beyond all limits.[35] The line about the plains of Troy is, on the level of language, a journey beyond limitation. W. David Shaw describes the unique quality of line 17 as follows:

> Because the termini of the chain—the windswept ruin and the ring of a proud and boisterous (a "windy") people—are overspecified, they free the mind from overelaboration of the intermediate stages. The space filled by years of war is collapsed into a direct confrontation of pride and ruin.[36]

As Shaw says, the line's rhetoric involves both "heroic" and "elegiac" styles: it images both Troy as heroic city and Troy in ruins after the fall. This combination of the heroic and elegiac, of pride and ruin, characterizes not simply this one-line depiction of Troy, but conveys the contradictory nature of Ulysses's mythic status as well. He is now a proud ruin, a king but an idle one, just as Troy is now a windy city because it is empty and fallen. The identity between man, language, and place is one followed throughout the poem and helps create its blend of heroism and melancholy. In the opening paragraph, Ulysses is bound up with images of Ithaca and with a style of realistic language that constitutes the diminishment of myth. Then in the second paragraph, the language assumes the heroism of myth, and Ulysses becomes that myth's hero, albeit only in memory. This stage reaches a tentative conclusion with line 17, which paradoxically signifies heroism at its height as it also figures heroism's demise and ruin. The powerful rhetoric of this line fails to hide the fact that "windy Troy" circles back to "idle king," as images of emptiness and powerlessness define both city and man. Ulysses himself is aware of this identity between man and place:

> I am a part of all that I have met;
> Yet all experience is an arch wherethrough

Gleams that untravelled world, whose margin fades
For ever and for ever when I move.

The first of the above-quoted lines reveals Ulysses's recognition
that his identity is bound up with the places of his mythic achieve-
ments; the latter three lines suggest how his identity is bound up
with the life and death of the language of myth itself. Matthew
Arnold first pointed out the unusual relation of the language of
these lines to epic and myth: "It is no blame to their rhythm, which
belongs to another order of movement than Homer's but it is true
that these three lines by themselves take up nearly as much time
as a whole book of the *Iliad*."[37] The slowness of time in these lines,
the enervation of the language itself, combines the heroism of epic
and myth with the melancholy sense of the fading away of life. The
fading "margin" projects future adventure, future journeys, but it
also images Ulysses's distance from the heroism of his past. The imagery suggests that while he may try to move, once again, toward
the "untravelled world" of myth, this world will continually recede
from his approach. Tennyson qualifies his attempt, in these lines,
at the grand epic style of the *Iliad* through the enervation of the
language, and the language mirrors Ulysses's own age and fading
power. Ulysses is as far from the adventures of the *Iliad*, as far from
his own past mythic stature, as Tennyson is from writing a new
classical epic. The heart of these lines lies in the elegiac sense of
both hero and poet as being outside of the myths they wish to in-
habit. The language of myth and epic is no longer within their
power, and they need to find other kinds of language, other conventions, to represent their experience. If one of Tennyson's principal concerns is, to use Richard Jenkyns's phrase, the "death of
poetry,"[38] this problem finds its literary analogue in Ulysses's concern for the death of his own myth, the fact that he has "become
a name." Ironically, his attempt to regain the power of myth through
the imagery of his travels, only serves to heighten the sense of elegiac distance from these past adventures. Yet, in one sense, Ulysses's
language is not distant from his own myth. Certain qualities of the
language and imagery prefigure the final journey described by Dante's
Ulysses: the "untravelled world" and the fading "margin" are figures for the limitations of heroism and knowledge beyond which

Dante's Ulysses will go in his final journey to death. As Shaw describes this passage: "It presents Ulysses engaged in the most strenuous activity of all – spectacularly envisioning his own deline."[39] This comment shows the direction in which Ulysses's heroism is going. Ulysses becomes a poet figure, a singer of his own elegy in which the language of adventure translates into a language of melancholy and grief. Dante's Ulysses, too, is in a sense a poet figure, and this fact explains Tennyson's interest in Dante's representation of the myth. For Dante's Ulysses speaks from the land of the dead and describes, in effect, how his own myth finally achieves its closure. And he, too, speaks in a language that is both heroic and elegiac, because he knows the final outcome of his own story.

Tennyson's Ulysses has not yet taken that final journey, but a sense of melancholy at the foreshadowed ending begins to emerge as the poem progresses:

> And this gray spirit yearning in desire
> To follow knowledge like a sinking star,
> Beyond the utmost bounds of human thought.

Tennyson combines Ulysses's heroic exhortation to his men with images of their death: the "sinking star" foreshadows the sinking of the ship that ends Ulysses's story in Dante. In alluding to Dante's treatment of the myth, Tennyson suggests how Ulysses' death is also the ending or death of the myth itself. Indeed, the final paragraph of the poem puts great emphasis on this sense of closure:

> Death closes all: but something ere the end,
> Some work of noble note, may yet be done,
> . . . .
> The lights begin to twinkle from the rocks:
> The long day wanes: the slow moon climbs: the deep
> Moans round with many voices. . . .

We see how reductive it is to view Ulysses as haughty or condescending toward the Ithacans, Penelope, or Telemachus. The earlier words were spoken by a Ulysses who was being false to himself, a Ulysses of literal language rather than of figurative power. Now we see that Ulysses can never exist at the literal level, but only on the level of a symbolic representation of heroism. He can exist only in myth, but now his myth confronts the final myth of death, which also brings the end of language and of myth itself. The melancholy of the final verse paragraph involves Ulysses's knowledge that the only mythical act of heroism left is one of actively seeking his own end.

> It may be that the gulfs will wash us down:
> It may be we shall touch the Happy Isles,
> And see the great Achilles, whom we knew.

We recall Carlyle's comment on the passage: "These lines do not make me weep, but there is in me what would fill whole Lachrymatories as I read."[40] The poignancy of the lines lies partly in our knowledge that his end will be to sink into oblivion beyond the world's limits. His destination will not be the Isles of the Blest but, if we follow Dante's account, the eighth circle of the Malebolge, for those guilty of deceit. And this knowledge gives the heroism of the closing a highly ambiguous quality:

> Though much is taken, much abides; and though
> We are not now that strength which in old days
> Moved earth and heaven; that which we are, we are;
> One equal temper of heroic hearts,
> Made weak by time and fate, but strong in will
> To strive, to seek, to find, and not to yield.

As Christopher Ricks points out, here is one of Tennyson's typically inconclusive conclusions.[41] We are not certain that Ulysses knows what his fate will be. Moreover, we are not certain that *we* know, in this particular rendering of the Ulysses myth, what his end will be. What we are certain of, however, is Ulysses's ironic sense of describing the life and death of his own myth. His is a language of elegiac self-consciousness, a language of melancholy, which stems from his recognition that he is now only capable of looking back retrospectively at the self that was a mythic figure, and he is incapable of existing as an active figure of power within the realm of myth itself. His myth has disinherited him. His separation from myth parallels Tennyson's separation from Hallam, and, most important, Tennyson's separation from the literary traditions of myth that he invokes in this group of poems written soon after the death of Hallam. A poem that explores the way the poet has become irrevocably detached from certain forms and conventions, "Ulysses" moves Tennyson further in the direction of his new idyll.

"Tithonus" is an expanded and revised version of "Tithon," which is one of a group of poems Tennyson wrote after the death of Hallam in 1833. "Tithonus" explores the nature of death and the possibilities of human resignation or action in the face of suffering and defeat. Tennyson drew upon the myth of the love between a mortal and Aurora, the goddess of the dawn. His probable source was the Homeric *Hymn to Aphrodite*. In the myth, Tithonus and Aurora are so much in love that the mortal asks the goddess for immortality so he can be with her forever. Aurora grants his wish, but gives him eternal life only, not eternal youth. Tithonus is thus fated to remain forever alive but forever aging. Tennyson describes the myth as follows: Tithonus was "beloved by Aurora who gave him eternal life but not eternal youth. He grew old and infirm, and as he would not die, according to the legend, was turned into a grasshopper."[42] Tennyson uses this last aspect of the myth in his poem "The Grasshopper," but he avoids such a conclusion in "Tithonus." It is easy to see why the story would appeal to Tennyson after the death of Hallam: the contrasts between man and the gods, mortality and immortality, youth and age, are central preoccupations of the poet at this period. The problem of immortality had been a concern of Hallam himself and one he dealt with in his *Theodicaea Novissima*.[43] Tennyson would return to the question of immortality again and again in the years following Hallam's death, as he wrote the lyrics that would eventually be brought together in *In Memoriam*.

The Tithonus story not only involves the problem of immortality but explores the difficulties of love and of human aspirations toward the divine. Both issues were in Tennyson's mind during this period of loss and grief; moreover, the story contrasts youth and age at a time when Tennyson began to see what age and loss of youth meant, having by now experienced the death of his father as well as of Hallam. Jowett comments on this transformation from youth to age in a letter to Tennyson, after the former had visited Hallam's grave: "It is a strange feeling about those who are taken young that while we are getting older and dusty they are as they were."[44] Hallam's death was bound up in the minds of his friends with the memory of youth. At the same time, Tennyson's thoughts of Hallam often involved the desire to be reunited with Hallam in death. The desire for death as escape had been one of the earliest and most intense preoccupations of Tennyson's poetry, and "Tithonus" is one of the most complex explorations of that desire that we have in his work. Again, the biographical detail is not irrelevant here: Tennyson's sister Emily was engaged to Hallam. During the time of mourning, she said, "What is life to me! if I die (which the Tennysons never do)."[45] Tennyson at times also felt the worthlessness of life and the attractions of death. The myth of Tithonus had the paradoxical quality of affirming and negating both of these feelings at the same time.

In addition to the biographical context, a word about the sources is in order. The principal source is the Homeric *Hymn to Aphrodite*. Ricks also points to two references to the Tithonus story in Horace's *Odes*.[46] Tithonus is mentioned in I.28, a meditation on the inevitability of death. In II.16, Horace uses Tithonus as an example of the type of suffering that all human beings must to some extent learn to bear. Despite the classical source and background of Tennyson's "Tithonus," in the language and imagery of the poem itself there are fewer actual allusions or echoes of classical literature than in some of the other Tennyson poems on classical mythological subjects. Nevertheless, in style and form "Tithonus" does resemble the classical idyll and epyllion (or little epic), and the principal debts here are to Theocritus and Virgil. Douglas Bush calls "Tithonus" "perhaps the most Virgilian of all Tennyson's poems. . . . The stately phrase and rhythm, the opulent but not profane decoration, the conscious art that governs the curve of the whole poem and weighs every syllable, all this is Virgilian. . . . [T]he pathos inherent in the simple cycle of human life is felt and rendered not only with Virgilian dignity and beauty, but with Virgilian pity and tenderness."[47] "Tithonus" is one of Tennyson's great poems of melancholy and mourning. It reveals its debts to Virgil in this regard.

The melancholy of "Tithonus" comes also by way of Keats and the Romantics. The desire for escape and immortality and the pattern of return to the poetry of the earth are quintessentially Keatsian. Bush notes the debt to Keats here, especially stylistically. He points to the similarity in these lines: "Man comes and tills the fields and lies beneath" ("Tithonus," 3) and "Of peaceful sway above man's harvesting" (*Hyperion*, I.110).[48] The concrete and sympathetic identification of man, the seasons, and the earth is one Tennyson gets in part from Keats. The melancholy of "Tithonus" has much in common with the moments of despair in the great Romantic crisis lyrics. The Virgilian aspect of the poem's melancholy is undoubtedly there, but "Tithonus" also contains the poet's melancholy relation to tradition, the latter stemming from Romanticism and the poet's wavering faith about the poetic task. As Dwight Culler observes, "Tithonus"

> is about a poet who feels his poetic powers failing. . . . For "Tithonus" is Tennyson's "Dejection: An Ode"; it is the negative part of his "Resolution and Independence," of his "Tintern Abbey" or "Immortality Ode." With the death of Hallam he lost Joy, that active, sacred power by which the poet creates worlds about him, by which he glorifies the earth. To the poet the loss of Joy is the loss of the imagination.[49]

One more point about the melancholy of "Tithonus" is related to a problem in the history of poetic truth as explored by W. J. Bate and Harold Bloom: the poet's sense of "the burden of the past." The melancholy of the poet, the fear of failing poetic power, is in part the result of his awe and admiration for the poets who have preceded him, and of his need to find the originality of his own voice within the many strands of earlier voices from which his own poetry is woven. As Bate puts it, "if you are exhorted to be 'original' at all costs, how do you take even the first step—especially if what you have been taught most to admire (and what in fact you really do most admire) is best typified by those very predecessors from whom you must now distinguish yourself?"[50] The melancholy so prevalent in Tennyson's work is bound up with this problem of originality, and the form taken by this problem within the language of the poems themselves is the transformation and development of certain types of poetic conventions. In "Tithonus," the exploration of certain themes such as death and immortality, youth and age, memory and the frustration of love, works along with the poet's melancholy exploration of poetic tradition, and the spiritual and aesthetic resolutions that it offers involve loss as well as gain.

We have been exploring Tennyson's poetics of melancholy in a group of poems that draw upon the conventions of the pastoral tradition. This seems the right approach to begin with in reading "Tithonus." "Tithonus" is both a pastoral love-lament with Virgilian and Theocritean elements, and an elegy (though here, paradoxically, an elegy for the "immortality" of the self rather than the mortality of another). In keeping with these traditions, "Tithonus" opens with a landscape from nature:

> The woods decay, the woods decay and fall,
> The vapours weep their burthen to the ground,
> Man comes and tills the field and lies beneath,
> And after many a summer dies the swan.
> Me only cruel immortality
> Consumes: I wither slowly in thine arms,
> Here at the quiet limit of the world,
> A white-haired shadow roaming like a dream
> The ever-silent spaces of the East,
> Far-folded mists, and gleaming halls of morn.

The grand style of these opening lines derives in part from the repetition, anaphora, and use of conjunctives. Tennyson emphasizes nature as repetition that terminates in death. He compresses within the image of each line a cycle of life that achieves its closure in the ground. Note the final words of the first three lines: "fall," "ground," "beneath." In terms of tone, here is a combination of a certain rhetorical elegance with simplicity and understatement. In line three, the poet conveys the entire life of a man, from birth to work to death: "Man comes and tills the field and lies beneath." This type of rhetorical economy, which resonates in the mind, produces the Virgilian pathos of the poem, and this form of language has more to do with the Virgilian epic than with the eclogues that most closely follow the pastoral idyll form.

Yet the opening does have affinities with elegy. The whole sense here is of closure, of ending, that the proper terminus of life in nature is death. In terms of pastoral tradition, the poem is both a meditation on and response to the image of death in Virgil's third *Eclogue*:

> Qui legetis flores et humi nascentia fraga
> frigides, o pueri (fugite hinc!) latet anguis in herba.

> (You who gather flowers and strawberries,
> away from here, boys; a snake lies in the grass.)

Even arcadia cannot preserve the innocent child from danger and death. Tennyson, however, transfigures pastoral elegiac conventions in his opening by having death be not something to be fled but something to be desired. One of the great ironies of "Tithonus" is that death itself becomes the arcadia or the pastoral pleasance from which the speaker is exiled and for which he mourns.

There is a sense of rightness about the representation of the cycle of death and life in nature at the opening of "Tithonus." The speaker perceives death as part of nature and as the proper end of life. The tone of voice here suggests not merely acquiescence but equanimity at this state of things. The speaker's perspective is a distant one, a perspective that can, at least for the moment, encompass a mythic sense of origins and ends. The opening four lines possess the mythic largeness of vision found in the two eclogues of Virgil which depart most radically from the Theocritean pastoral norm: *Eclogue* VI and the Messianic *Eclogue* IV. One of the ways Tennyson both responds to and transforms the Virgilian image of death is through its exploration as both cosmic myth of beginning and ending, and its prosaic relation to natural cycles of nature and of the life of man. In "Tithonus," death is both a natural fact and a type of mythic break with all experience that precedes it. The singer at the beginning of "Tithonus" sings of a world coming to an end in a manner that mirrors in reverse the mythic song of the world's beginning that Silenus sings in *Eclogue* VI:

> For he sang how, through the great void, were brought together the seeds of earth, and air, and sea, and streaming fire withal; how from these elements came all beginnings and even the young globe of the world grew into a mass. . . .

how next the earth is awed at the new sun shining and from the
uplifted clouds fall showers; when first woods begin to arise. . . . [51]

   Silenus sings of the trees beginning to rise for the first time.
Tithonus sings of their decay and fall. He sings of the ending of
things, not the beginning. In *Eclogue* VI, Silenus sings of the origin
of the world of which he is happily a part, but Tithonus sings of the
end of a world from which he is inalterably separated. His song
is about the desire for an ending that he will never achieve, and
his end or death is perpetual and unceasing: "Me only cruel immortality / Consumes: I wither slowly in thine arms." Line 5 is one
of the great ironic moments in Tennyson. Where one expects "cruel
love" or "cruel death," one finds instead a word that denotes a usually
desirable state: "immortality." The line shifts the mood and imagery
in a very different direction from lines 1 through 4: despite the
elegiac sense of ending in the first four lines, there is also a sense
of the substantiality of man, nature, and song. The language describing the cycles of time and nature in the first four lines grounds
human existence in a satisfying and sanctifying reality. This reality
is that of the song itself, as emphasized by the "burthen" that the
vapors weep and by the image of the dying swan. The paradox of
substantiality in the song or "burthen" of the vapors and in the
song of the swan lies in their being songs of ending and death, but
ones which are effected through the living processes of nature.
Mists and vapors and dying birds are real things in the living world.
Their reality contrasts with the disembodiedness of the immortal
world, and their language of song contrasts with, as Ricks points
out, the disquieting silence of the immortal realm in which Tithonus
now resides.[52]
   In contrast to the decaying woods and the death of the man
who works in the fields, the place Tithonus now inhabits is intangi-
ble, unreal, and silent. He is a "shadow" who lives in a "dream"
world of "mists" and "gleaming halls." Tithonus now lives at the
"limit of the world" where Aurora rises, bringing the dawn. But
the immortality he achieves is simply the hypostasis of nature's decay into an unending state of suffering. He is "consumed" by it.
He "withers slowly." He has become a "white-haired shadow."
The unnaturalness of this state contrasts with the appropriateness

of the natural cycle, imaged at the poem's opening, in which death
and life lead to each other in a relation of productive reciprocity.
This reciprocity defines, as well, the difference in language and
song between the two worlds.

Like the elegies of Bion and Moschus, the song of lamentation
in the opening four lines mourns the passing of life, but as an act
of communal affirmation of the order of things. Paradoxically, the
opening description of the inescapability of death in nature constitutes a language of life's affirmation that offers a sharp contrast
with the silence that characterizes the world of immortality. The
poet suggests here that when death is withdrawn from the world of
nature, pastoral song withdraws also. Tithonus's new pastoral retreat is at "the *quiet* limit of the world." "Limit" here means both
the edge of the world from which Aurora, as dawn, emerges, and
the way immortality limits the nature of the world and the nature
of pastoral song. The quietness is a sign of Tithonus's exclusion
from the community of nature, and the celebration of this exclusion in the language of pastoral. Tennyson equates his melancholy
exile from pastoral with Tithonus's exile from humanity, and Tithonus's nostalgia is very much the poet's own:

> Alas! for this gray shadow, once a man—
> So glorious in his beauty and thy choice,
> Who madest him thy chosen, that he seemed
> To his great heart none other than a God!
> I asked thee, 'Give me immortality.'
> Then didst thou grant mine asking with a smile,
> Like wealthy men who care not how they give.

One observes the nostalgic distance here, the contrast between
the "gray shadow" and the youth who was once "glorious in his
beauty." Ricks points out that Tennyson has the speaker describe
the imagery from his mortal youth in the third person to increase
the sense of distance between his present and former state: "his
beauty," "him thy chosen," "he seemed."[53] One also observes here
Tithonus's narcissism. The phrase "So glorious in his beauty" is a
surprising revelation of his self-love, when what would be more appropriate at this point would be a description of the beauty of
Aurora and his love for her. Tithonus will later describe with deep

feeling his youthful love for Aurora, but what he conveys here is a selfish sense of the loss of his own youth. Even more troubling is his description of youthful aspiration. His heart is "great" not with love for Aurora but with aspirations to divinity: "he seemed / To his great heart none other than a God!" With this yearning, he asks Aurora for immortality. In a curious way, however, the gods fail Tithonus. Despite the supposed love between Tithonus and Aurora, when she grants his wish she evinces a coldness and indifferent violence toward her mortal lover:

> Then didst thou grant mine asking with a smile,
> Like wealthy men who care not how they give.
> But thy strong Hours indignant worked their wills,
> And beat me down and marred and wasted me,
> And though they could not end me, left me maimed
> To dwell in presence of immortal youth,
> Immortal age beside immortal youth,
> And all I was, in ashes.

There is a metonymic connection between the cruelty of immortality and the cruelty of the goddess Aurora. Tennyson's description suggests Aurora is not only unthinking in her granting of his request, but may have actually known what the consequences of this request would be. Because the poem is a dramatic monologue spoken by Tithonus, there is an ambiguity in the description of Aurora. This ambiguity centers on the violence of his transformation: Is it her responsibility, or is his indulgent pathos in retrospect a reaction to the suffering he brought upon himself? The phrase "thy strong Hours" would seem to implicate Aurora as the cause of his suffering. It may well be, however, that he wishes to displace onto her his own guilt for the choice he made: he is the one who wished to be immortal, and if the terms of that wish's fulfillment are more than he bargained for, the responsibility rests with Tithonus, not Aurora. At least from his perspective, however, the gods and his own state of immortality have failed him, have not lived up to their envisioned promise. That the failure actually rests with Tithonus, and that this failure is analogous to a pattern of expectation and disillusionment, emulation and rebellion, in the poet's relation to literary history, constitutes Tennyson's larger meditation within the poem.

"Tithonus" contains a tension between sympathy and judgment, between identification and detachment, a tension that Langbaum considers characteristic of the dramatic monologue form.[54] This tension, moreover, helps to define Tennyson's consciousness of pastoral tradition within the poem. The fact that "Tithonus" is a dramatic monologue is one indication of the poem's formal debts to the classical idyll. Dwight Culler suggests the dramatic monologue is not as exclusively modern a form as Langbaum suggests: Culler argues that this form has roots both in the classical epistle, especially the *Heroides* of Ovid, and in the pastoral idyll of Virgil and Theocritus.[55]

In the pastoral idyll, a tension often exists between the longing of the singer and the poet's detachment from the singer through the artifice of the idyll's form and language. In "Tithonus," Tennyson pushes that tension further in the direction of the modern dramatic monologue but also toward a kind of aesthetic meta-language about his own relation to poetic tradition. In the character of Tithonus, he creates an ironic contrast between traditional expectations of naivete associated with the figures in the pastoral world and a more troubling sense that the speaker is both calculating and self-deluding.

Yet it would be a mistake to place too great an emphasis on the negative side of Tithonus's character and on the negative side of Tennyson's transformation of the pastoral idyll. Even in the second verse paragraph, there are hints of the genuine love between Tithonus and Aurora that partially redeem his overreaching egotism. In a subtle image, Tennyson conveys the pain Aurora feels at the irrevocability of Tithonus's state of exile: "those tremulous eyes that fill with tears / To hear me." However much Aurora may be implicated in his transformation, she does not wish for him to suffer. Tithonus's awareness of her sympathy is probably what enables him to state one of the central realizations of the poem:

> Why should a man desire in any way
> To vary from the kindly race of men,
> Or pass beyond the goal of ordinance
> Where all should pause, as is most meet for all?

Here is where "Tithonus" mirrors "Ulysses." Ulysses, of course, says the exact opposite. It is a measure of Tennyson's sophistication and of the complexity of both poems that neither of the views espoused by the two speakers is entirely "right." In "Tithonus," there is a sense of this desire for pause as a desire to return to the cycles of nature and human life. Tithonus wants to return to his proper place in the scheme of things. But his desire for an ending, a final closure, is another manifestation of the suicidal impulse for escape so often found in Tennyson's poems, as in, for example, "The Lotos-Eaters" and "The Two Voices." The true suicidal impulse for Tithonus is not his wish to pause and rest, but his initial desire to escape the limitations of human kind. Tithonus's perceptions about what he has lost are not sentimental distortions of the past, but constitute the painful recognition of the value of the limits that he wished to exceed.

Jacob Korg says "Tithonus" is about the dangers of fulfillment, but the real irony of the poem is not that fulfillment is dangerous, but that there are true and false ideas about what constitutes fulfillment and Tithonus has chosen a false idea.[56] The sophistication of the poem, however, centers on the fact that the true idea and the false idea are closely related and might even appear indistinguishable. As Robert Pattison points out, the state of fulfillment Tithonus yearns for is not dissimilar to the positive idyllic state represented in "The Gardener's Daughter."[57] In fact, it can be useful to compare passages from the two poems. The first passage from Tennyson's earlier English idyll shows the delicate balance required to achieve the pastoral world in the modern age:

> Not wholly in the busy world, nor quite
> Beyond it, blooms the garden that I love.

The second passage from "The Gardener's Daughter" presents one of the finest images of pastoral love in Tennyson:

> For up the porch there grew an Eastern rose,
> That, flowering high, the last night's gale had caught,
> And blown across the walk. One arm aloft—
> Gowned in pure white, that fitted to the shape—
> Holding the bush, to fix it back, she stood,
> A single stream of all her soft brown hair
> Poured on one side: the shadow of the flowers
> Stole all the golden gloss, and, wavering

Lovingly lower, trembled on her waist—
Ah, happy shade—and still went wavering down,
But, ere it touched a foot, that might have danced
The greensward into greener circles, dipt,
And mixed with shadows of the common ground!
But the full day dwelt on her brows, and sunned
Her violet eyes, and all her Hebe bloom,
And doubled his own warmth against her lips,
And on the bounteous wave of such a breast
As never pencil drew. Half light, half shade,
She stood, a sight to make an old man young.

These lines bear comparison with the following passage from
"Tithonus":

Ay me! Ay me! with what another heart
In days far-off, and with what other eyes
I used to watch—if I be he that watched—
The lucid outline forming round thee; saw
The dim curls kindle into sunny rings;
Changed with thy mystic change, and felt my blood
Glow with the glow that slowly crimsoned all
Thy presence and thy portals, while I lay,
Mouth, forehead, eyelids, growing dewy-warm
With kisses balmier than half-opening buds
Of April. . . .

Each moment creates a picture that stops time through the
power of pastoral love represented in art. But in both poems, in
different ways, there is a sense in which this type of immortality
or timelessness through pastoral love and art is doomed to failure.
Though "The Gardener's Daughter" is not a somber meditation
on death like "Tithonus," there is, nevertheless, an elegiac sense
of lost youth that qualifies the vision of timelessness in the garden
state, and thus, qualifies the power of love and pastoral art. This
qualification occurs in the final line of the passage, when the speaker
says, "a sight to make an old man young." It is an old man's vision of
remembered love.

In "Tithonus," the vision of pastoral love is also a remembered
one, though here not from a stance of old age and approaching death
but from the perspective of the eternally aging and never dying

Tithonus. His remembered vision of pastoral love constitutes an elegy on his lost youth, but it also constitutes his recognition of the danger of wishing to make that moment of pastoral love timeless and outside of death. Indeed, the poem closes not with the vision of love in the pastoral garden, but with Tennyson's great vision of Tithonus's longing to return to the cycles of seasons and the community of people from which he had earlier desired to escape:

> Coldly thy rosy shadows bathe me, cold
> Are all thy lights, and cold my wrinkled feet
> Upon thy glimmering thresholds, when the steam
> Floats up from those dim fields about the homes
> Of happy men that have the power to die,
> And grassy barrows of the happier dead.
> Release me, and restore me to the ground;
> Thou seest all things, thou wilt see my grave:
> Thou wilt renew thy beauty morn by morn;
> I earth in earth forget these empty courts,
> And thee returning on thy silver wheels.

"Tithonus" is Tennyson's ironic transformation of the melancholy of pastoral elegy, in which the melancholy derives not from the loss of another but from the inability to lose one's self. The poem divides into two pastoral worlds: the world of earth and death with its seasons of nature and the life of man, and the false pastoral of immortality that can only remember life as a kind of framed picture from which the deathless inhabitant is excluded. The melancholy in the pastoral world of earth inheres in death's necessity, but that inherence is also a kind of affirmation, as the poetry of the earth attests (the sympathetic response in language of nature to man's loss contributes to a community of human feeling). "Tithonus" begins and ends with this poetry of the earth. The false pastoral world involves the exile from nature and from language as exemplified by Tithonus's inhuman and silent habitation at the quiet limit of the world.

In such a world, the only art is one of elegiac remembrance, the framed "picture" of lines 50 through 63. In this passage, as in the picture of the beloved in "The Gardener's Daughter," the speaker is irrevocably detached from the remembered scene, the timelessness of which mirrors his exile from the temporality of human life and death. The scenes are emblems of the speaker's inhumanly deathless state, and his melancholy yearning is not for the scene's timelessness but for his return to time and mortality. The latter kind of pastoral is, then, false for all its attractions, and it serves as a reminder to the poet of his own detachment from the community of poetic tradition. The poet's melancholy, like that of Tithonus, is bound up with his invocation of pastoral conventions from the outside, as framed picture, rather than from the inside as lived experience. Tithonus's myth of exile is also Tennyson's.

"Demeter and Persephone" (1889) is one of Tennyson's best-known late poems based on classical myth. He wrote the poem after the death of his son Lionel. It therefore parallels poems like "Ulysses" and "Tithon" which Tennyson wrote after the death of Hallam. As in those poems of the 1830s (and the revised "Tithonus" of 1860), Tennyson uses a story from classical mythology to structure his representation of his own mourning and recovery in the face of great loss. The basic story of Demeter and Persephone concerns Persephone's ravishment and abduction by Dis, god of the underworld. Demeter, her mother, goes in search of her, and when she discovers her whereabouts, she, as goddess of the harvest, makes all living things fail and die. Zeus enacts a compromise in which Persephone will spend part of the year on earth with her mother and part of the year with Dis in the underworld.

There are numerous classical sources for the myth. The most important sources for Tennyson's poem are the Homeric "Hymn to Demeter," Ovid's *Metamorphoses* (Book V), and Ovid's recounting of the story in Book IV of his *Fasti* (April, the Games of Ceres). Douglas Bush points, as well, to Claudian's "Rape of Proserpine," a fragment of which Tennyson had translated in his youth.[58] In *A Memoir*, Hallam Tennyson says "Demeter and Persephone" "was written at my request, because I knew my father considered Demeter one of the most beautiful types of womanhood."[59] R. C. Jebb, a classicist, helped Tennyson with the sources, and Tennyson wrote a dedicatory poem to Jebb which precedes the longer poem. The dedication is worth quoting because it sheds light on Tennyson's attitude about the modern poet's handling of myth and the way modern poetry relates, in general, to poetic tradition.

> Fair things are slow to fade away,
> Bear witness you, that yesterday
>   From out the Ghost of Pindar in you
> Rolled an Olympian; and they say
> That here the torpid mummy wheat
> Of Egypt bore a grain as sweet
>   As that which gilds the glebe of England,
> Sunned with a summer of milder heat.
>
> So may this legend for awhile,
> If greeted by your classic smile,
>   Though dead in its Trinacrian Enna,
> Blossom again on a colder isle.

"To Professor Jebb" is a revealing poem. Tennyson sees Jebb as a fellow poet who uses classical sources: Jebb had written a Pindaric ode in Greek for the eight-hundredth anniversary of the University of Bologna, thus the reference to the "Ghost of Pindar." The jaunty wit, the cheerful camaraderie of fellow writers of poems based on classical models, fails to conceal the elegiac note, the note of Tennyson's abiding sense of disinheritance from the traditions he so admires. Even the opening line of "To Professor Jebb," which is meant to convey art's power to resist time, actually connotes its opposite: "Fair things are slow to fade away." It is an image of poetic diminishment, in that the classical stories and poetic forms may be slow to fade yet they do fade. The poet further emphasizes his sense of distance from poetic tradition through the words "Ghost" and "torpid," and by the final two lines, in which the myth may, "Though dead in its Trinacrian Enna, / Blossom again on colder isle." The myth in its classical form, says the poet, is dead, but he hopes that it will "blossom again" in the new form he has created; however, the poet qualifies this hope in the final two words. "Colder isle" evokes the barren ground in which the myth will have to take root: the words suggest that the land and the times are inhospitable to such efforts. The poem becomes a sign of Tennyson's consciousness that his relation to myth and to tradition is that of an exile.

In addition, the poem creates a parallel between death and rebirth in the myth itself, and poetic death and rebirth. This parallel implies that one of the attractions of the Demeter and Persephone myth, for Tennyson, was its complex tension between death and creation, a tension that mirrored his concerns about imaginative death and life as he tried to work out a balance between tradition and originality.

"Demeter and Persephone," then, is as much about the poet's relation to tradition (and about his poetics of melancholy) as it is about the thematics within the myth itself. Tennyson's comments about the poem suggest his awareness that the poem reflects his poetics and the relation between modernity and tradition: "I will write it, but when I write an antique like this I must put it into a frame—something modern about it. It is no use giving a mere *réchauffé* of old legends."[60] In this comment we begin to sense the connection between Tennyson's detachment from his subject matter and his sense of apartness from tradition. The fond superciliousness of the words used to describe the myth is a sign of the poet's troubled relation to the poetry of the past: "an antique like this," "old legends." Perhaps unwittingly, the condescension reveals Tennyson's awe before the power of the myths and poetry of the classical age, as well as his fear of being unable to create new and valuable poetry out of the earlier texts.

The idea of the frame exemplifies his modern sophistication but also his malaise at being outside the community of literature and myth upon which he draws. He is, as a modern, outside the frame; the myth lies within the frame, at the center of tradition. The frame is a poetic device used to bring the myth back to life. But it simultaneously suggests the slow fading away of the life of the legend, the imaginative death that inheres in it, as the poet can only represent myth in a detached and distanced way. Tennyson's use of the frame is one of the ways his re-creation of the myth of Demeter and Persephone comes to embody his poetry of melancholy, his own myth of exile and disinheritance.

Tennyson criticism has offered various interpretations of "Demeter and Persephone." Jerome Buckley sees the poem as focusing on the problem of identity and religious belief: "banished from love (typified by her mother, Demeter) Persephone has lost her true identity, and it is the burden of the idyll to demonstrate that love can restore the self and so transcend the force of death and hell."[61] In Buckley's view, the image of the "new dispensation" at the close serves for Tennyson a "deeply personal religious need."[62] Douglas Bush speaks of "Tennyson's mellow Virgilian sense of the rhythm of the seasons and the life of man."[63] Bush emphasizes, at the same time, the dark side of the poem: "Over Tennyson's less buoyant optimism lies the shadow of the hard eternities, of the Fates who spin the lives of men and know not why they spin."[64] On the other hand, in *The Alien Vision of Victorian Poetry*, E. D. H. Johnson views the poem more positively in terms of Tennyson's psychology of creative process:

> Persephone, appearing in dream, explains that her periodic with-drawal from the phenomenal world into the nether region of shad-ows does not really involve a loss, but is mysteriously necessitated by the process of creation. . . . When interpreted this way, "De-meter and Persephone" becomes a symbolic representation of Ten-nyson's entire poetic career. Beneath his artistic productivity lay dark depths of consciousness on communion with which, rather than any external stimulus, depended his will to create.[65]

Two critical essays, by G. Robert Stange and James Kissane, place the poem in the context of Tennyson and the Victorians' understanding of and attitudes about mythology. Stange points out the poem's similarities to Sir James George Frazer's discussion of the myth in *The Golden Bough* (the first volume of which did not appear until after the publication of Tennyson's poem). In Stange's view, all of Tennyson's poems on Greek and Roman themes are "symbolic narratives of separation, either from an object of love or from the natural course of life."[66] James Kissane, on the other hand, argues, in his essay "Victorian Mythology," that the poem has affinities with Pater's essay "Demeter and Persephone" in *Greek Studies*. In Kissane's view, the poem contains the three phases—natural, poetical, ethical—that Pater describes in the original myth.[67] Both Frazer's later work and Pater's earlier essay stress the dark and melancholy aspects of the myth of Demeter and Persephone.

Tennyson's poem begins near the end of the story. Demeter's dramatic monologue opens with a description of Persephone's re-turn from the underworld:

Faint as a climate-changing bird that flies
All night across the darkness, and at dawn
Falls at the threshold of her native land,
And can no more, thou camest, O my child,
Led upward by the God of ghosts and dreams,
Who laid thee at Eleusis, dazed and dumb
With passing through at once from state to state,
Until I brought thee hither, that the day,
When here thy hands let fall the gathered flower,
Might break through clouded memories once again
On thy lost self. A sudden nightingale
Saw thee, and flashed into a frolic of song
And welcome; and a gleam as of the moon,
When first she peers along the tremulous deep,
Fled wavering o'er thy face, and chased away
That shadow of a likeness to the king
Of shadows, thy dark mate. Persephone!
Queen of the dead no more—my child! Thine eyes
Again were human-godlike, and the Sun
Burst from a swimming fleece of winter gray,
And robed thee in his day from head to feet—
'Mother!' and I was folded in thine arms.

The structure of imagery and the quality of feeling and emotion
in Tennyson's opening qualify the idea of return and rebirth. We
see this qualification in the simile of the bird with which Demeter
describes Persephone's return. The simile involves an opposition
between "darkness" and "dawn," between "falls" and "flies," and it
is a subtle and complex image for Persephone's bewilderment as
she returns to life from death, after having lived in Hades with Dis.
But the image involves more. The figurative language depicts the
way her hope of return changes with the consciousness of death.
This consciousness of death makes the return itself a kind of "fall,"
as the bird "Falls on the threshold of her native land"; moreover,
the simile figures forth a state of exile. The fact that the bird is
"climate-changing" suggests moving from country to country, which
Persephone does, but it also suggests that the bird (like Persephone)
is no longer at home in any country.

Persephone exists in a permanent state of displacement. The
word "threshold" emphasizes this point. When the bird finally

does reach her home, she is still just outside of it. Her consciousness of death places her, spiritually, at the "threshold of her native land." This image for Persephone's return, then, implies that after having seen the realm of death she can never fully return to the upper world – she remains in a state of exile. The pattern of alliteration links the two sides of the rebirth/death relation: "*f*aint," "*f*lies," "*f*alls"; "*d*arkness," "*d*awn"; "*c*an no more," "*c*amest." There is an alternation here between verbs of action and verbs denoting the cessation of action, and between substantives suggesting hope and suggesting loss of hope. This pattern, in combination with the image of the "threshold," is the embodiment in language of Demeter's perception that Persephone's return is a partial one: the pattern of imagery and alliteration signifies the consciousness of exile.

Persephone is, moreover, in a state of confusion and passivity. Tennyson signals Persephone's passivity through the verbs for which she is the passive object. She is "led upward" by Hermes. She is "laid" at Eleusis by Hermes. And Demeter says to her, "I brought thee hither." Her sense of placelessness makes it impossible for her to act on her own; it also makes it impossible for her to speak. Not only is she confused or "dazed" by her "climate-changing," she is "dumb." While Persephone's silence is the measure of her loss, it also marks out her possession of a kind of inchoate power. Silence can be a kind of detachment, a kind of wisdom, that lies beyond language. In this, Persephone looks back to such silent figures as the "maid" of "Come Down, O Maid." One of the areas of concern in the poem centers on the power to be gained in life and language by "passing through at once from state to state." This sense of passing through different worlds describes the movement from death to the return to the middle state of earth, but it suggests also the movement of the poet between tradition and modernity. Like Persephone, the poet passes through a palimpsest, of times and of language, that gives these temporal worlds form. In this regard, it is curious and significant that Tennyson's representation of Demeter's effort to bring Persephone back into the world underwent three stages of revision, before he settled on the passage as it now stands. Here follow those three states:

1. I brought thee hither that a glance
   At thy last sight on earth, the flowery gleam

Of Enna, might have power to disentrance
Thy senses.

2. I brought thee hither, to the fields
   Where thou and thy sea-nymphs were used to roam
   And thy scared hands let fall the gathered flower,
   For here thy last bright day beneath the sun
   Might float across my memory and unfold
   The sleeping sense.

3. I brought thee hither, where thy hands
   Let fall the gathered flowers, that here again
   Thy last bright hours of sunshine upon earth
   Might break on darkened memories.

In his discussion of the revisions, Jerome Buckley notes the shift from prose-like explanation to concrete imagery in the second passage. Then follows the exclusion of irrelevancies and tightening in the third passage. This tightening, finally, leads to the shift from memory to the "lost self" of the passage in its last form. As Buckley observes, the changes are more than stylistic: there is a shift of emphasis from recovering the senses and recovering memories to recovering the identity of the self. Buckley interprets this shift as tying in with the religious theme of love overcoming the forces of hell and death.[68] But one can view the change to the "lost self" in terms of the nature of art itself. The image of the "lost self" constitutes an emblem of the poet's confused identity as he "gathers the flowers" of poetic tradition. Indeed, even Buckley notes how the second version of the passage enables Tennyson to incorporate an echo of an important passage from Milton.[69] In its first state, the passage contains the image of the "flowery gleam." But in its second state, Tennyson changes this to "thy scared hands let fall the gathered flower." This is an echo of *Paradise Lost*, Book IV:

> Not that faire field
> Of Enna, where Proserpin gath'ring flours
> Her self a fairer Floure by gloomie Dis
> Was gather'd, which cost Ceres all that pain
> To seek her through the world. . . .
>   might with this Paradise
> Of Eden strive.[70]

As G. Robert Stange points out, this passage from Milton was a favorite of Tennyson's, and he frequently read it aloud. Its importance to our reading of "Demeter and Persephone" is twofold: it is yet another example of Tennyson's debt to the pastoral tradition and his use of the *locus amoenus* topos. Stange offers one interpretation of the significance of this type of garden imagery in Tennyson's poetry:

> Imaginary places analogous to the Eden garden are abundant in Tennyson's poems; they usually suggest a refuge from active life, a retreat to the past (as in "The Hesperides" and *Maud*) or a sacred bower of poetic inspiration (as in "The Poet's Mind"). In Tennyson's poetry both heights and depths suggest danger and death; the valley, the sheltered plain, represent the fruitful life. The secluded valley of Enna is reminiscent of the enclosed, shadowy garden, or the tropical islands of the other poems.[71]

Stange's noting of the recurrence of the image is accurate, but his description of the image's function and meaning is too simple. Tennyson often qualifies the image of the garden or pleasance in negative ways, and while the images of heights and depths often appear to be places of danger and death, they can be places of power and creativity as well. Tennyson's representation of the vale of Enna and his allusion to the Miltonic description of it are not meant to suggest that the middle state to which Persephone returns is an Eden garden. The irony of Persephone's return rests in the darkness and danger she brings back with her into the upper world. At the same time, when the poet gathers the flowers of tradition and builds tropes on Milton's contrast of the Eden garden and the fields of Enna, he is, like Persephone, passing from one literary state of mind to another, yet he is not entirely at home in either.

The pleasance Tennyson describes here is not exactly the Enna of classical myth where nature "falls," nor is it the Garden of Christian myth where man falls. Just as Persephone is in between the state of hell and the state of earth, the poet's representation of the pastoral retreat suggests the tense poise of the artist between classical and Christian myths of fall and redemption. Simultaneously, on the level of literary history, this tension constitutes an image of the poet on the "threshold" of the community of poetic traditions that are his home, the place from which he originates as a poet, but from which he has fallen, and before which he can only look as at a place he has lost. Persephone "let fall the gathered flower" when the violent side of nature first manifested itself in her abduction by Dis. In Tennyson's parable of the poet, the poet lets fall the gathered flowers when he realizes that Enna or the pastoral retreat has become the emblem for his division into two opposing literary states of mind: the past of "old legends," and the present of a detached modernity in which the old conventions are distanced and framed. In this sense, the allusion to Milton's fields of Enna works as another framing device, a sign of the poet's fall from Milton's pastoral world and from a fixed identity within it. Tennyson is no longer within pastoral but on its threshold. The phrases "falls on the threshold" and "let fall the gathered flower" implicate the poet in a troubled relationship to poetic representation, just as Persephone's fall implicates all creative growth in the death force that lies in the underworld.[72]

The return of Persephone to the light of day is overshadowed by the darkness of death that she can never entirely abandon. This is analogous to Tennyson's sense that his modernity is overshadowed by the poetry of the past, a contrast that seems to signal, in Richard Jenkyns's phrase, the "death of poetry."[73] There is violence and melancholy in Persephone's return from Hades and in the poet's return and turning away from poetic tradition. The poet images this violence in the language of the opening passage of the poem: he describes Persephone as moving through and against a force of resistance that is in part her own passive inability to realize life again after having been in the world of the dead. Demeter brings her back to the fields of Enna so, as she tells her, the day "Might break through clouded memories once again / On thy lost self."

There is a subtle kind of violence in the very process of reviving life. The image of "breaking through" repeats the initial act that drew her down to Hades: Dis's act of rape. As W. David Shaw puts it: "When the goddess Demeter is first reunited with her daughter, she must revive painful memories of the rape, so that in their pastoral paradise the countervailing reflections of hell, like repressed material under psychoanalysis, may be brought into focus and dispelled."[74] Tennyson chooses to have Demeter bring Persephone back to Enna rather than simply to have them be reunited at Eleusis. It is a significant choice. The fields of Enna are not the paradise on earth but the place where this paradise is lost, where innocence is violated and violence "breaks through."

We see, then, the pastoral landscape itself is bound up with violence and suffering. The return to life and the reunion in love of mother and daughter are defined by that violence. In fact, the reunion cannot be brought about without a psychological violence analogous to the physical violence that occurred earlier in the same pastoral scene. The pastoral scene becomes (in both an emotional and an aesthetic sense) a place of violent confrontation from which both the protagonists and the poet wish to free themselves.

If, as Stange suggests, "Demeter and Persephone" is about the "penetration" to secret wisdom,[75] the poem holds out the troubling possibility that this wisdom may result from the breaking into and breaking away from the natural order itself. Tennyson metonymically transfers this penetration from Dis to Persephone. If he has unnaturally ravished her, she has, against the order of things, entered the depths of Hades and returned to the earth bearing within her the wisdom of that experience. Her initial act of gathering flowers leads to her acquiring a singular knowledge, and Tennyson sees a parallel between her initial act and the act of the poet, whose gathering of images and tropes from the past "breaks through" and disrupts tradition, though it enables him to return with a singular kind of language. Persephone's penetration, and the poet's, to wisdom is somber and melancholy because of their recognition of the violence enacted in the acquiring of this wisdom. In this sense, "Demeter and Persephone" is a melancholy poem, and it is no accident that Tennyson alludes to an iconographic symbol from the melancholy tradition in the passage that immediately follows the echo of Milton's description of the garden:

> A sudden nightingale
> Saw thee, and flashed into a frolic of song
> And welcome. . . .

There is a double-sidedness to this image, as there was earlier to the image of the fields of Enna. The song of the nightingale functions as a sign of happiness here at the return of Persephone. The nightingale can be a symbol of love, but it has strong associations with the idea of melancholy. In addition, the nightingale sings at night. Persephone initially emerges from the darkness of the underworld to darkness on earth. Her return, then, is bound up from the start with symbols having negative connotations. Darkness is one of these symbols; the nightingale is another.

One finds the Tennysonian nightingale in a early sonnet ("Check Every Outflash"), where he combines it in a very conventional way with love and "mild-minded Melancholy." The nightingale has a long-standing iconographic association with the melancholy tradition, and coming immediately after Tennyson's allusion to Milton, the bird brings to mind "Il Penseroso." In "Il Penseroso," Milton associates the nightingale with the "Goddess, sage and holy . . . divinest Melancholy." In "Il Penseroso," Milton links melancholy with the wisdom of the isolated thinker, and the nightingale becomes a type for the solitary artist. In introducing the image of the nightingale at this particular point in "Demeter and Persephone," Tennyson is associating the melancholy knowledge that Persephone has acquired in the underworld with the melancholy knowledge of the poet. The character of this knowledge assumes further definition in the second passage, which describes the return to the fields of Enna:

> So in this pleasant vale we stand again,
> The field of Enna, now once more ablaze
> With flowers that brighten as thy footstep falls,
> All flowers—but for one black blur of earth
> Left by that closing chasm, through which the car
> Of dark Aïdoneus rising rapt thee hence.
> And here, my child, though folded in thine arms,
> I feel the deathless heart of motherhood
> Within me shudder, lest the naked glebe
> Should yawn once more into the gulf, and thence
> The shrilly whinnyings of the team of Hell,
> Ascending, pierce the glad and songful air,
> And all at once their arched necks, midnight-maned,
> Jet upward through the mid-day blossom. No!
> For, see, thy foot has touched it; all the space
> Of blank earth-baldness clothes itself afresh,

And breaks into the crocus-purple hour
That saw thee vanish.

This is a powerful image of the violence that inheres in the pastoral pleasance in its fallen state. Persephone's return "again" to the "pleasant vale" is a fall: "as thy footstep falls" echoes the earlier "falls on the threshold" and "thy hands let fall the gathered flower." The pleasant vale is not as pleasant as it once was: it has undergone a violent transformation. Tennyson closely links Persephone's fall to the forceful appearance, the rising up, of the powers of the lower world. We see the violent disruptiveness in such lines as "dark Aïdoneus rising rapt thee hence." The complexity of image here mirrors the complexity of her achievement of wisdom. Now, for Persephone, myth signals man's irrecoverable fall from innocence and the ideas of rebirth and return are defined by that loss.

The imagery of the pastoral retreat in this passage suggests the need to open up to knowledge, but such a receptivity is complicatedly close to unwished-for ravishment. The vale of Enna undulates in a series of openings and closures: "one black blur of earth / Left by that closing chasm"; "lest the naked glebe / Should yawn once more into the gulf." These are images simultaneously of the pressures of violation and healing. In the world of fallen pastoral, the earth remains scarred: there remains a "black blur," a "space / Of blank earth baldness" that the returning flowers cannot cover.

Tennyson combines the negative aspects of violence and violation with the sorrowful death-consciousness that brings wisdom. This juxtaposition defines the pastoral retreat. Just as the return to the fields of Enna facilitates the "breaking through" of memories so that Persephone can reenter the middle state, the actual healing or recuperation of the pastoral *locus amoenus* involves intrusive violence. We note, as well, that the image of "breaking through" memories that Demeter hopes will heal Persephone parallels in this second passage the team of hell, which she fears will again "*pierce* the glad and songful air." The poet links both processes, that of ravishment and that of recovery, to the rebirth of nature in the pastoral garden: the "blank earth-baldness clothes itself afresh, / And *breaks* into the crocus-purple hour / That saw thee vanish." Tennyson does not equate Persephone's rape, in a positive sense, with her acquisition of wisdom or with the rebirth of nature (as imaged by the breaking forth of flowers), but the confluence of the three types of imagery, and the three processes, does suggest a dark and melancholy awareness on the poet's part that the innocence of human nature, and the innocence of the pastoral world, inevitably fall into a complex relation with evil. Demeter now recognizes that violence and pain are not only constituents of the pastoral world, but are actually necessary stages to be gone through in order to recover pastoral, albeit in a fallen form. This is one of the ways Tennyson emphasizes the melancholy in the myth of Demeter and Persephone. Sir James George Frazer would, a few years later, place a similar emphasis on the dark side of nature in the myth:

> We do no indignity to the myth of Demeter and Persephone – one of the few myths in which the sunshine and clarity of the Greek genius are crossed by the shadow and mystery of death – when we trace its origin to some of the most familiar, yet eternally affecting aspects of nature, to the melancholy gloom and decay of autumn and to the freshness, the brightness, and the verdure of spring.[76]

This transformation of pastoral, this recognition of violence and evil as an almost organic component of the pastoral scene, also describes in "Demeter and Persephone" the path out of which originates artistic vision. Persephone's return to the fallen pastoral world constitutes an image of the solitary artist who has seen evil and thereby attains a profound vision that can be translated into art. Her isolation, as Stange observes, and her new power are aspects of the poet's creativity.[77] Persephone's transformation from child to queen suggests her new power. Demeter's denial, "Queen of the dead no more," only serves to emphasize Persephone's magisterial presence. Yet this power isolates her from humanity: like the "climate-changing" bird, her passing from state to state has given her knowledge, but it also means she can no longer clearly locate her identity within one state. She has become the isolated artist on the "threshold." Even the description of her eyes as she recovers sight in the daylight world – "Those eyes / Again were human-godlike" – suggests the isolation that is the result of her ambiguous identity. Just as she passes from state to state, from Hades to Earth, her own identity wavers between the godlike and the human. Now, however, she can never be one or the other. Her journey to Hades and her return have forever set her apart from both men and gods:

> Child, those imperial disimpassioned eyes
> Awed even me at first, thy mother—eyes
> That oft had seen the serpent-wanded power
> Draw downward into Hades with his drift
> Of flickering spectres, lighted from below
> By the red race of fiery Phlegethon;
> But when before have Gods or men beheld
> The Life that had descended re-arise,
> And lighted from above by the Sun?

As Stange observes, the phrase "imperial disimpassioned eyes" not only conveys Persephone's power as a queen who has witnessed the realm of death, it is a telling description of the stance of the poet himself.[78] Like Persephone, the poet's detachment is not the result of complete absence of feeling but stems, rather, from his sense of being outside or between the ordinary realms of experience. The poet is "disimpassioned" because he has the melancholy wisdom that comes from being outside the exclusive knowledge associated with particular genres or types of figurative language (these being the literary equivalent of the states through which Persephone passes). The barriers that separate diverse worlds of experience have been broken in Persephone's journey, and the poet, as he shifts from classical myth to its representation from the perspective of the modern "frame," realizes in his work a similar breaking down of boundaries and conventions. What is especially interesting about Persephone as a figure for the poet (whose state of exile is both a source of melancholy and of power) is that Tennyson metonymically transfers the very same figure to Demeter, who undergoes a similar period of "climate-changing":

> Child, when thou wert gone,
> I envied human wives, and nested birds,
> Yea, the cubbed lioness; went in search of thee
> Through many a palace, many a cot, and gave
> Breast to ailing infants in the night,

And set the mother waking in amaze
To find her sick one whole; and forth again
Among the wail of midnight winds, and cried,
'Where is my loved one? Wherefore do ye wail?'
And out from all the night an answer shrilled,
'We know not, and we know not why we wail.'
I climbed on all the cliffs of all the seas,
And asked the waves that moan about the world
'Where? do ye make your moaning for my child?'
And round from all the world the voices came,
'We know not, and we know not why we moan.'
'Where?' and I stared from every eagle-peak,
I thridded the black heart of all the woods,
I peered through tomb and cave, and in the storms
Of Autumn swept across the city, and heard
The murmur of their temples chanting me,
Me, me, the desolate Mother!

We find the story of Demeter's wanderings in search of Persephone in the classical sources of the myth such as the *Fasti*, but
through compression and elision of detail, Tennyson emphasizes
her swift movement from place to place. Demeter imitates Persephone by becoming a wanderer between worlds. In this way,
Demeter comes to language through suffering in a manner that
parallels Persephone's return to language, as signalled by the song
of the nightingale. The language that Demeter now uses as she
searches for Persephone is the language of pastoral elegy. In the
images of her calling to the winds and to the sea-waves, Tennyson
draws on the Homeric Hymn and Ovid's *Metamorphoses*. However,
the language and imagery of this passage derive not from these
sources alone but from the classical pastoral elegy and its English
successors. Tennyson uses variants of the pastoral device of the refrain and of the call and response. In addition, the passage involves
the pathetic fallacy, which is used infrequently in Theocritus but
plays an important part in the elegies by Bion and Moschus:

'Alack for the Cyprian,' cry all the hills, and the oak trees, 'Alas for
Adonis.' The rivers wail for Aphrodite's sorrows; the springs weep
for Adonis on the hills. The flowers turn brown for grief.'[9]

That is from Bion's "Lament for Adonis," and here is the opening of Moschus' "Lament for Bion":

> Wail sorrowfully, ye glades and waters of the Dorians; weep rivers, for our beloved Bion. Now make lament, all green things; now moan, all groves, and, flowers expire with unkempt clusters. Now, roses and anemones, don mourning crimson; speak out thy letters, hyacinth, and add more cries of sorrow to thy petals. The fair singer is dead.[80]

When Demeter calls to the anthropomorphized nature, she does get a response, but it is not a response that validates her grief. Nor does the response provide the answer to her question. Tennyson uses the conventions of the pastoral elegy, but also makes some significant changes. In Bion and Moschus, the representation of nature through the pathetic fallacy emphasizes nature's sympathetic identification with man, the way the whole world grieves for the person who is gone. The language of nature's response confirms the speaker's sense that his language of grief has meaning. In Tennyson's poem, the pastoral conventions of elegy do not serve this purpose. The poet uses pathetic fallacy to represent nature's grief, but the grief of the winds and the waves is not the result of Persephone's disappearance. Their grief has some other cause, one they themselves are unaware of.

Variations of the call-and-response structure and the language of pathetic fallacy create, in Bion and Moschus, a community of feeling. In "Demeter and Persephone," however, the different parts of nature do not understand the meaning of their feelings, nor can they provide sympathy or answers for Demeter. The conventions that in the classical elegy create a bond between man's sorrow and nature, here emphasize man's exile from nature. Nature's response to man's grief describes not sympathetic identification, but a pessimistic expression of the meaninglessness of grief itself: "We know not, and we know not why we wail"; "We know not, and we know not why we moan." The language of nature does not relieve Demeter's sorrow but compounds the mystery of grief, suggests a frightening absence of meaning at the core of all natural life. Pathetic fallacy here signifies a separation of man from nature, and a separation of both man and nature from meaning.

Ultimately, Demeter's alienation from nature and her sorrow at Persephone's absence lead her to a wasteland and visions of hell on earth. In her journey, the sorrowing mother (*mater dolorosa*) moves from the simple, elemental landscape of the classical pastoral elegy, to a landscape that in certain respects is like the conventional eighteenth-century landscape of melancholy, and then to the modern wasteland which prefigures Eliot. Lines 58 through 67 constitute the classical landscape of pastoral elegy. Lines 68 and 69—"I thridded the black heart of all the woods, / I peered through tomb and cave"—contain iconographic elements of the melancholy tradition from Milton's "L'Allegro" and "Il Penseroso" right up to Gray. The emphasis in these lines is on the Gothic aspect of nature (with darkness and evil conveyed by the epithet "black heart"); and there is a nod toward the graveyard school in "I peered through tomb and cave." This passage exemplifies, in a compressed form, Tennyson's "journey" from the classical elegy to the melancholy descriptive poetry that comes to the fore in the middle and late eighteenth century. Demeter, as sorrowing mother and type for the poet, cannot stop there; for no answer has been provided as to Persephone's whereabouts. She moves on to the city as spiritual wasteland: "and in the storms / Of Autumn swept across the city, and heard / The murmur of the temples chanting me, / Me, me, the desolate Mother." Here she turns in maternal grief but also, like the poet turning from conventions which have provided no answers, to the city-jungle as hell on earth:

> And fled by many a waste, forlorn of man,
> And grieved for man through all my grief for thee,—
> The jungle rooted in his shattered hearth,
> The serpent coiled about his broken shaft,
> The scorpion crawling over naked skulls;—
> I saw the tiger in the ruined fane
> Spring from his fallen God. . . .

Just as Persephone's journey to knowledge involves the disruption of the pastoral *locus amoenus* symbolized by the fields of Enna, Demeter's journey moves from an order of nature from which she is now alienated—the winds, seas, eagle-peak—to a natural world characterized by violent disorder. Her journey is also a literary one from the conventions of pastoral elegy to the breakdown of those conventions, as they fail to provide the answer to Demeter's grief.

Demeter discovers that neither nature nor man's conventionalization of nature in traditional types of figurative language provides meaning in the face of her daughter's absence. Nature, language, and the gods, fail her. In terms of the last, the image of the "fallen God" prefigures the religious doubt that slowly emerges in Demeter as she discovers where Persephone is. If Demeter perceives a failure in nature to explain Persephone's absence, and a failure in the poetic conventions of pastoral elegy to mitigate and bestow meaning on her sorrow, she also perceives a failure in the religious structures and myths that have defined her entire world and even her identity. These three areas of failure define the melancholy of "Demeter and Persephone." Tennyson was drawn to the myth of Demeter and Persephone because it is a myth about the failure of myth itself to give order and coherence to the world. Pater refers to this sense of failure in Greek myth, and to where it eventually led, when he says in "Winckelmann": "Scarcely a wild or melancholy note of the medieval church but was anticipated by Greek polytheism."[81] Demeter confronts the limits of myth when she confronts the Fates (a passage almost Hardian in its pessimism):

> but trace of thee
> I saw not; and far on, and, following out
> A league of labyrinthine darkness, came
> On three grey heads beneath a gleaming rift.
> 'Where'? and I heard one voice from all the three,
> 'We know not for we spin the lives of men,
> And not of Gods, and know not why we spin!
> There is a Fate beyond us.' Nothing knew.

It is fitting that in this final realization of the failure of classical myth, the poet echoes Virgil's Messianic *Eclogue*:

> "Taelia saecla" suis dixerunt "currite" fusis
> concordes stabili fatorum numine Parcae.
> ("Ages such as these, glide on!" cried to their spindles the Fates,
> voicing in unison the fixed will of Destiny. [trans. Fairclough])

Eclogue IV has been interpreted as prefiguring the birth of Christ and can, thus, be viewed as an important turn in literary history (at least retrospectively) from the classical world of mythic gods to modern Christianity. The irony of Tennyson's allusion is that the Fates in Virgil give voice to hopeful prophecy: the years and Destiny are bringing the return of the Golden Age. In contrast, the Fates in "Demeter and Persephone" see the lives of men and even the larger Fate that controls those lives as inexplicable. They signal the end of an age, not a new beginning. In a sense, Tennyson chooses to divide in two his allusion to the Messianic *Eclogue* by having the Fates speak only of their lack of knowledge (this image constitutes the nadir of Demeter's journey and her realization that even the mythic gods are no longer of any use to her), and by displacing the prophecy of the new dispensation to a later point in the poem, when Demeter and Persephone have been reunited. Here, however, the prophecy is not of a new dispensation (Tennyson's modern "frame"), but of a spectral vision of evil and innocence bound up with each other:

> "The Bright one in the highest
> Is brother of the Dark one in the lowest,
> And Bright and Dark have sworn that I, the child
> Of thee, the great Earth-Mother, thee, the Power
> That lifts her buried life from gloom to bloom,
> Should be for ever and for evermore
> The Bride of Darkness."

The lines, "The Bright one in the highest / Is brother of the Dark one in the lowest," constitute, in epigrammatic form, the melancholy knowledge that Demeter has discovered in her journey. Nature has failed her, and so have the gods. She expresses her bitterness on realizing that failure (her sense of alienation from and emotional superiority to the gods, who have shown their violent and evil side in Persephone's ravishment) in the following passage:

> Then I, Earth-Goddess, cursed the Gods of Heaven.
> . . . .
> The man, that only lives and loves an hour,
> Seemed nobler than their hard Eternities.

Demeter's alienation from the gods increases her alienation from nature. Earlier, nature had failed her by being unable to tell her where Persephone had gone and by being unable to sympathetically grieve with and for her. There nature contained its own inexplicable sorrow. Now, Demeter, in turn, fails nature:

> My quick tears killed the flower, my ravings hushed
> The bird, and lost in utter grief I failed
> To send my life through olive-yard and vine
> And golden grain, my gift to helpless man.

When one of the gods loses faith in the efficacy of their own myths, the system of belief and the order of nature cease to function. As belief withdraws, the procreativeness of nature withdraws also. While the myth ultimately reestablishes the order of the gods in the compromise granted by Zeus (in which three-quarters of the year Persephone resides in the middle state of earth with her mother, and one-quarter is spent in Hades with her husband Dis), Tennyson's interest in the myth does not lie in the explanation of the cycle of the seasons and the growth, harvest, and decay of nature, all of which Frazer emphasizes in his discussion; rather, Tennyson's interest lies in the way the symbolic journeys of both mother and daughter are types of a loss of faith and innocence which qualify new belief through a consciousness of evil and suffering. This sense of loss contributes to Tennyson's modern "frame":

> Yet I, Earth-Goddess, am but ill-content
> With them, who still are highest. Those gray heads,
> What meant they by their 'Fate beyond the Fates'
> But younger kindlier Gods to bear us down,
> . . . . Gods,
> To quench, not hurl the thunderbolt, to stay,
> Not spread the plague, the famine. . . .

This is Tennyson's modern version of the prophecy of the golden age found in Virgil, *Eclogue* IV. Demeter's visions of a troubling sort of autumnal peace qualify this prophecy. The two autumn scenes toward the close of the poem contain within them a sense of withdrawal from the belief in the beneficence of nature, which the prophecy of a new dispensation does not dispel:

> Once more the reaper in the gleam of dawn
> Will see me by the landmark far away,
> Blessing his field, or seated in the dusk

> Of even, by the lonely threshing-floor,
> Rejoicing in the harvest and the grange.

The poet echoes Keats's "To Autumn," a poem that Tennyson returned to again and again. "To Autumn" takes as its subject the closure of pastoral, yet it does not so much close as fade slowly away. Its melancholy derives from the image of a creativity whose full achievement also constitutes its demise. In "Demeter and Persephone," Tennyson's imagery of the rebirth of nature, reunion of mother and daughter, and even the autumnal scenes of peace, work alongside the melancholy sense that as these events come, or may come, to pass they are also passing away. At the poem's close, Demeter expresses the hope that Persephone will "see no more" the "silent field of Asphodel." Even this hope suggests how the consciousness of evil and suffering has marked forever the pastoral scene of love and innocence. In Tennyson's melancholy idyll, the fields of Asphodel and the fields of Enna now define and determine each other.

III

Songs from *The Princess*

IN THIS CHAPTER WE WILL EXPLORE HOW TEN-nyson's sense of exile from tradition helps to determine the way he structures emotion (especially melancholy) in his poems. The emphasis here will be on the interaction in Tennyson's poetry between his sense of tradition and structures of emotion, how they shape each other. Two songs from *The Princess*, "Tears, Idle Tears" and "Come Down, O Maid," are to be examined from this perspective. The first of these lyrics contains less direct allusions to the pastoral tradition but exhibits connections to this tradition nevertheless, especially in terms of the poem's representation of melancholy: "Tears, Idle Tears" is the poem that best exemplifies the structures of emotion in the melancholy poetics of Tennyson. The second lyric, "Come Down, O Maid," is directly indebted to pastoral conventions and contains many echoes of the classical pastoral writers. It is probably Tennyson's most Theocritean poem, and it will be approached here in terms of how Tennyson adapts the idyll form to explore certain emotional states of mind, and how, in the process, he creates a new kind of melancholy idyll. In these two poems, Tennyson takes the form and feeling of both pastoral conventions and the melancholy mode in a new direction.

Several questions arise in regard to "Tears, Idle Tears." What exactly is the nature of the emotion it describes? How do the formal structures of language and image in the poem represent these emotions? What is the nature of the poem's relation to pastoral and melancholy poetry?

> Tears, idle tears, I know not what they mean,
> Tears from the depth of some divine despair
> Rise in the heart, and gather to the eyes,
> In looking on the happy Autumn-fields,
> And thinking of the days that are no more.
>
> Fresh as the first beam glittering on a sail,
> That brings our friends up from the underworld,
> Sad as the last which reddens over one
> That sinks with all we love below the verge;
> So sad, so fresh, the days that are no more.
>
> Ah, sad and strange as in dark summer dawns
> The earliest pipe of half-awakened birds
> To dying ears, when unto dying eyes
> The casement slowly grows a glimmering square;
> So sad, so strange, the days that are no more.
>
> Dear as remembered kisses after death,
> And sweet as those by hopeless fancy feigned
> On lips that are for others; deep as love,
> Deep as first love, and wild with all regret;
> O Death in Life, the days that are no more.

The nature of the emotion described here has been the subject of much debate among the critics. That the poem conveys strong emotion has not been disputed, however. The predominance of feeling has been the basis of objections to the poem, such as Leavis's: Leavis says the poem conveys "emotion for its own sake without a justifying situation."[1] But Douglas Bush links the strong emotion in Tennyson to Virgil: "Their best work is essentially elegiac, the product of a temperamental melancholy, a brooding wistful sense of the past."[2] Bush goes on to say of "Tears, Idle Tears": "It is at such moments that he writes as Virgil would have written."[3] Bush justifies Tennyson's emphasis on pure emotion, but we still need to inquire about the specific nature of this emotion in "Tears, Idle Tears." In his well-known essay on the poem, Cleanth Brooks observes the ambiguity and paradox in the poem, and describes the emotion as "the sense of being irrevocably barred out from the human world."[4] Graham Hough says, "the theme is an almost objectless regret."[5] Spitzer considers the "divine despair" of the poem to be the despair of the God of Death in Life, which, he goes on to say, reveals Tennyson's "intense disharmony with reality."[6] Despite the differences among these critics, they all agree that Tennyson's achievement here lies in his ability to embody this emotion, as difficult to describe as this emotion is, in language and imagery that constitute a sophisticated and complex poetic structure.

Brooks was the first to observe the elements of paradox and ambiguity in the poem, and they are nowhere more evident than in the way Tennyson represents emotion. The key description of emotion in the first stanza is the near oxymoron of "divine despair." This, the speaker says, is the source of the tears. But what sort of feeling is described by "divine despair"? The word "despair" comes from the Latin *desperare* and denotes reversal of hope, yet hopelessness is not the best way of describing the emotion and mood of "Tears, Idle Tears." Tennyson has linked "despair" with the word "divine," which suggests, as Spitzer argues, a deity but also something sacred and good. The emotion is not simply sadness or resignation; it involves a power that sanctifies human experience, and such power is the opposite of despair. Tennyson even qualifies the image of the tears, which ought to be a clear sign of sadness, with the adjective "idle." Even without knowledge of its classical source, "idle" reverberates with meaning. Various critics have asked why the tears are "idle." "Idle" can mean worthless or useless; in Middle English it means void or empty. The word may connote that the tears are without signification—are a kind of cipher. The apparent lack of meaning is itself part of the image's significance. In the first stanza, the speaker does not know the tears' meaning; the inability to define this sign, to articulate this mood, is the emotional and intellectual crux of the first stanza. To understand the meaning of this gesture and image requires that the speaker actively pursue a series of thoughts. The poet emphasizes the speaker's active search for meaning in stanza one through the verbs: "know," "rise," "gather," "looking," and "thinking." This mental activity is the effort to fill in the absent meaning in the void for which the tears are an emblem. Furthermore, the verbs suggest that the speaker's experience produces something other than resignation or hopelessness. Resignation would bring with it passivity, not the kind of active, curious attention that the speaker evinces. Even to say "I know not" shows an awareness of an absence of meaning that needs to be filled. The negative construction suggests its desired opposite: the speaker's need to know what the tears mean. The opening stanza of "Tears, Idle Tears" does not simply represent a vague sense of melancholy, but shows the speaker's rigorous acts of thought and inquiry into the significance of this mood.

The inquiry into melancholy's meaning constitutes a type of creative power, a source of poetic inspiration for Tennyson. This power and inspiration is nowhere more in evidence than in "Tears, Idle Tears." At the same time, while Tennyson is drawn to the poetic conventions associated with the representation of melancholy, he also feels apart from them. Consequently, his poetry about melancholy is also about the melancholy of poetic disinheritance. In order to understand the emotion in "Tears, Idle Tears" and to understand the way the poet structures this emotion through language and image, it is not sufficient to speak of the loss of Hallam or the poet's "passion of the past," as important as these are. One must look at the conventions of the poetry of melancholy, conventions which constitute the poet's inheritance and, simultaneously, his sense of alienation. J. W. Mackail has a brief but illuminating discussion of the relation of Tennyson to Theocritus in his *Lectures on Greek Poetry*. Mackail says that "Tears, Idle Tears" is "completely in the Theocritean manner . . . the style, the movement, the enriched, subtilised, and refracted embodiment of emotion, though applied to a different subject, are precisely those of the twelfth idyll."[7] Given Tennyson's debts to Theocritus, it may seem inconsistent to go against Mackail's judgment on "Tears, Idle Tears." However, while elements of the classical pastoral elegy, love-lament, and the Greek *pothos*, or longing, that we associate with Theocritus clearly influence the general form of "Tears, Idle Tears," the true emotional debts here lie with the Romantics, especially Wordsworth and Keats.[8] In glancing at the poem's relation to these poets, we can see the meaning of the poem's melancholy.

Tennyson says of the poem: "This song came to me on the yellowing autumn-tide at Tintern Abbey, full for me of its bygone memories. It is the sense of the abiding in the transient."⁹ As commentators have pointed out, Tintern Abbey is near Clevedon, where Hallam was buried. The memories have a personal basis in Tennyson's mourning over the death of Hallam. Hough notes that section 19 of *In Memoriam* was also written at Tintern Abbey:

> The Wye is hushed nor moved along,
>   And hushed my deepest grief of all,
>   When filled with tears that cannot fall,
> I brim with sorrow drowning song.¹⁰

"Tears, Idle Tears" is about this personal grief, but it is also about a more general sense of memory, the past, and, specifically, the poetry of the past. The poem that informs Tennyson's song is, of course, Wordsworth's "Tintern Abbey." Wordsworth describes the loss of the elemental communion with nature experienced in his youth, but there is little sense of "deepest grief" here:

>   other gifts
> Have followed; for such loss, I would believe,
> Abundant recompense.

The recompense is the ability to look on nature and hear the "still, sad music of humanity." In "Tintern Abbey," memory of the past, in a manner that looks ahead to Proust, creates a deeper spiritual bond between man and world than can be experienced in the present. The "green pastoral landscape" becomes dearer as the poet's sense of the past deepens. This is a different configuration of emotion than that found in "Tears, Idle Tears." As James Kissane says, there is a "deep incongruity" between Wordsworth's poem and Tennyson's: "there is in Tennyson's poem none of his predecessor's serene confidence that the 'wild ecstasies' of the past 'shall be matured / Into a sober pleasure' and that memory is but 'a dwelling place / For all sweet sounds and harmonies.'"¹¹ Kissane's point fits in with our general argument about Tennyson and melancholy; memory becomes the "dwelling place" where the melancholy poet meditates on his distance from "all sweet sounds and harmonies." In Wordsworth, poetry and song still validate the poet's place within the world and within poetic tradition. In Tennyson, the attenuation of song and the distance from the world are the signs of the poet's placelessness. Contrasting "Tintern Abbey" and "Tears, Idle Tears," Kissane remarks that the latter

> perhaps typifying a later stage of the Romantic sensibility, comes from an imaginative world where the self cannot know communion or continuity save in the unmitigable need to experience them.[12]

In Tennyson, it is not simply the sense of continuity that the poet needs to experience but even the sense of grief itself. This is the significance of the "tears" being "idle"; they connote an absence of meaning and an emotional absence. The speaker cannot even experience a sense of continuity with his grief, and he desperately needs to. Wordsworth's "green pastoral landscape" evokes a sense of sadness in the speaker, but also joy. The tenuous and vague imagery in Tennyson's song implies, on the other hand, that nature can evoke neither sadness nor joy in the speaker. The depth of feeling in the poem arises from his inability to feel a part of the world, including the natural world, that surrounds him. We can see the difference with Wordsworth, if we look at one more passage from the latter, this time from "Intimations of Immortality":

> To me the meanest flower that blows can give
> Thoughts that do often lie too deep for tears.

Wordsworth here describes a complex relation between nature ("flower") and mind ("thoughts") and emotion ("tears"). The green world (i.e., the pastoral world) has an effect on the mind that goes beyond emotion. But this "sinking" pattern, which Hartman has shown to be pervasive in Wordsworth, gives way to a rising up, not of tears, but of language.[13] In Wordsworth the deep thoughts that occur in the mind's relation to world are a source of poetic inspiration. The complex relation between world, mind, emotion, and language ultimately suggests a reciprocity between man and nature that subsumes the grief man feels. This reciprocity is missing in "Tears, Idle Tears," because the speaker experiences the emotion but not the thoughts that should go with the emotion. His tears reverse Wordsworth's formula. Tennyson's speaker experiences tears that are too deep for thoughts.

The Wordsworthian speaker looks on the landscape of pastoral and this landscape gives rise to thoughts, thoughts he then puts into language. Keats is more aware of the way nature can limit the poet's powers of language: the sadness the poet feels before nature's limiting power in "To Autumn" involves a diminution of song that is his final paradoxical statement of poetry's decline when the poet is at the apex of his powers. In both of these Romantic poets, however, nature is the form the imagination takes in the process of poetic creation. The representation of nature becomes a way of structuring the representation of emotion in the Romantic lyric. Does Tennyson use the representation of nature to structure the emotions in "Tears, Idle Tears" in a way similar to the Romantics, and what sort of emotion does that structure produce? We are back to that question again, but this time it can be approached via the representations of nature. Brooks says the principal structure in "Tears, Idle Tears" is one of paradox, meaning that the representation of nature in the poem is paradoxical. One can see the double-sided pull in the images of nature in the opening stanza, where the tears rise

> In looking on the happy Autumn-fields,
> And thinking of the days that are no more.

W. David Shaw, in his discussion of the poem, speaks of the "pastoral oxymorons of inner weather."[14] The phrase "happy Autumn-fields" is an example of such a "pastoral oxymoron." The poet describes the Autumn-fields as "happy." Yet autumn is usually associated in poetic tradition with other emotions, especially melancholy. There is a great passage in *The Seasons* by James Thomson, a poet Tennyson knew well, that, in the pastoral melancholy tradition, brings together the season, the landscape, and the relation of melancholy to the powers of poetic creativity.

> Fled is the blasted Verdure of the Fields;
> And, shrunk into their Beds, the flowery Race
> Their sunny Robes resign. Even what remain'd
> Of bolder Fruits, falls from the naked Tree;
> And Woods, Fields, Gardens, Orchards, all around
> The desolated Prospect thrills the Soul.
> He comes! he comes! in every Breeze the Power
> Of Philosophic Melancholy comes!

His near Approach the sudden-starting Tear,
The glowing Cheek, the mild dejected Air,
The softened Feature, and the beating Heart,
Pierc'd deep with many a virtuous pang, declare.
O'er all the Soul his sacred influence breathes!
Inflames Imagination; thro' the Breast
Infuses every Tenderness; and far
Beyond dim Earth exalts the swelling Thought.[15]
                                   ("Autumn," ll.998–1013)

While one cannot prove Tennyson had this specific passage in mind when he wrote his own song of autumnal melancholy, Thomson lies behind Wordsworth and is an important representative of the melancholy tradition being addressed in "Tears, Idle Tears." Though marred by such things as the ornate periphrasis of "Their sunny Robes resign," the passage looks ahead to what M. H. Abrams has described as the "correspondent breeze" in Romantic nature poetry.[16] The "desolated prospect" of the autumn landscape yields a "sacred influence" that "inflames imagination." "Philosophic Melancholy" with his "sudden-starting Tear" is a force of poetic inspiration. The sharp differences between the autumnal melancholy in Thomson and in Tennyson's "Tears, Idle Tears" are a measure of the distance Tennyson has traveled from Romanticism in his understanding and representation of nature, melancholy, and the language of the poet.

The representation of nature in "Tears, Idle Tears" is not simply paradoxical; it is ironic. When the poet speaks of the "happy Autumn-fields," he is making an ironic comment about the landscape, the quality of his emotion, and his relation to poetic tradition. In the passage from Thomson, looking at the "Prospect" leads to the emotion ("Philosophic Melancholy"), which, in turn, leads to the "influence" that "inflames Imagination." Sight, emotion, and thought work with each other in the act of poetic creation. A similar structure was seen in the passages from Wordsworth. But there is a division in Tennyson. As Kissane points out, there is a "dramatic contrast between *looking* on the happy autumn-fields and *thinking* of the days that are no more. Sensation and reflection are disconnected."[17] There is a two-fold irony in this. First, it is the irony of alluding to a season conventionally associated with melancholy (both in life and literary history) as "happy." Second, there

is an irony in that the happy natural landscape produces the opposite feeling within the speaker: he is sad. Just as there is an absence of meaning in the tears that are idle or void, there is an absence of continuity between perception and emotion. Finally, this
absence of continuity defines the poet's relation to Romantic melancholy. The poet alludes to the conventions, but he does not feel
them: they are only empty forms, like the cipher-tears. The speaker's relation to nature is comparable to his relation to traditions of
melancholy poetry. Just as there is, in Kissane's words, a "disparity
between the plenitude of external nature and the desolation of the
conscious self," there is a disparity between the rich poetic traditions upon which Tennyson bases the poem and the poet's inner
sense of impoverishment as he faces those traditions and attempts
to give them new meaning and new feeling.[18] Assad has shown
with great care how the pattern of rhythm in the lyric moves from
despair to hope and back to despair. In his view, Tennyson's use
of stress structures the poem as a tension between opposites.[19] We
have just seen how this tension works on the thematic level in the
contrast between poetic plenitude and impoverishment.

This tension of opposites—emotional, metric, literary, historic—
serves as a paradigm for this overall argument about the specific
nature of Tennysonian melancholia. It is a sadness that is aware of
itself as a sadness. Thus, the poet begins to represent the emotion
through a language of convention, a system of literary codes, that
can then be manipulated, by the detached poet, in sophisticated
ways. In "Tears, Idle Tears," as with some of the other Tennyson
poems we have examined, the melancholy tradition begins to ac-
quire a sophisticated sense of the artifices of its own langauge.
Behind stanza one, in terms of literary history, lie primarily Wordsworth and Keats, and secondarily, the whole line of melancholy-
descriptive poets of which Thomson is one example. But Tennyson's
literary debt and its ensuing melancholia are not simple things to
define. In "Tears, Idle Tears," Tennyson does not simply draw upon
the Wordsworthian meditation on nature viewed from a temporal
retrospect. The wildness the speaker feels in the final stanza has a
vague kinship to the Wordsworthian sense of power that comes
from nature and "rises" and "gathers" in the poet. The "despair"
is "divine" because it is power, not simply passivity.

From Keats, Tennyson gets his sense of natural process as the prefiguration of the poet's ending. Thus, "happy Autumn-fields" signifies both the abundance of nature and the austerity that swiftly follows the season's harvest. Moreover, the emblem of natural process is, too, a figure of the poetic process. For the poet, the cessation of creativity is the greatest source of melancholy, greater even than the memories of time lost. The end of creativity is a sign of the poet's mortality. If, however, "Tears, Idle Tears" is Keatsian in its emphasis on the diminishment inherent in both natural and poetic process, as in the final stanza of "To Autumn," it is also Keatsian in its antithesis of death and deathless song, as in, of course, the "Ode to a Nightingale":

> Ah, sad and strange as in dark summer dawns
> The earliest pipe of half-awakened birds
> To dying ears, when unto dying eyes
> The casement slowly grows a glimmering square;
> So sad, so strange, the days that are no more.

In Keats's poem, the "charm'd magic casements" open on "faery lands forlorn," and the word "forlorn" brings the speaker back from oblivion and potential death to the world of process. Keats intertwines two sides of human consciousness: passive lack of consciousness versus conscious creativity, and death versus process—these define each other. In Tennyson's stanza, however, the two sides do not so much define each other as ironically negate each other. This irony works on a small scale in the phrase, "so sad, so strange," which Shaw calls a "pastoral oxymoron." The sadness and strangeness are the result of awakening life being perceived through the eyes of death. Shaw notes that the grammatical structure of the poem is a series of similes, and this stanza is the second in the series.[20] The speaker uses the simile to describe the emotion experienced in looking at the landscape and thinking of times past. Unlike Keats's poem, however, the antitheses are not united in this simile. Brooks says of the passage, "the dead past seems to the living man as unfamiliar and fresh in its sadness as the living present seems to the dying man."[21] His view neglects the diminishment of sound and sight in the imagery. This diminishment of the world heard through "dying ears" and seen through "dying eyes" (a diminishment that Assad shows to be at work in the actual stress patterns of this line, with its fading ending) suggests the radical separation the speaker feels from the world.[22] The diminishment is yet another sign of the speaker's sense of disinheritance from the world; we can see that the nature of his disinheritance is different from the Keatsian fusion of oblivion and consciousness. In Keats, these differences blend; in Tennyson, they remain in a state of tension.

In the first line of stanza three, Tennyson describes the slowly emerging light of the early morning with the phrase, "dark summer dawns." The phrase is, like "divine despair" and "happy Autumn-fields," a near oxymoron. "Dawn" connotes light, the opposite of "dark." The symbolic opposition is apparent. The poet represents nature here as embodying hope and beginnings, but also as embodying sadness and despair. The dawn is a beginning, but in its darkness it is also an ending; the image prefigures the crucial "Death in Life" of the fourth stanza. The tension of opposites, the way death and life, passivity and process, are juxtaposed but never fused, constitutes the form of language that Tennyson's poetics of melancholy takes. The tension is, moreover, analogous to the tension of Tennyson's consciousness of the poetic past as he tries to create for himself a poetic present. In stanza three, the poetic tension centers on how Tennyson moves beyond Keats's nightingale of oblivion and the magic casement that draws the earlier poet back into the world of time. It is no accident that this stanza contains an image of birds' song: "The earliest pipe of half-awakened birds." If we take Keats's "Ode to a Nightingale" as an analogue, we observe crucial differences. In Keats, the song of the bird lures the speaker away from the world to a pastoral retreat of darkness, where he tastes the sensation of being "half in love with easeful death." The song of the "half-awakened birds" in "Tears, Idle Tears" works in the opposite way. The song constitutes not the seductiveness of death, but the struggle for life. There is an antithetical energy between the awakening life of the birds and the fading away of the dying man, yet there is no need to emphasize the dying person; indeed, the poet himself does not. His emphasis is on the arc of sound in the song, from its source to its conclusion. The poet stresses the birds' song's earliness and "half-awakedness." From this perspective, the song of the bird is a type for poetic song, and it suggests the origin and priority of poetic song in the face of death. This affirmation, however, is one that remains aware of the signs of mortality imprinted on the very character of its song. The song will fade because the life of man will fade, and even the meter embodies this "fading" at the line-endings.

In "Tears, Idle Tears," the "earliest pipe of half-awakened birds" is an emblem of pastoral beginnings, and the "dying ears" is an emblem of a poetic consciousness sadly aware of how the moment of first awakening in the life of the poet is irretrievably past. The sense of distance between man and song in stanza three serves as a figure for Tennyson's distance from the pastoral tradition he is alluding to here. Tennyson creates ironic pastoral through such devices as what Shaw calls the "pastoral oxymoron," and through the diminishment of sight and sound as a way of conveying the poet's ending. In terms of the latter, "Tears, Idle Tears" looks back to the closing stanza of "To Autumn." There is a melancholy poetics in Keats's work, but what distinguishes the two poets in terms of the melancholy tradition and the melancholy of poetic creation is that Keats quite sincerely discovers the sober facts of process and mortality *within* his poems. For Keats, these discoveries are a question of emotion as well as of thought. In contrast, Tennyson realized from the start that there was no pure song outside of mortality. In addition, he was far more conscious of poetic conventions as images from the past that can never again be present; thus, he was far more melancholy about his own originality.

It is in this sense that much of Tennyson's poetry contains a secondary level of meaning, an allegory about the poet's uneasiness: the fear that his aesthetic "medley" of mixed genres, conventions, and figures is the result of an acute awareness of tradition, which diminishes the sincerity of the emotion being expressed. The melancholy irony of "Tears, Idle Tears" is a result of the sense of the past in life and poetry as being irretrievable. But the melancholy comedy, to borrow Kincaid's terms, of the poem rests in the sense that the very awareness of the inability to recover the past can be life-affirming.[23] This is, perhaps, what Tennyson means when he says the poem conveys the "abiding in the transient." "Thinking of the days that are no more" is a different statement from simply saying "these days are no more." The poet's active search for the meaning of the past, his attempt to fill in the absent meaning emblematized by the image of the tears, brings the past into the present, and turns convention into new creation. Stanza three suggests the pathos of mortality and the pathos of the poet's sense of disinheritance from literary history. Even so, the stanza also suggests the hope that lives in song and poetry. The apparent fading of vision also implies a more positive vision within it: "The casement slowly grows a glimmering square."

In one sense, the image is the objective correlative for the fading strength of the dying person. In another sense, however, it is an image of vision coming back to life: the "glimmering light" slowly "grows." What appears initially to be a sign of death can be interpreted as a sign of the rebirth of hope which points to a central fact about the melancholy in "Tears, Idle Tears." While the poem contains a sadness which originates in the recognition of mortality, there is also a movement toward hope. For example, the near oxymorons are ironic, but they also transform seemingly negative words into potentially positive ones. We have just looked at one example, in the images that seem to signal despair but contain a measure of hope, such as the song of the awakening birds and the glowing light in the casement.

Part of the more hopeful emotion that lies within the poem's melancholy has to do with Tennyson's understanding of memory. He describes it as follows:

> It is what I have always felt even from a boy, and what as a boy I called "the passion of the past." And it is so always with me now; it is the distance that charms me in the landscape, the picture and the past, and not the immediate to-day in which I move.[24]

We see the strong sense of nostalgia in his comments, and how that nostalgia fits in with this poem. Nostalgia, as Laurence Lerner has shown, is an important component of the melancholy tradition.[25] The pastoral nostalgia of "Tears, Idle Tears" is part of a complex of emotion related to Tennyson's understanding of memory's significance to the act of poetic creation. Nostalgia becomes a form of creative power rather than passive despair. The poet evinces this power in the final stanza of the poem:

> Dear as remembered kisses after death,
> And sweet as those by hopeless fancy feigned

On lips that are for others; deep as love,
Deep as first love, and wild with all regret;
O Death in Life, the days that are no more.

The passage involves a series of similes in which the speaker compares the melancholy imagination to love. The similes themselves constitute the first level of this imaginative activity. The phrase "hopeless fancy feigned" connotes the second level of the imaginative act. The speaker describes a person who loves someone who does not respond in kind, but rather who loves another. This person then imagines the kisses that will never actually take place. The structure of emotion, then, in this stanza involves two acts of the imagination: first, the simile "dear as remembered kisses" that links the love idea to the initial movement of feeling that gives rise to tears in stanza one; and second, the person imagining love that will never actually occur. The phrase "hopeless fancy feigned" is important because it suggests something about the relation of melancholy and the imagination in the poem as a whole. Remembered moments are like "fancy." They are acts of the imagination that bring pleasure as well as sadness. This notion is behind Tennyson's comments about "the passion of the past," as well. The sense of distance Tennyson speaks of, and his view of the past as a "picture," suggest how the passion of the past is bound up with imaginative re-creation. It is this imaginative re-creation of the past which constitutes its true source of fascination for Tennyson. The passion of the past is also the passion of the poet. In this sense, "Tears, Idle Tears" possesses a kind of dark humor in which sadness is both real and a feigned fancy. As imaginative constructs, the images from the past are poetic images, conventions that Tennyson consciously alludes to, and this constitutes their charm and their distance. Despite the appearance of deeply felt sadness, there are always levels of artifice in Tennyson's poems about melancholy. Such artifice is far less evident in Keats because of his relative lack of self-consciousness of genre conventions, in the sense of feeling at home with those conventions rather than apart from them. In Tennyson's case, it is not a question of false sentiment, but of a willingness to explore the nature of poetic tradition in ways that do not always take its conventions entirely seriously. Tennyson, then, is between the nonironic melancholy poetry found in the Romantics, except for Byron, who is a special case, being as much a neoclassicist as a Romantic, and the dark irony of Hardian melancholy.

We have yet to look at the classical source for the most important image in the poem: the "tears." While we have looked at the poem's melancholy primarily from the perspective of Tennyson's relation to Romanticism, and to certain images from Keats and Wordsworth, a strong case can be made that the poem's emotion has deep affinities with one of the classical writers. Douglas Bush (and before him W. P. Mustard) points out that the "idle tears" come from Virgil's *Aeneid*.[26] The most telling instance of the image, in terms of Tennyson's poem, comes in Book II, when Aeneas looks at the pictures of the Trojan War on the walls of Carthage. He weeps over the images of his city's destruction:

> "Here, too, the honorable finds its due
> and there are tears for passing things; here, too,
> things mortal touch the mind. Forget your fears;
> this fame will bring you some deliverance."
> He speaks. With many tears and sighs he feeds
> his soul on what is nothing but a picture.[27]

Aeneas's tears are for passing things, but they are also for the way the work of art honors what has past. This is one of the great examples in Western literature of *ecphrasis*, in which the literary representation of something is figured forth as a work of art. Ecphrasis has affinities with the epyllion, or little picture, which is a variant of the pastoral idyll genre. Both ecphrasis and the epyllion involve the Theocritean framing of the picture being described. Theocritean framing is a device Tennyson uses frequently: we find it in such different works as the "Morte d'Arthur" and "The Gardener's Daughter." As in Theocritus, the principal function of framing in Tennyson is to create a sense of detachment between poetic voice and subject; however, this moment of ecphrasis in Virgil combines the element of detachment derived from the framed representation of the picture and the pathos that comes from Aeneas's deep feeling. The moment is exemplary of a similar combination of detachment and deep feeling in "Tears, Idle Tears." Martin Dodsworth describes this aspect of framing in Tennyson:

The frame has a special attraction to Tennyson because it marks not merely the discontinuity of the poem with the world of everyday experience but also of the inward nature of its subject matter. The poems tend to center on states of mind and on dramatic changes of heart, the action takes place within the speaker as much as outside him.[28]

But what Dodsworth describes is the opposite of the effect Theocritus achieves through framing and ecphrasis. And Tennyson is very close to Theocritus in many ways. In Tennyson, framing can suggest the inner state of mind of the subject, but it can also define the poet's distance from that state. Such is even the case with the moment from Virgil that he alludes to through the image of the tears. The pathos created by the scene of Aeneas before the pictures of the fall of Troy involves certain kinds of detachment. Aeneas looks at the representation of a place that no longer exists, a place that he cannot return to. In this instance, the device of ecphrasis is the sign of his state of exile. In alluding to Aeneas's tears, Tennyson also alludes to his sense of exile from the meaning of his own grief – the "idle" tears constitute the absence of that meaning. He is also alluding to his sense of poetic disinheritance; however, this moment of ecphrasis in the *Aeneid* prefigures Aeneas's building of a new city. This prefiguring is analogous to Tennyson's attempt to forge out of his poetic disinheritance a place within tradition. He achieves that place through the creation of his new idyll, of which "Tears, Idle Tears" is itself one of the finest examples.

"Come Down, O Maid" is a poem about female sexuality, male perception of women, and a dialectic of melancholy and joy mediated by the language of poetic tradition. The lyric represents a struggle between male power and female power through language, and addresses a number of the themes dealt with throughout *The Princess*. As with many of his idylls, Tennyson frames this song. The narrative context in which Princess Ida nurses the Prince back to health after the battle creates the frame. First she read "Now Sleeps

the Crimson Petal," and then "she found a small Sweet Idyl, and
once more, as low she read:"

> "Come down, O maid, from yonder mountain height:
> What pleasure lives in height (the shepherd sang)
> In height and cold, the splendour of the hills?
> But cease to move so near the Heavens, and cease
> To glide a sunbeam by the blasted Pine,
> To sit a star upon the sparkling spire;
> And come, for Love is of the valley, come,
> For Love is of the valley, come thou down
> And find him; by the happy threshold, he,
> Or hand in hand with Plenty in the maize,
> Or red with spirted purple of the vats,
> Or foxlike in the vine; nor cares to walk
> With Death and Morning on the silver horns,
> Nor wilt thou snare him in the white ravine,
> Nor find him dropt upon the firths of ice,
> That huddling slant in furrow-cloven falls
> To roll the torrent out of dusky doors:
> But follow; let the torrent dance thee down
> To find him in the valley; let the wild
> Lean-headed Eagles yelp alone, and leave
> The monstrous ledges there to slope, and spill
> Their thousand wreaths of dangling water-smoke,
> That like a broken purpose waste in air:
> So waste not thou; but come; for all the vales
> Await thee; azure pillars of the hearth
> Arise to thee; the children call, and I
> Thy shepherd pipe, and sweet is every sound,
> Sweeter thy voice, but every sound is sweet;
> Myriads of rivulets hurrying through the lawn,
> The moan of doves in immemorial elms,
> And murmuring of innumerable bees."

    Critics have differed over the lyric's interpretation. Valerie Pitt
says that in its juxtaposition with the sexual awakening symbolized
by "Now Sleeps the Crimson Petal," the poem is "not so much an
address to an idealist as to a virgin."[29] In Pitt's view, "Maid" is a
celebration of the "fruitfulness of marriage."[30] Gerhard Joseph views
the poem, and *The Princess* as a whole, as a sexual contest and a

contest of genres. The entire work is, in his view, a "barely disguised psychomachy."[31] Of Ida's reading of this song, Joseph says:

> Her egosim approaches the haughtiness of the soul ensconced in
> her mountainous Palace of Art and of Lady Clare Vere de Vere
> among her halls and towers. In her song at the conclusion of *The
> Princess* she beautifully recapitulates that by now familiar descent of
> the proud artist's psyche from the heights in Tennyson's early poetry
> into the valley of Victorian love in his later work.[32]

James Kincaid further pursues this idea of the lyric as a contest of
styles but in terms of his scheme of comic and ironic patterns:

> The poem presents most clearly the opposition between two kinds
> of comedy: the heroic world of the cold and splendid mountain,
> and the domestic pastoral world of the valley.[33]

We will be less interested in the marriage theme than in the idea
of sexual contest and contests of styles, and how the two relate to
Tennyson's understanding of the traditions of pastoral and melancholy poetry.

   It is important to stress the qualifying irony in the very context
of the poem's reading. Ida reads a poem which is a song sung by
a male voice—a shepherd. The shepherd sings to the female figure
of the maid. Ida is giving voice to what is a male song of courtship
and also a male commentary on female aspirations and independence. There is an interesting irony here in that a male writer (Tennyson) is describing a female reader (Ida), who is reading a song
in which the principal speaker is male (the shepherd) singing to or
wooing a female (the maid). The complexities of sexual dialogue
and intertwining of voices imply, as Joseph suggests, a sexual contest, but one that is very much related to poetic language and poetic
voice. The song involves sexual struggles in three senses: first,
defining what it means to be male and female; second, defining
and apportioning power between the two; and third, defining female and male relationships to poetic language and poetic conventions. The poet undertakes all three tasks in "Come Down, O Maid."

   Tennyson comments, "'Come down, O maid' is said to be taken
from Theocritus, but there is no real likeness except perhaps in the
Greek Idyllic feeling."[34] The denial—like many of Tennyson's com-

ments on questions of influence—needs to be taken seriously but not necessarily accepted. Pattison has shown how, in many instances, Tennyson's denials of influences ascribed to his works by critics are then later assimilated into his own accounts of the poems.[35] In this specific case, it is fair to say there is a strong Theocritean element to the poem. In his *Lectures on Greek Poetry*, J. W. Mackail says that "Come Down, O Maid" is very similar to the songs of Lycidas and Thyrsis in Theocritus.[36] Christopher Ricks's edition of the *Poems* notes echoes of Theocritus, Virgil, Ovid, and Milton, among others. Paul Turner says the song is "pervasively Theocritean, but most closely related to *Idyll* XI, where Polyphemus, seated on his high rock beneath the white snows of Mount Etna, tells the sea-nymph Galatea that he will learn to swim, in order to discover 'what pleasure you can find in living in the deep.'"[37] The notion of the song as both love-lament and act of seduction derives from the idyll and pastoral tradition. In addition, Theocritus and Virgil often incorporate the song within a contest between singers. In Tennyson's new idyll, however, the contest has as much to do with the relative powers of female and male as it has to do with the power of the singer, yet the two are intimately related. They are related through the idea of voice, and it is with the question of voice that we must begin.

The poem opens with the shepherd's voice. His voice utters words that are ambiguous in tone and meaning: "Come down, O maid, from yonder mountain height." In one sense, the opening line is hortatory. The verbal construction of the opening clause is in the imperative mood. However, the second half of this first sentence is interrogatory. The sentence is a mixture of command and question. Even the apostrophe "O maid" is a mixture of emotions and meanings. On the one hand, the shepherd's apostrophe is a diminutive, a gesture of condescension. From that perspective, the shepherd utters the first clause in a voice of superiority. But the apostrophe is double-sided, as is the complete sentence. The voice of the shepherd, and his apostrophizing of the maid, is slightly worshipful in tone. The mixed emotion and mixed tone are not at all dissimilar to the qualities of voice found in Polyphemus's song to Galatea in *Idyll* XI. In "Come Down, O Maid," the maid is not simply a diminutive creature but a powerful figure before whom the shepherd bows down in awe: it is worth observing that he is looking up at her as she stands on the mountain heights. From this second perspective, then, the first clause takes on the quality of a request rather than a command. This tension in the voice between request and command, between the apostrophe as diminution or idolization, is one key to the poem. Does the shepherd view the maid as a small, helpless creature or as a figure of power? Within the context of the narrative of *The Princess*, the maid serves as a central image for Tennyson's exploration of female identity and female power. Tennyson is asking, "What does it mean for the maid to come down from the mountain height?" On the most basic narrative level, to come down from the height means that Ida will now abandon her dream of a woman's college completely apart from men. Her descent is the recognition of her need for the companionship and love of men. One could even carry this line of interpretation so far as to say, as Kissane does, that "this descent involves a change in Ida from feminist to female."[38] Such would seem to be the basic meaning of the song, and the voice of the shepherd then becomes a voice of male censoriousness advocating female submission; however, as John Killham has demonstrated in his study of the feminist and political background to *The Princess*, Tennyson's position in the poem is not as unqualifiably anti-feminist as initially appears.[39] As a paradigm for the sexual contest and the related contest of poetic styles in *The Princess*, "Come Down, O Maid" qualifies the anti-feminist view in a number of ways.

The first type of qualification within the song has to do with the relative power of speaker and subject. If we look at the language of the opening sentence, we see that the voice of the shepherd evinces powerlessness as well as power before the maid. The speaker links the substantive words of power with the maid. He emphasizes her power through the emphatic repetition of the word "height": "height" is the closing word of the first line, the closing word of the second line before the parenthetical comment, and one of the nouns in the prepositional phrase in line three. In its association with the noun "maid," the word "height" transforms the former from a descriptive diminutive to a substantive word of power. The language of the shepherd's song bestows power on the female figure. To be on the mountain height is to be power-ful, to be above the common realm in a positive as well as negative sense.

The shepherd's song stresses the negative connotations of the maid's distance and aloofness; however, through the language of his song, we do not feel that her distance is necessarily a negative at-tribute. Rather, it is a power to be desired. And her silence strength-ens the impressiveness of her power. In terms of the dramatic struc-ture of the lyric, she is the silent listener. Her silence accrues to her power. As there is a sublimity in her "height," there is a sub-limity in the way she is beyond language itself. Indeed, there is an important reversal in terms of the contest of literary styles played out in the larger narrative text. Within "Come Down, O Maid," the female figure is *not* the figure of gentle lyricism but of epic heroism. She is a woman of few words.

The poem's pastoral melancholy lies within the shepherd's voice – his need, in effect, to plead with her. When he sings, "What pleasure lives in height . . . / In height and cold, the splendour of the hills?" he intends the question to be rhetorical, a statement of a negative fact. The answer is supposed to be that no pleasure lies there. But is the voice of the shepherd persuasive? Probably not. When we change the clause from the interrogative mood to declarative state-ment, we are struck by how weak a statement it is. The shepherd's statement is weak to just that degree that the image he evokes is actually one of an admirable strength. Although he wants his ques-tion to suggest that the maid in her isolation cannot experience pleasure, the image he uses to describe her place of isolation con-notes pleasure rather than displeasure. The "splendour of the hills," because it is an image of power and strength, signifies the pleasure the maid derives from the space she inhabits. In the first sentence of the lyric, the shepherd's argument, then, is as follows: the maid, in order to be fully human, must descend from the position of power (the "height" and "splendour of the hills") to one of weak-ness ("down" in the valley where Love is). He urges her to give up the "cold" aloofness that is a sign of her power and independence, and to accept a lower position of dependence and powerlessness. The very terms of his argument, however, suggest a counterargu-ment: the female should maintain this desired position of "splendour." The language and imagery of the opening sentence function as a thematic and stylistic prelude to the entire lyric.

The opening question receives fuller elaboration in the following twenty-eight lines, lines that constitute one lengthy sentence made up of a complex series of phrases and clauses. The second sentence, like the first, opens in the imperative mood:

> But cease to move so near the Heavens, and cease
> To glide a sunbeam by the blasted Pine,
> To sit a star upon the sparkling spire. . . .

As the shepherd begins to give voice to his plea in more elaborate and specific terms, the language continues to undermine his argument. The first clause begins with the conjunction "but." This is significant for two reasons: first, it suggests elaboration, and second, it implies qualification. As with the shepherd's first sentence, the emotion and meaning here continue to be a mixture of command and question. The imagery contained within his first rhetorical question undercuts his line of reasoning. Here, as the second sentence opens, the conjunction "but" looks both back to that first sentence, as if to further qualify it, and forward, as a subtly negative factor in the ensuing clause; furthermore, the conjunction combines with the negative denotation of the verb "cease." This combination makes the shepherd's meaning in the ensuing series of clauses one that is strong in its denunciations but weak in its affirmations. The shepherd questions the pleasures of the mountian heights in the first sentence, but in the following clauses he offers no alternative. The singer's expressive language involves a type of limitation; specifically, the limitation of the powers and freedoms of the maid. The imperative "cease," however, paradoxically emphasizes its opposite. The literal meaning of the verbal constructions denotes a sense of movement being closed off, but the true emphasis falls on the infinitives: "to move," "to glide," "to sit." At the same time, the elision of "like" in clauses two and three turns the figure from simile to metaphor, producing a strong metonymic identification between the female figure and certain aspects of the natural world. Together, the emphatic infinitives and the elided similes associate the maid with a powerful and agile sense of movement through a sublime and picturesque landscape. We begin to observe a strong contrast between the melancholy lament of the shepherd and the powerful heroism of the maid.

From the seventh line on, however, the tone begins to change.

> And come, for Love is of the valley, come,
> For Love is of the valley, come thou down
> And find him. . . .

The quality of tone in the verb "come" is here no longer the mixture of command and plea that the same verb signified in the opening line. Nor does the verb have the harshly negative connotations of "cease." In lines seven and eight, the verbal repetition has the rhetorically formal dignity of a gracious invitation. The poet develops this graciousness through the lyricism of the parenthetical clause to which the verb is joined: "for Love is of the valley." The elegiac note is tempered by the light mellifluousness of the verse produced by the vowel sounds and assonance: *o, i, a,* combined with the labial *m* and the *l*. At this moment, the voice of the shepherd turns from negation to affirmation. The gentle lyricism is the equivalent in language of the warm domesticity that lies in the valley. It is no accident that as the shepherd begins to sing of the descent into the valley, the song assumes a Keatsian autumnal richness: the poet signals this Keatsian quality by a subtle modulation from the repeated verb "come," with its parenthetical clause ("for Love is of the valley"), to the more active imperative "find," and its direct object "him." At this moment, we realize the poet is not simply speaking of love as an abstraction but as a personification, and it is in this moment that the song takes a Keatsian turn:

> by the happy threshold, he,
> Or hand in hand with Plenty in the maize,
> Or red with spirted purple of the vats,
> Or foxlike in the vine. . . .

This is the language of Keats's autumn pastoral, with the rhetorical formality, which is Keats by way of Milton, in the inversion of subject and phrase in "by the happy threshold, he," and also with the anaphora in lines 10 through 12: Or . . . Or . . . Or. In addition to the formal tone, there is the Keatsian sense of natural abundance, of organic plenitude, as Love walks "hand in hand

with Plenty in the maize." Even the grammar of the passage, with
a series of phrases, conveys the effect of abundance both of place
and activity.

We begin to see the value of the alternative the shepherd offers
the maid, for the passage serves to counteract with its own kind
of gentle power the sublimities of the mountain heights. Yet almost
in spite of itself the description turns back to those very same mountain heights:

> nor cares to walk
> With Death and Morning on the silver horns,
> Nor wilt thou snare him in the white ravine,
> Nor find him dropt upon the firths of ice,
> That huddling slant in furrow-cloven falls
> To roll the torrent out of dusky doors. . . .

The shepherd says, this is a place where Love does not care to walk.
But, as in the opening lines, the supposedly negative description
has a kind of power that makes it seem desirable for the maid to
remain there, rather than descend. Ruskin spoke of the passage with
admiration: "Perhaps one of the most wonderful pieces of sight in
all literature is–Nay, that's just it; I was going to say a bit of Tennyson–the piece of Alp in *The Princess*."[40] Hallam Tennyson
comments that the song "is descriptive of the waste Alpine heights
and gorges and of the sweet rich valley below."[41] These adjectives
do not fully describe the tension that results from the attractiveness
of *both* of these worlds. Tennyson associates Love and Plenty with
a landscape of Keatsian autumnal abundance. At the same time,
however, he associates Death and Morning with the sublime landscapes found in Romantic songs to the awful power of nature, such
as section one of *The Prelude*, "Kubla Khan," and "Mont Blanc."
The shepherd's language of pastoral love continues to work against
itself by invoking an opposite world of nature that is sublime and
powerful. Furthermore, this powerful natural world is, by metonymic association, the austere power of the female figure in the
poem. This is not a simple opposition, in either ethical or aesthetic
terms. The qualities of language, image, and voice in the shepherd's
song enable Tennyson to avoid simplistic formulas. We can see this
in the next passage, in which he associates the female figure with
the power of nature:

let the wild
Lean-headed Eagles yelp alone. . . .

Earlier, the shepherd's song had identified the maid with a star and with the light of the sun. Now he links her with the formidable power of the eagles. The lines possess that peculiar Tennysonian quality of being preternaturally realistic and, at the same time, symbolic. The image also shows how the poet avoided the patronizing didacticism that marred an earlier juxtaposition of this image and theme. In "Rosalind," Tennyson also used the eagle as a sign of female freedom but in a much more supercilious way:

> Come down, come home, my Rosalind,
> My gay young hawk, my Rosalind:
> Too long you keep the upper skies;
> Too long you roam and wheel at will;
> But we must hood your random eyes,
> That care not whom they kill. . . .
> . . . .
> When we have lured you from above,
> And that delight of frolic flight, by day and night,
> From North to South,
> We'll bind you fast in silken cords,
> And kiss away the bitter words
> From off your rosy mouth.

What saves the shepherd's use of the wild bird image from this kind of saccharine conventionality is the unsentimental opposition between pastoral domesticity and the romantic sublime. No longer is the female figure a "young hawk" who "frolics" in "delight." On the contrary, the maid is linked with eagles that are "wild" and "yelp alone" amid the height and cold. Hallam Tennyson's description of the "waste heights" of the poem suggests the way the song is allied to the British tradition of sublime and frighteningly solitary descriptive poetry. "Come Down, O Maid" is not only a sexual contest, but a contest in poetic styles and genres. The stress on the sublime picturesque saves the melancholy love-lament from insipid sentimentality. The tension of opposites allows the poet to draw upon the conventions of pastoral melancholy without falling prey to them. As James Kincaid puts it: "The poem . . . revivifies

pastoral clichés. The new comedy, in fact works by asking that clichés
be deliberately accepted as such."[42] One of the ways that Tennyson
does this in the song is through the confluence of sexual contest
and stylistic contests. Through this conjunction, there is an ironic
reversal in which the poet associates melancholy passivity with the
male figure, and sublime heroism with the female figure. Melancholy passivity has often been associated with male figures in the
traditional pastoral love-lament, but in the context of *The Princess*,
it affords a startling thematic and stylistic reversal, nevertheless.
Just as there are two sexual identities in the song, there are two
kinds of landscape and two kinds of poetic language, and the poet
is hesitant about designating the relative value of each term in
these three paired relationships. There is a language of pastoral
melancholy here, but also a language of sublime picturesque. The
intertwining of the two transcends the conventions of both.

After the image of the eagles, the poet continues to explore the
interrelation of melancholy passivity and sublime power through
the representation of the natural scene:

> and leave
> The monstrous ledges there to slope, and spill
> Their thousand wreaths of dangling water-smoke.
> That like a broken purpose waste in air:
> So waste not thou. . . .

Hallam Tennyson's comment is especially appropriate here in his
contrast between the "waste Alpine heights and gorges and the
sweet rich valleys below." The contrast in this comment and in the
song seems patently clear in its designation of relative value to the
two landscapes, but in the song, that clarity is apparent rather than
actual. Once again, there is an attractiveness to the landscape he
is urging her to abandon. The adjective "monstrous" might seem
pejorative, but again, it suggests the power of nature and the power
of the female. The verbs "slope" and "spill" also connote powerful
activity. "Dangling" could be understood as softening or diminishing the sense of active force described in the previous line, and the
verb "waste" further strengthens the sense of a cessation of activity
and the idea of dwindling power. When we think carefully, though,
about the picture the speaker describes here, we realize it is not

one of wasted action without purpose or force. We need to pause and remind ourselves of what exactly the speaker describes. The description is of a waterfall, with the many streams cascading over the rocks and through the air. The shepherd makes a parallel between the "broken purpose" of the waterfall and the maid's isolation: the maid is wasting her life on the mountain heights. But the waterfall is not an image of a "broken purpose." While the ledges and rocks divide the waterfall into many streams, the waterfall is still a continuous flowing. Like Heraclitus's problem about putting one's foot into a stream at two different moments, the waterfall images the paradox of the continuity and discontinuity of time. The waterfall is never the same from moment to moment. Yet it is not wasting itself. It is continuous. The image of the waterfall, then, is not one of wasted action but of powerful stability, like the maid herself in her isolation. There is, moreover, a sexual connotation to the image. In identifying the female figure with the waterfall, the poet links her with a natural force that is actively outgoing rather than passive and receptive. The words "spill" and "waste" suggest qualities one tends to associate with masculine activity; however, in lines 22 through 24, the image of the waterfall and the verb "spill" are associated with the woman. She assumes the activity here, activity that is sexual in nature. The maid is like the "torrent," and one can understand the "torrent" as representing sexual energy as well as a more general energy associated with the natural world. The image, then, represents something very different from "broken purpose."

The language of the shepherd's song can be misleading. There is a manipulative quality to his song. His figurative association of maid and waterfall supposedly suggests her wasted life, but the figure turns back against itself. His attempt to transform the sublime power of the woman and her active sexual force into a picture of desolation and waste fails. Through his song, elemental forces of nature, such as sexuality, death, time, (all mysterious primitive energies that he paradoxically associates with the diminutive little "maid") are defused and civilized. The shepherd's pastoral art works against the primitive, natural world in which the female figure resides. In this lyric, the pastoral impulse describes not so much a withdrawal to the pastoral pleasance as a withdrawal from it. In his study of Theocritus, Thomas Rosenmeyer says that the lyricism of Theocritean pastoral is "distributive," "disengaged," "cool."[43] The lyricism of the pastoral singer in "Come Down, O Maid" is different from this: it is engaged in seducing the maid, and instead of a cool detachment, the language offers, in W. David Shaw's words, "pastoral warmth."[44] The shepherd's song, far from promising a revitalization of the maid's life, offers, in disguise, its diminishment. The pastoral of marital domesticity here displaces the promise of the retreat to nature. Apart from the context of *The Princess*, within the world of the lyric, this poem is ultimately a false pastoral of sentimental melancholy:

>   pillars of the hearth
> Arise to thee; the children call, and I
> Thy shepherd pipe, and sweet is every sound. . . .

The shepherd's pastoral song is, finally, an argument for marriage and domesticity. The argument is entirely appropriate in the context of the narrative. Ida will give up her scheme for a woman's college apart from men and will marry the Prince. Many critics view this outcome as a victory of healthy love over proud isolation. Thus, Kissane comments: "the Prince and Princess, in taking possession of each other, and of their true selves, represent unity and wholeness."[45] One can, moreover, read this marital and sexual unity as a type for the larger unity Tennyson sought in the world and through his art. This is Pitt's argument: "Marriage, then, the relationship between man and woman, was fast becoming Tennyson's symbol of relationship with the world. It was his escape from isolation."[46] Finally, Culler sees the arc of relationship in *The Princess* and in this lyric as closely tied to Tennyson's aesthetic development:

> Princess Ida, then, though a figure in a fable about the education
> of women, is also a symbol of the development of Tennyson's
> poetry. . . . When he melted her heart and persuaded her to come
> down into the valley, marry, and have a child, he was essentially
> asking her to take up her abode in the English Idyl.[47]

The lyric is more ambiguous than these comments would lead us to believe. Killham's study has shown that Tennyson's position on the "woman question" in *The Princess* is highly equivocal.

Numerous passages in the narrative suggest that female independence and power are ideas that need to be taken seriously.[48] At the poem's close, moreover, it is far from certain that Ida has made the right choice. The poet suggests alternative possibilities for the future of female/male relationships. Such qualifications about the nature of female identity and the extent of female power are clearly evident within "Come Down, O Maid."

Tennyson qualifies the shepherd's image of domestic bliss and love in the valley in several ways: first, by the attractiveness of the representation of the alternative world in the mountain heights; second, by the sense of power the speaker associates with the maid as she resides in those heights; third, by the ambiguous nature of the envisioned pastoral domesticity at the close. The poem's closure is central to the lyric's meaning, because it involves an important transformation of the previous images and ideas. It is the shepherd's most specific representation of the world that he has offered to the maid throughout, but now he conveys it through positive statement rather than negative commands. The closure also involves a subtle shift from a direct address to the maid to a more seemingly neutral kind of description:

> and sweet is every sound,
> Sweeter thy voice, but every sound is sweet;
> Myriads of rivulets hurrying through the lawn,
> The moan of doves in immemorial elms,
> And murmuring of innumerable bees.

The final two lines are justly famous. As Ricks observes, however, there is a "sense that such mellifluousness is too gratified, too limited, a skill."[49] The beauty of these lines should not distract us from the entire picture the shepherd's song creates. In this closure, the singer finally names himself a "shepherd," and that emphasizes the sense of artifice that surrounds the song. We begin to feel that the singer is not a shepherd at all, but one who is simply using a poetic convention; we recall that in the context of the narrative, it is Ida who reads this "sweet Idyl." Artifice has always been a part of the idyll form, but in "Come Down, O Maid" it is so extensive that it raises doubts about the nature of the singer's invitation to the maid. There is something not only artificial about the shepherd's invocation of the "pillars of the hearth," but cloying in its domesticity as well. Once again, the shepherd's language, his rhetorical elegance, belies his picture of domestic simplicity, signals the dangerous seductiveness of his song. The clause, "and sweet is every sound" follows "and I / Thy shepherd pipe." The next line contains a variant of "sweet" and then, in a chiasmic reversal of the clause in the preceding line, "every sound is sweet." The rhetorical artifice casts a shadow of falseness over this picture of domestic happiness and love: the sounds are too sweet. When compared to the earlier mountain heights and rolling torrent, the description seems insipid. Toward the closure of the song, the shepherd returns to earlier images but deprives them of their power (just as he wishes to deprive the maid of hers). In the mountain heights, there is a "torrent" and a "thousand wreaths of dangling water-smoke." The shepherd produces a diminutive double of this image in his domestic scene: "Myriads of rivulets hurrying through the lawn."

We feel a sense of diminishment in the shepherd's voice as he turns from the mountain heights to the "pillars of the hearth" and the domestic "lawn." One of the ironies of "Come Down, O Maid" is that the shepherd speaks as if the maid ought to be sad and lonely in her isolation, but the song actually becomes sad when he descends to the valley.

The poem opens with, "she found a small / Sweet Idyl, and once more, as low, she read," and closes, "So she low-toned." The frame reveals Ida's implicit unhappiness with the shepherd's view. On the one hand, her low voice does signal acquiescence: her realization that she "had failed / In sweet humility." On the other hand, her "low-tone" is an imitation of the shepherd's melancholy, especially of the lyric's close, an imitation that reveals her desire to reject it. Ida unconsciously identifies with the maid on the mountain heights, with the eagles that "yelp alone," with the torrential waterfall. This helps explain why the shepherd's scene of pastoral domesticity is tinged with melancholy, a scene which ought to be joyful if pleasure really does lie in the valley. The melancholy also belongs to Ida; she is unhappy, perhaps without even being aware of it, about capitulating to the Prince. The final two lines evoke an aura of defeat. Tennyson's use of vowel sounds, alliteration, labials, and assonance produces a closure of "sweet" rich sound, but it is a closure that is attenuated. The voice of the shepherd moves from a lively lyricism to a tonal quality associated with elegy. The slow withdrawal of human presence from the scene qualifies the image of domestic happiness. In the earlier description of the mountain heights, the shepherd directed a monologue at the maid; both maid and shepherd were part of the scene. In the final lines of the song, this is no longer the case. After the words "I / Thy shepherd pipe," there is a shift from human voice to sound. We could even say pure sound, without human voice. The shepherd's voice withdraws. The phrase "Sweeter thy voice" signals the last moment in which the speaker and his subject meet. After this, the voice of the shepherd moves away from the maid, and the natural scene moves away from the voice of the shepherd. One feels a sense of distance between voice and scene, and the voice itself fades. The diminishing voice of the singer serves as a contrast to the more energetic "yelp" of the eagles, and also to the actively agile verbs associated with the maid early on in the song. The nouns at the close, "moan" and "murmuring," are passive and tinged with sadness. As human presence withdraws, the description of nature becomes elegiac. One of the important ironies of "Come Down, O Maid" is that the loneliness and distance the shepherd explicitly ascribes to the maid in her splendid isolation are the very qualities that implicitly define the domestic pastoral scene in the valley at the poem's closure.

Tennyson's lyric "Come Down, O Maid" constitutes a paradigmatic moment in the history of the transformation of melancholy as a literary idea. We can best see this in a comparison with another crucial moment in this history – Keats's "To Autumn." The comparison tells us much about Tennyson's relation to Keats, to tradition, and to certain developments in the poetry of melancholy.

There are other poems by Tennyson that are more deeply indebted to Keats. George Ford, in *Keats and the Victorians*, demonstrates the strong presence of Keatsian language, especially in the early work of Tennyson.[50] Why, then, compare "Come Down, O

Maid," a poem of Tennyson's middle years, with "To Autumn"? Tennyson's song constitutes one moment of culmination in the poet's exploration of melancholy, the poet, and tradition. It is closely tied to "To Autumn," a poem that represents a transitory ending moment in the melancholy tradition, but that also turns that tradition in a new direction. There are deep and strong affinities between the two poems.

"To Autumn" is Keats's greatest evocation of the natural world of "process," to use the term of Bate and Perkins, and humanity's close kinship to this process.[51]

> Season of mists and mellow fruitfulness,
>   Close bosom-friend of the maturing sun;
> Conspiring with him how to load and bless
>   With fruit the vines that round the thatch-eves
>   run;
> To bend with apples the mossed cottage-trees,
>   And fill all fruit with ripeness to the core;
>   To swell the gourd, and plump the hazel shells
>   With a sweet kernel; to set budding more,
> And still more, later flowers for the bees,
> Until they think warm days will never cease,
>   For summer has o'er-brimmed their clammy cells.

Douglas Bush notes an echo of Theocritus's *Idyll* VII in the opening line.[52] There are numerous echoes of classical pastoral throughout: *Idyll* VII is especially important, because it is a celebration of the abundance of nature, as is Keats's "To Autumn." While both "To Autumn" and *Idyll* VII celebrate the harvest of autumnal abundance, there are as many differences as there are similarities between the two poems. In Keats's opening stanza, the mood is subdued, the voice muted. In Theocritus, the tone is lively and even celebratory: the speaker and his friends are on their way to a thanksgiving festival in honor of Demeter. In terms of the development of melancholy pastoral, the differences between the two poems are significant. In Theocritus's *Idyll* VII, the figure of melancholy does not appear, but other goddesses associated with nature do. The way Theocritus structures the representation of nature, man, and gods is relevant to our understanding of melancholy in Keats's poem. In *Idyll* VII, the jaunty light-heartedness

of the human figures separates them from the potential sadness of
the natural landscape:

> I and Eucritus however, resuming our way to the homestead
> Of Phrasidamus—and with us diminutive, pretty Amyntas—
> Soon were outstretched at full length on deep couches of sweet-
>   smelling rushes,
> And were enjoying ourselves at our ease amid newly-cut vine leaves.[53]
> (11.130–33)

The poet positions the human figures within the natural setting,
but there is little sense of the Romantic subject/object relation. As
Rosenmeyer says, the "paratactic naiveté sees to it that the lyricism, such as it is, does not turn private or ego-centered."[54] Rosenmeyer also suggests that Theocritean pastoral involves "perception
of a world that is not continuous, but a series of discrete units."[55]
We see in *Idyll* VII that the human figures are separate from the
landscape; moreover, man and landscape are each separate from the
gods:

> Just such a drink as you goddesses mixed for us then at the picnic
> Next to the altar of Deo the queen of the threshing floor? Let me
> Also implant once again the great winnowing-shovel atop the
> Pile as She smiles, holding poppies in one hand and sheaves in the
>   other.[56]
>
>   (11.152–55)

Demeter is an allegorical figure here. While she does possess human
attributes, there is a great distance and difference between her and
the people who worship her, and between her and the natural
world to which she stands as figure.

The structure between man, nature, and the gods is very different in "To Autumn." There are no human figures to begin with,
apart from the figure of the poet as conveyed by the poetic voice.
The personifications of natural forces possess human attributes,
but possess also the very real qualities of the natural world itself.
The poetic voice (or human presence), the personified god and
goddess figures, and the natural world, exist in a much closer and
more ambiguous relation than in *Idyll* VII. The poet figures forth
this intimacy right at the opening, with the poetic voice directly
addressing the season. The speaker does not name Autumn in the

first stanza, but she is the figure addressed and is, therefore, brought onto almost the same level as the speaker. This levelling effect makes the goddesslike figure an almost human one as well. Autumn is one of the final goddess figures in Keats, and as with the others, Keats allies her in subtle ways to the figure of melancholy. These figures constitute a crucial point of transition from the personified Melancholy of the eighteenth century, such as the sentimental "goddess of the tearful eye" of Joseph Warton. The figure in Keats is something other than a personification of a state of mind. At the same time, Keats's goddesses are not as completely separate from human concerns as the abstract and emblematic Demeter of Theocritus.

Keats naturalizes and incorporates the goddess figure within organic process, and the figure also becomes an aspect of the poet's mind as he works with tradition and moves beyond it. In the second line of "To Autumn," the phrase "Close bosom-friend of the maturing sun" suggests the season possesses one of the most human qualities of all: the ability to engage in friendship. The word "maturing" likewise endows the sun with a human quality. The poetic voice at the opening of "To Autumn" speaks to a female goddess figure who is also extremely human in her various qualities. This involves a different approach from that of Theocritus in *Idyll* VII. In Theocritus, the goddess of nature is a ritualistic emblem in the context of a social and public event—the harvest festival. In Keats's poem, nature is the object of solitary communion with the poetic voice. These two differences (that Keats's goddess is more human and more natural; that the poetic voice exists in a much closer relation to the goddess figure) help to account for the greater sense of melancholy in Keats's poem, despite the fact that both he and Theocritus celebrate nature's plenitude.

Keats allies the figure of Autumn, like the other female goddesses of power in his poems, to the idea of melancholy. His Autumn is a figure of melancholy in part because she is no longer part of a social ritual within a community (as in *Idyll* VII), no longer an aspect of rites that give a sense of continuity in the midst of change. The poem is a solitary act of homage to the season, not a communal festival; however, what Keats represents is not simply the season and natural process: he explores the end of a tradition. "To Autumn" is a poem of an emphatically austere closure. It is a poem about endings. When compared with *Idyll* VII, it offers a curious reversal of sequence. In *Idyll* VII, the images of the bees and the wood-dove suggest subdued song; along with Lycidas's lament, this moment achieves the idea of pastoral melancholy. The poet follows these images, however, with the lively picture of abundant harvest. Finally, the poem closes with the personified goddess of the harvest. "To Autumn" uses similar elements, but arranges them in a different way. Stanza one opens with the address to the season, and this address builds to a rich description of autumnal abundance. Then in the second stanza, the personified figure of Autumn goes through actions and gestures associated with the season. This is the closest the poem comes to the emblematic image of the goddess Deo at the end of *Idyll* VII. Stanza three contains the muted sights and sounds of the season. The stanza echoes in a special way these lines from Theocritus's idyll:

> Far off
> Out of the thick-set brambles the tree-frog croaked in a
>   whisper;
> Linnets and larks were intoning their tunes, and the wood-
>   dove made moan.
> Busy and buzzing, the bees hovered over the musical waters.[57]
>   (ll.138–41)

Virgil's first *Eclogue* also contains lines that may have been in Keats's mind when he wrote "To Autumn." The wood-dove's moan in both Theocritus and Virgil, however, is a soothing reassurance of the peace to be found in the pastoral retreat. In contrast, the quiet sounds that bring "To Autumn" to a close are intimations of mortality. "To Autumn" begins with the imagery of plenitude that ends *Idyll* VII, and it ends with the austere music that is just barely hinted at in middle passages of Theocritus's poem.

Keats draws here upon the imagery of pastoral celebration, but shifts those images toward the melancholy found in pastoral elegy. In addition, Keats structures the poem so that the isolated poetic voice directly addresses the personified season. Through the device of personification, the poet makes the season into a female figure of power, one allied to the other powerful females in Keats's work. As Kermode and Vendler argue in different ways, these female figures are closely related, both to each other and to the idea of melancholy.[58] We can view Autumn as the final transformation of the goddess Melancholy in Keats, and this signals a crucial shift in his conception of melancholy itself. "To Autumn" exemplifies the division that the figure of melancholy undergoes in Keats's work: one half of the figure is internalized into the poet's mind; the other half is reassimilated into the natural world of process. In terms of the former, the division involves not only the poetic voice addressing Autumn, but a dialogue of the mind with itself. Autumn/Melancholy is an aspect of the poet's mind. Bate says the theme of the first stanza is "ripeness, of growth now reaching its climax."[59] True enough, and this ripeness is also the poet's sense of the culminating ripeness of his poetic powers and the power of literary tradition itself. The sense of fruitful abundance is troubling in its nearness to decay and death, and the imagery comes close to being a metaphor for the poet's fear of failure before the plenitude of tradition.

Here in stanza one, the pastoral impulse turns inward, and the pastoral scene works as an emblem for the melancholy of the poet who both admires the plenitude of experience embodied in tradition, and who suffers the consciousness of how fragile and transient is all human experience before the fact of death. Nature and tradition here reach a point of surfeit; only decay and death lie beyond it. In "To Autumn," the Keatsian pastoral moment is no longer the place where the poet goes to escape death; it is the place he comes to in order to face it. There is something stifling about the imagery in stanza one. Its fullness is burdensome. This burdensomeness parallels the poet's fear of the stifling of his own voice retrospectively before tradition, and proleptically before impending death. Keats's Autumn is a displaced figure of Melancholy, because autumn affords the perfect complex of images of ripeness perilously close to dissolution that defines the moment in his own poetics of melancholy. Rather than being an escape or a retreat, rather than being the place where the singer revives, the pastoral landscape is both the cause and the representation of the singer's burden. There is a fragile balance here, though, because Keats so closely associates Autumn with the landscape, that the allegorical personification recedes before the richly descriptive imagery of process in nature. Ultimately, the personified Autumn, who is also the final form that Melancholy takes in Keats, becomes the poet in his relation to nature and to poetry. The allegorical goddess withdraws, to be replaced by the solitary figure within the landscape who confronts the potential cessation of all poetic sound. In the figural progression of the poem, personified Autumn disappears or dissolves into her voice or "song," and then that, too, fades away.

Tennyson's "Come Down, O Maid" continues Keats's transformation of the idea of melancholy in poetic tradition. Like "To Autumn," Tennyson's song draws upon the pastoral of Theocritus and Virgil and the British traditions of pastoral and melancholy poetry. While Tennyson does not invoke the actual figure of Melancholy in the poem, the emotions and themes associated with the figure constitute an important subliminal presence. Just as Autumn is one of a series of female goddess figures associated with melancholy in Keats's mind, Tennyson associates the personifications in "Come Down, O Maid" through the language and imagery that describe them with the poetry of melancholy.

We have already noted the Keatsian imagery in Tennyson's poem, and the general critical recognition of Tennyson's debt to Keats. The similarities, however, are not simply a matter of echoes in language and imagery. Both poems are meditations on the pastoral idea. Keats and Tennyson incorporate a strain of melancholy that underlies Theocritean pastoral within the epistemology of their poetic practice. The parallels and divergences in their use of pastoral melancholy are illuminating not only for what these tell us about the two poets: they show us how certain literary conventions are passed from one poet to the other. There are differences between the two poems, certainly. Tennyson's lyric is, on the primary level, a love song; Keats's ode is a descriptive nature poem (though to say that is to be very reductive).

By definition, a lyric gives voice to personal emotion, while an ode is a more public form of utterance. Even these differences, however, when looked at in terms of the two specific poems, yield similarities. Tennyson himself describes "Come Down, O Maid" as a "sweet Idyl." As the term suggests, the poem draws on the idyll form as created largely by Theocritus. It is a song, but held within a frame. Unlike the conventional lyric, the Theocritean idyll involves a certain distancing of emotion and a simultaneous recognition of levels of artifice involved in the lyric performance. This aspect of the poem moves Tennyson's lyric closer to the more public, formal poetic forms, such as the ode. The Theocritean idyll, which lies behind "Come Down, O Maid," is a public performance and not simply a private utterance of deeply personal emotion. On the other hand, Keats's odes move that genre away from formal public verse, to verse that embodies the poet's personal concerns; Keats further moves the ode away from public celebration to private introspection.

After Romanticism, Tennyson moves the short poem back toward a more public form. The Tennysonian idyll and the Keatsian ode are not as disparate generically as they at first appear; moreover, while "Come Down, O Maid" is a type of love song, it is one that locates its figures within a natural landscape that the speaker describes with care and in great detail. Like "To Autumn," Tennyson's song is a descriptive nature poem, of a sort. Furthermore, in both poems the landscape works as a symbolic field in which various aspects of the poet's task interact, as it were. Finally, one of the most crucial areas of shared concern and shared conventions centers on the two poets' use of personification. Personification, as Rosenmeyer notes, is almost wholly absent in Theocritean pastoral,[60] but it is a standard feature of eighteenth-century pastoral and melancholy poetry. In stanza two of "To Autumn," Keats creates a personified season without even resorting to the name itself.

> Who hath not seen thee oft amid thy store?
> Sometimes whoever seeks abroad may find
> Thee sitting careless on a granary floor,
> Thy hair soft-lifted by the winnowing wind;
> Or on a half-reaped furrow sound asleep,
> Drowsed with the fume of poppies, while thy hook
>   Spares the next swath and all its twinéd flowers;
> And sometimes like a gleaner thou dost keep
> Steady thy laden head across a brook;

> Or by a cyder-press, with patient look,
> Thou watchest the last oozings hours by hours.

If stanza one is largely tactile, stanza two is largely visual. Through a series of closely described visual details and scenes, the poet represents Autumn as a figure with human attributes and as a process within nature itself; however, this personified Autumn is subtly ambiguous. Unlike, say, Theocritus's Demeter, Autumn is not an allegorical figure: Autumn is not an emblem for the season, but the season itself. The personified figure's relation to the season is not one of correspondence between two different levels of meaning (i.e., allegorical figure with its abstract meaning/actual season in its concrete detail); rather, the poet actually constitutes the personification through these concrete details. Keats's use of personification suggests human moods and attitudes: he conveys the figure's humanness through such details as the word "careless" modifying "thee." Such descriptive details shift the figure from allegory to realism, and from abstract concepts to the embodiment of human emotion. Another example is the phrase "Thy hair soft-lifted." It is almost too delicate and too human an image to fit within the category of personification. In a similar manner, the ensuing visual scenes describe acts that are more human than allegorical. Autumn is sound asleep on a half-reaped furrow (the noontime rest is a standard pastoral trope). Autumn walks across a brook balancing her harvest-laden head. Finally, Autumn sits beside the cider press watching "with patient look." When we paraphrase the stanza this way, it sounds almost comical. There is a reason for that. Keats is pushing the allegorical concept in the direction of human motivations and moods. In so doing, the poet is making the personified figure not only in the image of nature but in his own image. What happens to personification in "To Autumn" is the internalizing of the female figure of power and melancholy into the poet's self. We observe the strong intimacy between the poetic voice and the figure the voice describes. In this way, the eighteenth-century philosophical allegory of nature is rehumanized. There are two aspects to this transformation. First, the personification is so realistically human, so endowed with the emotions and motivations we associate with people, that it is hard to see the figure of Autumn as an abstract symbol. Second, in using the ode as a vehicle for personal lyric utterance, there is a strong sense of intimacy between voice and subject when the voice addresses Autumn.

In "To Autumn," the act of personification is, for Keats, the confrontation with his muse and with the powerful and melancholy realization of the limits imposed on his poetic voice by time and nature. The poem is Keats's reconciliation with Melancholy as his true muse. Ultimately, then, "To Autumn" traces a path, from the philosophical and moral allegories found in the eighteenth-century writers of pastoral, to the allegories of nature in Romanticism, which in turn become allegories of art. We locate the melancholy of "To Autumn" in the poet's awareness of the limits to his art, and it is this type of melancholy that Tennyson and Hardy would continue to explore.

Personification and its relation to the melancholia of the poet assume a slightly different form and function in "Come Down, O Maid." In the Keats ode, the figure of personification is also the silent figure addressed by the poetic voice. In Tennyson's song, the shepherd does not address a personified figure, though the maid's status hovers ambiguously between the figurative and the literal; however, the shepherd's description of the landscape involves a series of personifications that he closely associates with the maid. Here follows the central passage:

> For Love is of the valley, come thou down
> And find him; by the happy threshold, he,
> Or hand in hand with Plenty in the maize,
> Or red with spirted purple in the vats,
> Or foxlike in the vine; nor cares to walk
> With Death and Morning on the silver horns. . . .

There are four personified figures in the passage: Love, Plenty, Death, Morning. The central figure is Love. As figurative language and as idea, this personification serves as the mediating form between the shepherd and the maid. There is an element of duplicity in the shepherd's use of personification. Love becomes a mask; the shepherd and his desire lie behind it. The function of personification in the lyric is thus very different from that of "To Autumn." The voice in Keats's poem discovers through the form of figurative language his own fulfillment as a poet, as well as the cessation of this fulfillment. In "Come Down, O Maid," though, personification is not a discovering but a covering over of the shepherd's will before the maid whom he wishes to seduce. In one sense, Tennyson returns to a more traditional conception of personification, in which there is a fairly sharp distinction between the figure and the reality the figure represents. The figure of personified Love is a consciously manipulated symbol used for a specific purpose by the singer. This explains, in part, Love's lack of attributes: there is a lack here of the details that make Keats's Autumn so human.

The picture in the passage just quoted resembles stanza two of "To Autumn" in its broad outlines, but the specific function and effect of the language and imagery are different. Love walks "hand in hand with Plenty," just as Autumn conspires with his "close bosom-friend the sun." But Tennyson's figures stand out; they are disconnected from the scene. The speaker does not address the figures in a tone of intimacy, nor do their qualities merge with the external reality they are meant to represent. Rather, we get a sense of the arbitrary placement of the figures in the scene. This discontinuity, this emphasis on the separateness of voice and subject, and of figure and landscape, is very Theocritean; it is also an important departure from the Romantic fusion of subject and object. There is a symbolic structure to the passage: Love joins with Plenty on one side, and Death joins with the Morning on the other. Tennyson separates out aspects of life and nature that Keats joined together. In "To Autumn," the abundance of the harvest is bound up with time and death. The poem's formal structure, as Bate points out, is one of "stasis" and "process."[61] In "Come Down, O Maid," on the other hand, the poet separates death and time (the latter signified by Morning) from birth and unity (Love) and from fruitful growth (Plenty).

The shepherd creates this miniature allegory. He chooses to place the aspects of mortality on the mountain heights, where the maid stands. In his song, he creates a false dichotomy between the powers of birth and growth, and the powers of decay and death. The falseness of this division (a falseness signalled by the very way he uses personification) reveals the duplicity inherent in the language of his song. Keats's complex union—of growth and decay,

birth and death, poetic sound and poetic silence—through a personified figure (in which figurative and literal language, and figurative and literal experience, merge) is replaced in Tennyson's poem
by a sense of disunity. The poet produces this disharmony through
the use of personification for the personal ends of the shepherd:
Tennyson emphasizes the artifice of the literary figure as the singer
uses it as part of his attempt to seduce the maid through language.
If "To Autumn" is an allegory of nature humanized by personified
Autumn as an image of the poet, "Come Down, O Maid" is an
allegory of the dehumanization of a poet figure who is too self-
consciously aware of the artifice of all language, and who then
chooses to manipulate these artifices to further mystify others. The
shepherd is a poet in bad faith.

The shepherd is Tennyson's image for a false kind of poet (an
aspect of his own poetic self that he feared) who uses language to
escape from reality into cliché rather than to enter fully into this
reality in all its complexity—the latter being Keats's achievement
in "To Autumn." At their deepest level, both of these works are
allegories about the poet's task. That this task can involve types of
seductive inauthenticity is figured in the closure of the shepherd's
song:

> and I
> Thy shepherd pipe, and sweet is every sound,
> Sweeter thy voice, but every sound is sweet;
> Myriads of rivulets hurrying through the lawn,
> The moan of doves in immemorial elms,
> And murmuring of innumerable bees.

Like "To Autumn," "Come Down, O Maid" ends with an emphasis on song and sound. There is an echo here of Virgil *Eclogue*
I: *nec gemere aeria cessabit turtur ab ulmo* (Nor will the turtledove
cease moaning in the high elm). Tennyson also alludes to Theocritus's seventh *Idyll* here; however, Tennyson's echoes of key
texts in the pastoral tradition only serve to point out the extent to
which the shepherd's song distorts and overturns the pastoral ideal.
The plangent tones of this close contain the implication that the
pastoral retreat to the "pillars of the hearth," where the singer
hopes to lure the maid, cannot shelter anyone from time and

death. This fact was, of course, a principal cause of the vague melancholy in Theocritean and Virgilian pastoral, but the great irony here is that the shepherd is either unaware of or chooses to ignore the signification of his closure. When the shepherd sings, "I / Thy shepherd pipe," he means to welcome the maid to the valley. The gesture typifies one aspect of the pastoral tradition, but its meaning here is atypical. This moment should be the most celebratory, the happiest, in the song: the maid has come down to the valley, has passed the "threshold," and has become part of the community of love and "sweet" domesticity. The shepherd has attained his end. The structure of feeling and emotion at the close, however, seems somehow different from the promise he initially held out to her. It is ironic that when the shepherd finally turns from the negative exhortations to abandon the mountain wastes and heights, and actually describes this valley he has promised her, his song becomes less forceful, less sure of itself. The final three lines of the song represent a scene that qualifies in important ways the shepherd's allegorical division of Love, Plenty / Death, Morning. The symbolically structured landscape held within it the hope that in the valley love and growth could escape time and death. The song's close tells a different story:

> Myriads of rivulets hurrying through the lawn,
> The moan of doves in immemorial elms,
> And murmuring of innumerable bees.

The power and energy of the waterfall cascading down the mountains have been tamed and domesticated into "rivulets" moving through the "lawn." As the waterfall was an image of the maid's power and independence, this line inevitably constitutes a major diminution of her power. It also implies, however, the diminution in the shepherd's power to deceive both her and himself about the nature of his pastoral song. There is an acknowledgement, however unwilling and unwitting, that the pastoral retreat he holds out to her does contain unpleasurable things such as death. The close brings forward through the language of his song the shepherd's melancholy recognition of his own duplicity. An exemplary passage in the traditions of pastoral and melancholy poetry, it also reveals Tennyson's internalization—and in this he goes further than Keats—of such melancholy ideas as the poet's self-conscious recognition of the limitations of his art.

The closing sounds in "Come Down, O Maid" image the shepherd's diminishing powers of song. This is, of course, not the same thing as the power of the poem or of Tennyson, because the paradox here is that the lines of poetry representing this diminishment constitute a poetic achievement of great strength. The dove's "moan" and the "murmuring" of the bees echo the now-subdued voice of the shepherd. At this moment, the song quietly descends toward stasis and death. Even the adjectives "immemorial" and "innumerable" contain within them the implication of their opposites: dwindling numbers and mortality. In the final lines, then, the shepherd discovers to the maid that the valley is a place not only of love but of melancholy. Love and melancholy meet here as they once did in an early poem of Tennyson's:

> speak low, and give up wholly
> Thy spirit to mild-minded Melancholy;
> This is the place. Through yonder poplar alley,
> Below, the blue-green river windeth slowly,
>   But in the middle of the somber valley,
> The crispèd waters whisper musically,
> And all the haunted place is dark and holy.
> The nightingale, with long and low preamble,
> Warbled from yonder knoll of solemn larches
> . . . .
> When in this valley first I told my love.

In this early sonnet ("Check Every Outflash, Every Ruder Sally"), Tennyson closely and somewhat unimaginatively follows the traditional topoi of seventeenth- and eighteenth-century melancholy poetry. There is the dark and secluded natural scene. The poet also suggests supernatural presences with the words "haunted place." Along with the owl, the nightingale is one of the iconographic figures in the seventeenth- and eighteenth-century poem of melancholy. The most important example of the last is in "Il Penseroso": "Sweet Bird that shunn'st the noise of folly, / Most musical, most melancholy." We find the romantic response to this emblem of melancholy in Coleridge's "The Nightingale" and, of course, in Keats's ode. Most important of all here, is the personified figure of Melancholy herself: "give up wholly / Thy spirit to mild-minded Melancholy." The figure of personified Melancholy within this type of iconographic landscape constitutes a central aspect of the idea of melancholy in English poetic tradition. In addition to Milton's "L'Allegro" and "Il Penseroso," one later finds this complex of images in such representative eighteenth-century poets as Thomson, Thomas and Joseph Warton, and Gray.

Tennyson's early sonnet shows us some of the ways the poet changed his handling of the theme of melancholy in a later meditation on the pastoral tradition. What transformations occur in the development from "Check Every Outflash" to "Come Down, O Maid"? The key change involves the shepherd's conscious attempt to hide the melancholy nature of love in the valley. In the early sonnet, the connection between love and melancholy is clear, and it follows the tradition of love-melancholy going back to Burton. The shepherd's song of seduction, on the other hand, involves the elision of the figure of melancholy from the landscape associated with love (i.e., the valley). Nevertheless, the figure comes back to haunt the scene at the close of the song. In "Check Every Outflash," the personification of melancholy makes the idea a philosophical abstraction that exists apart from the voice of the poet or the landscape that the voice describes. In this respect, the treatment of melancholy is much like that of Thomson or the Warton brothers. On the other hand, in "Come Down, O Maid" what initially appears to be the abandonment of the idea entirely, turns out to be a highly significant transformation of it. In the poem's closure, Tennyson naturalizes the figure of melancholy into the landscape; the moaning doves and buzzing bees are conventions of classical pastoral melancholy. But at the same time, Tennyson internalizes the figure of melancholy into the singer's voice. The "moan" and "murmuring" are signs of the singer's melancholy awareness of the diminishment, the fading, of his song. In other words, Tennyson does not really elide the personification of Melancholy but merely displaces it onto the voice of the poet, and, finally, onto the poet's consciousness of his work. There is one more aspect to this transformation. In the traditional poem of melancholy, the speaker directly addresses the personified figure. In Tennyson's song, the shepherd does not address a personification but an actual female figure, and one does not associate this person with the iconographic landscape of melancholy, but with the sublime and picturesque landscape that connotes power and freedom. He transfers the idea of melancholy from the female figure to the male poet figure. His pastoral landscape at the end closely follows the iconography of the melancholy tradition. The shepherd's song tries to elude melancholy, just as it tries to avoid time and death, but all three forces return at the poem's closure. The form the language takes at the end suggests the inevitability of the very idea that the singer wished to evade; the somber tones of the shepherd's melancholy in the last three lines of the poem are the result of a literary idea's returning in spite of itself.

There is a sense of return here. In Keats and Tennyson, the conventions of melancholy become associated with and even become the images for the poet figure's troubling sense of the limitations of his voice when confronted by mortality and by the daunting heritage of literary history itself. "Come Down, O Maid" is not simply a sentimental love lyric; it is one of Tennyson's more somber meditations on how a poet can go astray or be false to his art through the conscious manipulation of traditional figures, tropes, and genre conventions. Tennyson's sense of the artifice of these conventions enables him to explore certain themes and emotions in new ways, and to explore the nature of his own poetics.

IV

Victorian Pastoral and the Poetry of Hardy

TURNING FROM TENNYSON TO HARDY, WE turn, most would agree, to a writer who is different in many ways from the earlier poet. Yet for all their differences, both poets share a thematic concern with love, loss, and the burden of memory. And there is a deeper thematic connection between Tennyson and Hardy: the thematics of a subversion and renewal of forms worked out through figurative language.

A paradoxical and interesting irony lies in the extent to which, on a certain level, the relation between Tennyson and Hardy in terms of style and form is one almost solely of difference. The irony is that, on a deeper level, the two poets cancel these disparities through their concern with problems of figuration and through the way they both foreground the rhetoric of tradition as a problem.

The connection between Tennyson and Hardy in terms of this thematic struggle is nowhere more evident than in Hardy's pastoral poetry. As we read Hardian pastoral, we see that like Tennyson, Hardy is daunted by the rhetoric of tradition. His pastoral language seems to mean what he does not wish it to say. In terms of themes such as love, loss, and memory, Hardy's pastoral figures say too little and too much: they say too little to the extent that the force of traditional pastoral forms has been emptied out, and they say too much about the task of representing these experiences within the framework of a language imposed on and inhibited by the rhetoric of tradition. Again like Tennyson, however, Hardy's deliberate exaggeration or foregrounding of pastoral rhetoric allows the problem of tradition itself to be an enabling source of poetic power. The more we read Hardian pastoral, the more we see that Hardy's irony is as much about the subversion and renewal of the rhetoric of tradition, as it is about the thematic incidents he represents by means of this rhetoric.

Tennyson and Hardy share the concern with the space of pastoral as being produced by figurative language, and as the area within which the duplicity of such figures is explored. Like Tennyson, Hardy subverts existing pastoral forms through the ironies of the genre's rhetoric, in order to create new pastoral forms. As we begin to read specific poems, we see Hardy employing pastoral figures and strategies only to disrupt them in ironic reversals as striking as the more readily observable ironies on the level of thematics.

"In a Wood" is from Hardy's *Wessex Poems* (1895). Although he based the poem on a prose passage in *The Woodlanders*, it is not a poem from that novel.

> Pale beech and pine so blue,
>   Set in one clay,
> Bough to bough cannot you
>   Live out your day?
> When the rains skim and skip,
> Why mar sweet comradeship,
> Blighting with poison-drip
>   Neighbourly spray?
>
> Heart-halt and spirit-lame,
>   City-opprest,
> Unto this wood I came
>   As to a nest;
> Dreaming that sylvan peace
> Offered the harrowed ease –
> Nature a soft release
>   From men's unrest.
>
> But, having entered in,
>   Great growths and small

Show them to men akin –
    Combatants all!
Sycamore shoulders oak,
Bines the slim sapling yoke,
Ivy-spun halters choke
    Elms stout and tall.

Touches from ash, O wych,
    Sting you like scorn!
You, too, brave hollies, twitch
    Sidelong from thorn,
Even the rank poplars bear
Lothly a rival's air,
Cankering in black despair
    If overborne.

Since, then, no grace I find
    Taught me of trees,
Turn I back to my kind,
    Worthy as these.
There at least smiles abound,
There discourse trills around,
There, now and then, are found
    Life-loyalties.[1]

J. O. Bailey discusses this poem in terms of Hardy's progression from the Romantic understanding of a beneficent nature to a post-Darwinian understanding of nature: "the poem presents his development from the period of his youthful Wordsworthian view of nature to his mature, Darwinian view."[2] But one can look at "In a Wood" in terms of Hardy's development and transformation of pastoral conventions. One can read this poem in the context of a literary tradition that goes back through Thomson, Spenser, Virgil, Theocritus, and Homer.

We find one of the pastoral conventions that Hardy uses in "In a Wood" in Spenser. Critics have not usually read Hardy in the light of Spenser, but Spenser was an early influence. In the *Early Life*, Florence Emily Hardy describes Hardy's youthful interest in Spenser: "He also began turning the Book of Ecclesiastes into Spenserian stanzas, but finding the original unmatchable abandoned the task."[3] Robert Gittings tells us that Hardy owned the works of Spenser in Moxon's Popular Poets series; Gittings suggests also that in 1871 Hardy put Tryphena Spark's initials next to a stanza from the "Epithalamium."[4] This suggests Hardy's interest in Spenser continued past his earliest adult years. Spenser may have been more of an influence on Hardy's poetry, especially his descriptions of nature and his use of pastoral topoi, than is generally thought to have been the case. Spenser provides, at the very least, a valuable analogue in terms of Hardy's use of pastoral topoi. "In a Wood" may not be a Spenserian poem, but Hardy's use of literary conventions in this poem draws on his knowledge of Spenser and of classical writers of pastoral.

The first stanza of "In a Wood" describes the trees "pale beech and pine so blue" in terms of potential violence – a violence that can destroy "sweet comradeship." This opening landscape is a traditional *locus amoenus*. But it is one in which the unity and friendship described in nature turn to division and hostility. The words "mar," "blighting," and "poison-drip" imply a nature filled with antagonistic forces. In stanza two, Hardy most clearly alludes to the idea of the pastoral bower:

> Heart-halt and spirit-lame,
> City-opprest,
> Unto this wood I came
> As to a nest;
> Dreaming that sylvan peace
> Offered the harrowed ease –
> Nature a soft release
> From men's unrest.

The imagery here is similar to the descriptions of bowers in the early poetry of Keats. Images and phrases such as "nest," "sylvan peace," and "soft release" in Hardy's poem are similar in quality of thought and feeling to descriptions in early Keats poems, such as "To Solitude," "To George Felton Mathew," and "Sleep and Poetry." The Keatsian bower derives from Spenser; the Keatsian contrast between city and country derives from Virgil and Horace. These are Hardy's models also. The city/country contrast becomes even sharper in Hardy than in Keats or his classical models: Hardy's hyphenated words stress the speaker's sense of weariness with city life: "heart-halt"; "spirit-lame"; "city-opprest."

As do the speakers in early Keats, Hardy's speaker enters the bower hoping to escape the city's oppressiveness. But there is an important difference between the early Keatsian bower and this *locus amoenus* in "In a Wood." In Keats, the ambivalence of the bower image centers on the deception and escapism that qualify the pleasure experienced within the pastoral scene. When Hardy's speaker enters within the wood, however, his problem is not escapism: the problem he faces is that there is no pleasure, no possibility of escape. The *locus amoenus* is a negative one. In Hardy's "In a Wood," the "ease" afforded by the pastoral world is illusory.

The poet suggests this illusiveness in lines five and six of stanza two: "Dreaming that sylvan peace / Offered the harrowed ease." He conveys the sense of illusion in two ways in these lines. First, "dreaming" connotes ideas that have no basis in reality, or hopes that may not be fulfilled. Second, Hardy's syntax is ambiguous. The words "the harrowed" can be read as a prepositional phrase with the preposition "to" elided. In this case, "ease" is the indirect object offered to the harrowed city-dweller. But "harrowed" could be read as adjectival, modifying "ease" as direct object. In other word, the city-dweller may be offered "harrowed ease." "Harrow" means to plunder or spoil, and the ambiguity of syntax and phrasing suggests that the "sylvan peace" may not offer escape. This bower may actually rob or spoil the person's ease who enters within it.

The dream of sylvan peace gives way to the harrowing or spoiling of the bower world in stanza three:

> But, having entered in,
>   Great growths and small
> Show them to men akin—
>   Combatants all!
> Sycamore shoulders oak,
> Bines the slim sapling yoke,
> Ivy–spun halters choke
>   Elms stout and tall.

Here the speaker defines the ironic kinship between man and the natural scene in terms of strife: "to men akin— / Combatants all!" On a thematic level, this passage shows Hardy's turn from the Romantic view of nature to the Darwinian view. But in terms of pastoral conventions, the passage involves the return to past literary traditions and the transformation of those traditions. The bower in "In a Wood" contains evil and destruction. It is comparable to the false bowers in Spenser. But Hardy is drawing upon an even more specific pastoral topos: the catalogue of trees. In Ovid's *Metamorphoses*, Orpheus retires to a grove after the death of Eurydice:

> There was a hill, and on it
> A wide-extending plain, all green, but lacking
> The darker green of shade, and when the singer
> Came there and ran his fingers over the strings,
> The shade came there to listen. The oak-tree came,
> And many poplars, and the gentle lindens,
> The beech, the virgin laurel, and the hazel
> Easily broken, the ash men use for spears,
> The shining silver-fir, the ilex bending
> Under its acorns, the friendly sycamore,
> The changing-colored maple, and the willows
> That love the river waters, and the lotus
> Favoring pools, and the green boxwood came,
> Slim tamarisks, and myrtle, and viburnum
> With dark-blue berries, and the pliant ivy,
> The tendrilled grape, the elms, all dressed with vines,
> The rowan-trees, the pitch-pines, and the arbute
> With the red fruit, the palm, the victor's triumph,
> The bare-trunked pine with spreading leafy crest,
> Dear to the mother of the gods since Attis
> Put off his human form, took on that likeness,
> And the cone-shaped cypress joined them, now a tree,
> But once a boy, loved by the god Apollo
> Master of lyre and bow-string, both together.[5]

We also find the catalogue-of-trees topos in Spenser. Here is the Spenserian grove:

> Enforst to seeke some covert nigh at hand,
>   A shadie grove not far away they spide,
>   That promist ayde the tempest to withstand:
>   Whose loftie trees yclad with sommers pride,
>   Did spred so broad, that heavens light did hide,
>   Not perceable with power of any starre:
>   And all within were pathes and alleies wide,

With footing worne, and leading inward farre:
Faire harbour that them seemes; so in they entred arre.

And foorth they passe, with pleasure forward led,
    Joying to heare the birdes sweete harmony,
    Which therein shrouded from the tempest dred,
    Seemd in their song to scorne the cruell sky.
    Much can they prayse the trees so straight and hy,
    The sayling Pine, the Cedar proud and tall,
    The vine-prop Elme, the Poplar never dry,
    The builder Oake, sole king of forrests all,
The Aspine good for staves, the Cypresse funerall.

The Laurell, meed of mightie Conquerours
    And Poets sage, the Firre that weepeth still,
    The Willow worne of forlorne Paramours,
    The Eugh obedient to the benders will,
    The Birche for shaftes, the Sallow for the mill,
    The Mirrhe sweete bleeding in the bitter wound,
    The warlike Beech, the Ash for nothing ill,
    The fruitful Olive, and the Platane round,
The carver Holme, the Maple seeldom inward sound.
        (*The Faerie Queene* I. 1. 7–9; Yale Univ. Press edition)

The development of the catalogue-of-trees topos from the grove of Orpheus in Ovid, to Spenser's wandering wood, and then to the "sylvan peace" in "In a Wood," tells us something about Hardian pastoral. Curtius observes the place of rhetoric in the Ovidian grove.[6] Ovid's long list of trees is a formalized description, but it is also a classical example of pathetic fallacy. Orpheus's song is a pastoral elegy, and Ovid uses pathetic fallacy to describe nature's response. As in the classical elegies the "Lament for Adonis" and the "Lament for Bion," Ovid's rhetorical "placing" of the natural scene involves the reciprocal sympathy between the poet figure and the landscape. The landscape responds in an anthropomorphic way to the person's sorrow: when Orpheus sings, the "shade came there to listen."

The speaker in "In a Wood" hopes to discover reciprocal sympathy within the pleasance. He hopes to find a "sweet comradeship" in nature; instead, he discovers a negative kinship. It is the idea of a negative *locus amoenus* which relates Hardian pastoral to

Spenser. Unlike the sympathetic kinship between man and nature in Orpheus's grove, the Spenserian grove is a place of deceit and evil. The Redcrosse Knight and Una enter the wood to escape "an hideous storme of raine." As was the speaker in Hardy's "In a Wood," they are looking for a nest and place of "ease":

> Enforst to seeke some covert nigh at hand,
> A shadie grove not far away they spide,
> That promist ayde the tempest to withstand. . . .

What Hardy's speaker discovers about the nature of the wood bears comparison with the description of the Spenserian grove. The sheltering aspect of the bower is illusive in this *locus amoenus* in Spenser. And it harbors evil.

> And all within were pathes and alleies wide,
> With footing worne, and leading inward farre:
> Faire harbour that them seemes; so in they entred arre.

The Spenserian "seemes" signals the deceptive aspect of this *locus amoenus*: what seems to Redcrosse and Una to be a "faire harbour" is actually an evil place designed to lead the knight from the path of "holienesse." Hardy's poem may not be directly based on the Spenserian grove, but it is broadly based on the traditional pastoral topos of the catalogue of trees. And the Spenserian analogue reveals some interesting points of comparison: Spenser's "faire harbour" is like Hardy's dream of "sylvan peace."

Spenser hints at the falseness of the wandering wood through the word "seemes." Hardy hints at the strife in his *locus amoenus* through the syntactical ambiguity of "Offered the harrowed ease." Spenser emphasizes further the wood's deceptive quality at the catalogue's closure: "the Maple seeldom inward sound." By ending the description of trees on this note, Spenser suggests that the outer appearance and the inner reality of the wood are not the same. There is something "unsound" about the wood. And that is what Hardy discovers in his bower also:

> Sycamore *shoulders* oak,
> Bines the slim sapling *yoke*,
> Ivy-spun halters *choke*
> Elms stout and tall.
> [my emphasis]

But Hardy's negative *locus amoenus* contains even more somber implications than does Spenser's. Spenser's wandering wood leads to Errour's den. And when Redcrosse slays Errour, that slaying holds out the possibility that evil can be localized, contained, and vanquished. Alternative pastoral bowers that are good rather than evil remain possibilities; Redcrosse and Una follow a path out of the wood and may reach one of these better places. The speaker in Hardy's "In a Wood" leaves his negative bower also. But the alternative place, the human community to which he returns, contains the same kinds of deceit and strife:

> Since, then, no grace I find
>   Taught me of trees,
> Turn I back to my kind,
>   Worthy as these.
> There at least smiles abound,
> There discourse trills around. . . .

Redcrosse and Una leave the wandering wood and eventually find "grace" within a larger human community. The speaker of "In a Wood" turns from the negative *locus amoenus* to people who, in his view, are as worthy as the trees—i.e., not very worthy.

The comparison of this Hardian bower, specifically the catalogue-of-trees topos, with Orpheus's grove in Ovid and with Spenser's wandering wood suggests several points about Hardy's development of pastoral. Unlike Orpheus's grove, Hardy's pleasance does not involve a sympathetic relation between the human figure and the landscape. As with Spenser's wandering wood, Hardy's bower is false and deceptive. But in Spenser there are positive bowers also. And there are possibilities of moral affirmation that are apparently denied Hardy's speaker. Hardy's human community is as unsound as his forest.

One final point about "In a Wood" and Hardy's development of pastoral: the opposition between country and city derives from classical sources, but it stems also from Wordsworth and Keats. In these two Romantic poets, this opposition is usually bound up with the poet figure's search for inspiration and for his poetic subject. Hardy's speaker is also such a poet figure. When the speaker turns from the woods, he turns from poetic tradition. Even more than Keats and Tennyson, the Hardian poet is outside of the pastoral community, and when Hardy turns to the larger world for inspiration and for a new sense of community, the larger world also fails him: "There at least smiles abound, / There discourse trills around." Unlike Keats, Hardy does not place himself back within pastoral through concrete, sensuous descriptions of natural process. Nature is too discontinuous and arbitrary. Unlike Tennyson, Hardy does not fully re-create the idyll form and attain a place within the tradition that way. More than either of these poets, Hardy establishes pastoral that involves a melancholy sense of the poet's disinheritance from the tradition. Hardy's sense of exile from pastoral tradition means that, even more than in Tennyson, the distant framed perspective of the idyll form becomes one of fragmentation and discontinuity.

"To Flowers from Italy in Winter" is from the volume *Poems of the Past and the Present* (1901).

> Sunned in the South, and here to-day;
>   – If all organic things
> Be sentient, Flowers, as some men say,
>   What are your ponderings?
>
> How can you stay, nor vanish quite
>   From this bleak spot of thorn,
> And birch, and fir, and frozen white
>   Expanse of the forlorn?
>
> Frail luckless exiles hither brought!
>   Your dust will not regain
> Old sunny haunts of Classic thought
>   When you shall waste and wane;
>
> But mix with alien earth, be lit
>   With frigid Boreal flame,
> And not a sign remain in it
>   To tell man whence you came.

J. O. Bailey says Hardy's "extension of compassion to organic nature" is "whimsical."[7] But the poem seems much more elegiac than whimsical. On the simplest level, one can type the poem as a description of the frailty of all natural life: the poet wonders if flowers can feel the pain of exile as people do. Yet the poem addresses more interesting questions than simply that of the nature of organic life. "To Flowers from Italy" is about pastoral tradition and Hardy's relation to classical writers of pastoral such as Virgil and Theocritus. In the *Early Life*, we are told that Hardy read Dryden's translation of the *Aeneid* in his youth; Hardy's interest in Virgil continued throughout his life.[8] Hardy's friendship with Reverend William Barnes strengthened his interest in Virgilian pastoral (Barnes's dialectal poems show the strong influence of Virgil's *Eclogues*). Hardy was also interested in Theocritus. Here is one of his notes for a poem: "Cf Theocritus & the life at Bockn when I was a boy—in the wheatfield, at the well, cidermaking, wheat weeding, &c."[9]

Flowers are a traditional symbol of pastoral poetry and an iconographic element within the pastoral world of Theocritus and Virgil. One of the nearest sources for Hardy's pastoral flowers could be William Barnes. Here is a passage from Barnes's "Tweil," a poem included in the selection of Barnes's work that Hardy would later make for publication in 1922:

> In wall-zide sheädes, by leafy bowers,
>   Underneath the swayèn tree,
> O' leäte, as round the bloomèn flowers,
>   Lowly humm'd the giddy bee,
> My childern's small left voot did smite
> Their tiny speäde, the while the right
> Did trample on a deäisy head,
> Bezide the flower's dousty bed,
> An' though their work wer idle then,
>   They a-smilèn, an a-tweilèn,
> Still did work an' work ageän.[10]

Barnes's poem, like Hardy's "To Flowers from Italy," is about the fragility of natural life and about the maintaining of this life. It is also about the fragility of the pastoral world and pastoral poetry. Hardy makes the point in his introduction to his edition of Barnes. Hardy speaks of Barnes's poems as "idylls." And in his discussion of Barnes's use of traditional Dorset dialect, Hardy observes the "silent and inevitable effacements" of the language of tradition: "In the villages that one recognizes to be the scenes of these pastorals the poet's nouns, adjectives, and idioms cease to be understood by the younger generation."[11]

Hardy's melancholy sense of the fragility of tradition is not limited to the Dorset dialect and the folk life of rural England. This melancholy sense of the passing away of the language of tradition, and of the conventions of literary tradition, involves Hardy's knowledge of English and Western literary history. We sense this awareness of history even in the way Hardy talks about Barnes's achievement. In Hardy's view, Barnes is not a minor dialectal poet; he is a part of the great British tradition. Barnes "really belonged to the literary school of such poets as Tennyson, Gray, and Collins, rather than to that of the old unpremeditating singers in dialect."[12] The three poets Hardy mentions wrote pastoral and are a part of the transformation of the classical pastoral tradition. Hardy's interest in Barnes's work stems from the younger poet's interest in the pastoral tradition and his own place within it.

This is the problem addressed in "Tweil" and "To Flowers from Italy." Barnes resituates himself in pastoral through the use of dialect. Hardy's attitude is more complicated; it is an attitude that bears comparison with Tennyson. "To Flowers from Italy" echoes uncannily Tennyson's introductory poem for "Demeter and Persephone," "To Professor Jebb":

> Fair things are slow to fade away,
> Bear witness you, that yesterday
>   From out the Ghost of Pindar in you
> Rolled an Olympian, and they say
> That here the torpid mummy wheat
> Of Egypt bore a grain as sweet
>   As that which gilds the glebe of England,
> Sunned with the summer of milder heat.
>
> So may this legend for awhile,
> If greeted by your classic smile,
>   Though dead in its Trinacrian Enna,
> Blossom again on a colder isle.

This poem expresses Tennyson's sense of exile from the classical writers. In "Demeter and Persephone," which this poem introduces, Tennyson uses flowers as a symbol of poetic creativity, but also as a symbol of a fall from innocence. Hardy may or may not have been familiar with these two Tennyson poems, but his "To

Flowers from Italy" uses similar images to address similar problems. Both poets use images of organic death and birth. Both use images of the "translation" of flora from the warm south to the coldness of England. And if Tennyson's poem suggests implicitly that he is a melancholy exile from classical pastoral and myth, Hardy's does so explicitly.

Hardy's identification with the flowers constitutes a statement of his own poetic situation: "Frail luckless exiles hither brought! / Your dust will not regain / Old sunny haunts of Classic thought." Even more than Tennyson, Hardy feels disinherited from the "haunts of Classic thought," and Hardy expresses this disinheritance through the use of pathetic fallacy. Tennyson uses pathetic fallacy and language that is both literal and figurative to create his new idyll form; Hardy's use of pathetic fallacy is ironical. Just as the bower in "In a Wood" is expressly false and characterized by strife, pathetic fallacy in "To Flowers from Italy" is false to the values of pastoral.

Hardian pathetic fallacy produces the opposite effect to the sympathetic response of nature in the "Lament for Bion":

> Wail sorrowfully, ye glades and waters of the Dorians; weep, rivers, for our beloved Bion. Now make lament, all green things; now moan, all groves, and, flowers, expire with unkempt clusters. Now, roses and anemones, don mourning crimson; speak out thy letters, hyacinth, and add more cries of sorrow to thy petals. The fair singer is dead.[13]

In "Demeter and Persephone," Tennyson uses a similar thematics involving pathetic fallacy when Demeter searches for Persephone. The difference between Tennyson and the classical pastoral elegy lies in nature's not responding sympathetically to Demeter's sorrow. Nature is unable to tell her where Persephone is. Nature provides no answers: "We know not, and we know not why we moan." The poet uses pathetic fallacy to connote the very distance from the pastoral world of innocence that both Demeter and Tennyson feel. But Tennyson still uses figurative language seriously. Nature is really endowed with human attributes.

Hardy represents his more severe sense of poetic disinheritance in "To Flowers from Italy" by raising the *idea* of pathetic fallacy and then interrogating it, as an idea. In lines 2 through 4, he uses the tentative and interrogatory conjunction "if" and the adverbial "as." Hardy does not create a picture of flowers that think and feel; he presents that possibility as a question. Bailey sees the tone as whimsical, but it is really skeptical and ironic. Pathetic fallacy is figurative language to be questioned, rather than a language of pastoral affirmation. Tennyson's "To Professor Jebb" images the rebirth of classical literature and myth through the "translated" and transplanted seed of grain. Hardy describes the end of this possibility through the flowers that end in dust and silence. Their dust will "mix with alien earth . . . / And not a sign remain in it / To tell man whence you came."

Hardy continues his exploration of pastoral through flower imagery in the fine poem "The Last Chrysanthemum" (this poem is also from the *Poems of the Past and the Present* volume of 1901):

> Why should this flower delay so long
>   To show its tremulous plumes?
> Now is the time of plaintive robin-song,
>   When flowers are in their tombs.
>
> Through the slow summer, when the sun
>   Called to each frond and whorl
> That all he could for flowers was being done,
>   Why did it not uncurl?
>
> It must have felt that fervid call
>   Although it took no heed,
> Waking but now, when leaves like corpses fall,
>   And saps all retrocede.
>
> Too late its beauty, lonely thing,
>   The season's shine is spent,
> Nothing remains for it but shivering
>   In tempests turbulent.
>
> Had it reason for delay,
>   Dreaming in witlessness
> That for a bloom so delicately gay
>   Winter would stay its stress?
>
> —I talk as if the thing were born
>   With sense to work its mind;

> Yet it is but one mask of many worn
> By the Great Face behind.

As with "To Flowers from Italy," "The Last Chrysanthemum" describes the fragility and transience of organic life. J. O. Bailey says the poem is about "ecological adaptation," but this view is a bit too literal.[14] The last flower appears and remains very late in the year; the season is now late autumn, "When flowers are in their tombs." "To Flowers from Italy" addressed the problem of "translating" or carrying over the flowers of Italy and "classic thought" to England. In "The Last Chrysanthemum," Hardy addresses the problem of literary exile from a slightly different angle; from the perspective of being too late: "Too late its beauty, lonely thing, / The season's shine is spent." There is a strong elegiac note to the poem: "Now is the time of plaintive robin-song."

Part of the poem's pathos stems from autumnal sadness and the image of the lone flower that will soon die. But the pathos is also related to pastoral elegy and to Hardy's sense of disinheritance from its conventions. Unlike "To Flowers from Italy," there is no specific reference to "classic thought" in this poem. Here classical thought means literature as well as philosophy. But there is an allusion to a classical writer of pastoral who was very important to Hardy. We know that Hardy read Dryden's Virgil as a youth, and Donald Davie has shown us the influence of Virgil on Hardy's work.[15] The melancholy way death impinges on life in "The Last Chrysanthemum" seems Virgilian.

There is a specific image in the poem that suggests Virgil:

> It must have felt that fervid call
> Although it took no heed,
> Waking but now, when leaves like corpses fall,
> And saps all retrocede.

These lines are an allusion to a famous passage in the *Aeneid*. In Book Six, as Aeneas travels through the underworld to see his father, he witnesses the shades hoping to cross the river Cocytus in Charon's boat.

> Hither rushed all the throng, streaming to the banks; mothers
> and men and bodies of high-souled heroes, their life now done,

boys and unwedded girls, and sons placed on the pyre before their father's eyes; thick as the leaves of the forest that at autumn's first frost dropping fall, and thick as the birds that from the seething deep flock shoreward, when the chill of the year drives them over- seas and sends them into sunny lands. They stood, pleading to be the first ferried across, and stretched out hands in yearning for the farther shore.[16]

As with the shades on the banks of the Cocytus, spirits which the poet compares to falling autumn leaves, this last flower has not yet found its rest in burial. The other flowers "are in their tombs." Hardy stresses the feeling of melancholy exile from home and tradi- tion. Paradoxically, burial in the earth is the yearned-for home for these shades in the underworld. The earth is implicitly the place of rest for the chrysanthemum also. The loneliness and desolation of the last flower is the result of its not being where the other flow- ers are: in their tombs.

After witnessing the sad spectacle on the shores of Cocytus, Aeneas asks the priestess to explain the scene. She does as follows:

All this crowd thou seest is helpless and graveless; yonder warden is Charon; those whom the flood carries are the buried. Nor may he bear them o'er the dreadful banks and hoarse-voiced waters ere their bones have found a resting-place.[17]

The wandering of these souls who wish to be buried is a figure for the wandering hero in exile, hoping to find a new home. This sec- tion of the *Aeneid* is an apt expression of Hardy's situation as a poet in exile from the home of pastoral. As with the chrysanthemum, Hardy senses that it is "too late" for pastoral.

The melancholy feeling of exile and of being "too late" is bound up with Hardy's use of language in "The Last Chrysanthemum." The poet uses figurative language to represent nature: the sun "*called*," the chrysanthemum "must have *felt* that fervid call." Not only does the flower feel as a person does, it even thinks:

> Had it reason for delay,
> Dreaming in witlessness
> That for a bloom so delicately gay
> Winter would stay its stress?

Hardy pushes the pathetic fallacy to an extreme degree. In "To Flowers from Italy," the speaker distanced himself from pathetic fallacy and pastoral elegy by situating the figurative language within conditional and interrogative modes. In "The Last Chrysanthemum," the speaker distances himself from pathetic fallacy by developing it to an improbable degree. We saw that Tennysonian pathetic fallacy has a way of becoming a very accurate transcription of nature, even as it looks ahead to the discontinuities and fragmentation of symbolism. Hardian pathetic fallacy is much more disembodied.

The speaker in "The Last Chrysanthemum" is alienated from nature and literary tradition. And pathetic fallacy functions as an idea rather than as a vehicle for achieving a concrete description of the world. The development of the poet's attitude toward pastoral in Tennyson involves an increasing sense of an allegory of the exiled artist. This type of allegory achieves an even more sardonic vision in Hardy's pastoral poems. Hardy uses figurative language, but it does not work to convey an image of what it attempts to describe. Instead, he foregrounds figurative language and pathetic fallacy as ideas to be questioned. In "The Last Chrysanthemum," pastoral nature becomes an idea, and Hardy is really addressing the failure of this idea:

> –I talk as if the thing were born
> With sense to work its mind;
> Yet it is but one mask of many worn
> By the Great Face behind.

In this final stanza, pathetic fallacy as a vehicle of natural description fails. Hardy turns to a larger and more abstract type of allegorical fiction. One critic calls this stanza "an embarrassing bit of gaucherie" that mars an otherwise excellent poem.[18] No doubt, the final stanza of "The Last Chrysanthemum" exemplifies Blackmur's criticism that Hardy is a "sensibility violated by ideas."[19] But we can also understand the stanza as Hardy's conscious sense of exile from poetic tradition. The poet acknowledges here the failure of his pathetic fallacy and his failure to reground his language in the pastoral mode. As the souls yearn to return home in Book VI of the *Aeneid*, the poet yearns to return to pastoral innocence but finds himself in a state of poetic exile and disinheritance.

Hardy continues to explore the pastoral topos of flowers and of generative natural life and decay and death in the poem "Transformations," from the volume *Moments of Vision*, published in 1917:

> Portion of this yew
> Is a man my grandsire knew,
> Bosomed here at its foot:
> This branch may be his wife,
> A ruddy human life
> Now turned to a green shoot.
>
> These grasses must be made
> Of her who often prayed,
> Last century, for repose;
> And the fair girl long ago
> Whom I often tried to know
> May be entering this rose.
>
> So, they are not underground,
> But as nerves and veins abound
> In the growths of upper air,
> And they feel the sun and rain,
> And the energy again
> That made them what they were!

Hardy said the scene was Stinsford Churchyard. J. O. Bailey comments on the poem as follows:

The concept of the poem is imaginatively a very old one. It appears in Fitzgerald's "Rubáiyát of Omar Khayyám": "I sometimes think that never blows so red / The rose as where some buried Caesar bled" (Stanza XIX). Besides this imaginative concept, Hardy had read such scientific essays as T. H. Huxley's "The Physical Basis of Life," which says that animal life may live in other forms only by feeding upon protoplasm that has lived, but died. In this scientific law, "There is a sort of continuance of life after death in the change of the vital animal principle, where the body feeds the tree or the flower that grows from the mound."[20]

It is curious that Bailey, after saying the concept is a very old one, then restricts himself to Hardy's near contemporaries. We find the idea of "transformations" in many of the classical writers, especially of pastoral. Hardy is as interested in the idea of "transformations" as a literary concept, as he is interested in it as a biological and ecological one.

On one level, the poem is an attempt at a pastoral *locus amoenus* and a figurative language that produce a pastoral scene involving sympathy between man and nature. Unlike "To Flowers from Italy" and "The Last Chrysanthemum," "Transformations" involves an emphasis on the rebirth and generation that emerge from death: the deaths of the people lead to the rebirth of nature. The way the speaker involves death and life with each other in this poem bears comparison with the fields of Enna in Tennsyon's "Demeter and Persephone." In that poem, the flowers in the field were, in part, the cause of Persephone's fall from innocence: Dis ravishes her while she is picking flowers. And when the flowers re-emerge, shooting up from the underworld, they are a sign that the world of pastoral innocence has been inalterably bound up with violence, evil, and death.

Hardy's poem is more positive in its attempt to naturalize death as the beginning of new life. But the ultimate sense of the poem is even more somber than Tennyson's "Demeter and Persephone." The positive side to this pastoral scene lies in the emphasis on new organic life: "green shoot," "grasses," "rose." The convoluted pathetic fallacy, in which human beings become plants and then the plants possess the feelings of human beings, affords an affirmative pastoral vision:

> So, they are not underground,
> But as nerves and veins abound
> In the growths of upper air,
> And they feel the sun and rain,
> And the energy again
> That made them what they were!

Here is a positive but ironic sympathy between man and nature. The moment looks back to the beginnings of pastoral elegy in the "Lament for Adonis" and the "Lament for Bion." And the transformation of the "underground" into the pastoral landscape looks back to Virgil's Elysium in Book VI.

But there is also a dark side to the transformations in this poem.

There is an ambivalence in "Transformations" which has its source in Ovid. Hardy emphasizes the grotesque side of this close kinship between man and the pastoral landscape. The metamorphosis in the poem, from human body to plant or tree, is comical but also strange and unpleasant. The ambiguous identity of both man and nature, the lack of definition or articulation between the two is unnerving:

> Portion of this yew
> Is a man my grandsire knew,
> Bosomed here at its foot. . . .

Is the yew a tree or a man? Is the subject of "bosomed" man or yew? The corporal punning of "bosomed" and "foot" is comic but also strange. As the passage continues, the phrasing and syntax become even more ambiguous: "This branch *may be* his wife"; "These grasses *must be* made / Of her who often prayed." The tentativeness of the verbal constructions belies the notion of a sympathetic and healthy reciprocity between man and nature; the transformations are not unqualifiably good.

The ambivalence of this kind of Hardian pastoral scene goes back to Ovid. The Ovidian metamorphoses often produce beautiful and lively natural phenomena, such as springs, trees, and flowers, but the conditions which usually bring about these changes are evil and violent. The transformation becomes a necessary means of escape from the threatening situation, but the nonhuman state of the transformation is not to be wished for. A good example is the story of Hyacinthus. Apollo and Hyacinthus were discus-throwing; Hyacinthus is hit in the head by a discus. Here is how Ovid describes Hyacinthus's dying:

> but all the arts were useless,
> The wound was past all cure. So, in a garden,
> If one breaks off a violet or poppy
> Or lilies, bristling with their yellow stamens,
> And they droop over, and cannot raise their heads,
> But look on earth, so sank the dying features,
> The neck, its strength all gone, lolled on the shoulder.[21]

To commemorate his love and sorrow for Hyacinthus, Apollo has him turned into a flower:

> "You will be
> With me forever, and my songs and music
> Will tell of you, and you will be reborn
> As a new flower whose markings will spell out
> My cries of grief, and there will come a time
> When a great hero's name will be the same
> As this flower's markings." So Apollo spoke,
> And it was truth he told, for on the ground
> The blood was blood no longer; in its place
> A flower grew, brighter than any crimson,
> Like lilies with their silver changed to crimson.
> That was not all; Apollo kept the promise
> About the markings, and inscribed the flower
> With his own grieving words: *Ai, Ai*
> The petals say, Greek for *Alas!*[22]

The Ovidian flower becomes, in this instance, a sign for the language of pastoral elegy: as it is made by Apollo, the flower is an emblem of poetic song. Most of the Ovidian metamorphoses turn human beings into natural objects that are, in turn, figures for the processes of artistic transformation. The Ovidian metamorphosis makes a work of art ambiguous in its moral status, and it suggests the poet's ambivalent attitude about the nature of his work. The implicit message is that generative and creative work, both organic and aesthetic, necessarily involves violence, pain, and loss. Hardy's "Transformations" contains a similar message. The grotesque imagery of bodily dismemberment and transformation into "portion" of a yew, or branch, or green shoot, is not a reassuring statement about man's relation to the natural landscape. Nor is it a reassuring statement about the poet's relation to literary tradition. These images of dismemberment signify organic and aesthetic discontinuity: natural process has become violently disruptive. "Transformations" is Hardy's sardonic transformation of the literary idea of pastoral innocence.

The tone that characterizes Hardy's poems of pastoral flowers and landscapes is ironic. But it is also rueful. This tone measures the poet's distance from the pastoral world. Hardy explores this rueful quality in the poem "A Backward Spring" from the volume *Moments of Vision*.

The trees are afraid to put forth buds,
And there is timidity in the grass;
The plots lie gray where gouged by spuds,
    And whither next week will pass
Free of sly sour winds is the fret of each bush
    Of barbary waiting to bloom.

Yet the snowdrop's face betrays no gloom,
And the primrose pants in its heedless push,
Though the myrtle asks if it's worth the fight
    This year with frost and rime
    To venture one more time
On delicate leaves and buttons of white
From the selfsame bough as at last year's prime,
And never to ruminate on or remember
What happened to it in mid-December.

J. O. Bailey's comments on the poem are short and to the point:

"A Backward Spring" presents Hardy's observation of trees and flowers. He attributes to some of them emotions like fear and timidity
in the face of hostile weather, though the aggressive snowdrops and
primrose blossom promptly with no apparent "gloom."[23]

This poem exemplifies the true voice of Hardian pastoral. Here
Hardy uses pathetic fallacy in a way that is neither purely descriptive nor purely an abstract idea. He does not use figurative language in this poem to convey concrete sensuous description as do
Keats and Tennyson, but neither does he invoke pathetic fallacy
just to mock it as an empty figure.

The tone of "A Backward Spring" is sad but accepting and is
best described by the word "rueful." A slight hesitancy of tone
evokes the backwardness, the hesitancy and reticence, that the
spring trees and flowers feel about blooming. The speaker neither
judges nor mocks. He accepts the world as it is. The quality of feeling and imagery is different from the grotesque in "Transformations," and from the allegory and self-criticism of the final stanza
of "The Last Chrysanthemum." It is different also from the bleak
sense of exile from nature and poetic tradition in "To Flowers from
Italy." These three earlier poems constitute negative pastoral scenes
in Hardy; "A Backward Spring" is a positive pastoral moment in

Hardy. The poem has deep affinities with the Keats of the Odes, especially "To Autumn."

Like Keats, Hardy is one of the great poets of autumnal melancholy. Here follows "The Later Autumn," from the volume *Human Shows* of 1925. This poem is a good example of Hardy's singular and idiosyncratic transformation of autumn pastoral.

> Gone are the lovers, under the bush
> > Stretched at their ease;
> > Gone the bees,
> Tangling themselves in your hair as they rush
> > On the line of your track,
> > Leg-laden, back
> > With a dip to their hive
> > In a prepossessed dive.
>
> Toadsmeat is mangy, frosted, and sere;
> > Apples in grass
> > Crunch as we pass,
> And rot ere the men who make cyder appear.
> > Couch-fires abound
> > On fallows around,
> > And shades far extend
> > Like lives soon to end.
>
> Spinning leaves join the remains shrunk and brown
> > Of last year's display
> > That lie wasting away,
> On whose corpses they earlier as scorners gazed down
> > From their aery green height:
> > Now in the same plight
> > They huddle; while yon
> > A robin looks on.

Like "The Last Chrysanthemum," "The Later Autumn" explores seasonal and poetic lateness. Hardy is highly conscious of the pastoral tradition he is indebted to here: the textual debts begin with William Barnes and can then be traced back to Keats, Thomson, and Virgil. The pastoral meditation on death through the imagery of falling leaves in the first stanza goes back to the *Aeneid*. But the contemporary source is Barnes. Here is stanza two of "Leaves A Vallèn" from Hardy's selected edition of Barnes:

> There dead ash leaves be a-toss'd
>   In the wind, a-blowèn stronger,
> An' our life-time, since we lost
>   Souls we lov'd, is woone year longer,
> Woone year longer, woone year wider,
>   Vrom the friends that death ha' took,
> As the hours do teäke the rider
>   Vrom the hand that last he shook.[24]

Hardy does not use the heavy Dorset dialect, but the imagery and quality of feeling are similar in the two poems.

J. O. Bailey points out that in stanza two, Hardy draws upon the cider-making of *The Woodlanders*.[25] But Hardy also draws upon stanza two of Keats's "To Autumn," with the picture of Autumn beside the cider-press: "The Later Autumn" becomes Hardy's meditation on that poem. Hardy takes further the melancholy sense of ending and death contained within Keats's imagery of seasonal plenitude. In Hardy's poem the bees are gone. The apples rot. In the pastoral grove "shades far extend / Like lives soon to end." This year's leaves "join the remains shrunk and brown / Of last year's." Last year's leaves are "corpses" that "lie wasting away." In "The Later Autumn," Hardy fulfills the potential organic and poetic decomposition implied in Keats's "To Autumn."

We can note the probable influence of James Thomson here also. Hardy's biographer, Robert Gittings, notes that Hardy owned the complete works of Thomson.[26] Thomson's *The Seasons* was one of the most influential descriptive poems in English literary history. In terms of imagery and thematics, the following passage from "Autumn" is relevant:

> The pale descending year, yet pleasing still,
> A gentler Mood inspires; for now the Leaf
> Incessant rustles from the mournful Grove,
> Oft startling such as, studious, walk below,
> And slowly circles through the waving Air.
> But should a quicker Breeze amid the Boughs
> Sob, o'er the Sky the leafy Deluge streams;
> Till choak'd and matted with the dreary Shower,
> The Forest-Walks, at every rising Gale,
> Roll wide the wither'd Waste, and whistle bleak.[27]
>   ("Autumn," 986–995)

And here is Thomson's description of man's disruption of the civic order of bees:

> The happy People, in their waxen Cells,
> Sat tending public Cares, and planning Schemes
> Of Temperance, for Winter poor; rejoiced
> To mark, full-flowing round, their copious Stores.
> Sudden the dark oppressive team ascends;
> And, us'd to milder Scents, the tender Race,
> By Thousands, tumbles from their honey'd Domes,
> Convolv'd, and agonizing in the Dust.[28]
>
> ("Autumn," 1174–1181)

These two passages reveal how, in Thomson, the elegiac sadness of season's end is bound up not only with the descriptive mode of pastoral, but also with the idea of work in nature that is dealt with in the georgic. The image of the falling leaves connotes the mood of pastoral elegy. But the work of the bees and man's work in collecting the honey derive as much from the georgic as from the pastoral impulse. The bees, the cider-making, and the burning of couch-grass are generically part of the georgic. These images are not only images of work in nature; they serve as figures for the work of the poet. The difference between Thomson's civic bees and Hardy's lies in the function of work in nature. Thomson places the pastoral work within a larger philosophical order, an order that derives, in part, from Shaftesbury's view of a beneficent nature. Thomson suggests the continuity between man, nature, and God when he invokes "Philosophic Melancholy" ("Autumn," 1003). In the passage on the bees, Thomson subsumes and makes affirmative the sadness and even violence (e.g., the disruption of the bee-hive) in this larger philosophic order. One finds this affirmation of civic and, simultaneously, poetic order in Thomson's classical model, Virgil's *Georgics*. In the *Georgics*, the poet makes the potential disorder in nature orderly by human knowledge and work:

> In fear of this, mark the months and signs of heaven; whither Saturn's cold star withdraws itself and into what circles of the sky strays the Cyllenian fire. Above all, worship the gods, and pay great Ceres her yearly rites, sacrificing on the glad sward, with the setting of winter's last days, when clear springtime is now come.[29]

The same sense of knowledge and order characterizes the community of bees in Book IV:

> [they] hold the dwellings of their city jointly, and pass their life under the majesty of law. They alone know a fatherland and fixed home. . . . [30]

The pastoral/georgic work of "The Later Autumn" is different from this affirmation of peace and order: the sense of spoiled nature conveyed by "mangy," "sere," and "rot" suggests work gone bad. And the images of "shades" and "corpses" imply that death will make all work futile. The closing line of "The Later Autumn"–"A robin looks on"–is the final sign of the futility of man's work in nature. It signals also the futility of the poet's work. In poetic tradition one associates birds with song and poetry. Hardy transforms this association. This robin *looks* but does not sing. It is Hardy's way of describing his own sense of lateness and his sense of the futility of poetic work, with the breaking down or decomposition of georgic and pastoral conventions. The bird's silence withholds testimony to nature; the silence seems to be a refusal to affirm a beneficent natural order or community. The final line is a more severe comment on the end of pastoral song than even the final stanza of Keats's "To Autumn."

Hardy's pastoral poems of flowers and leaves involve a melancholy sense of poetic disinheritance that is greater than that found in the pastoral of Tennyson and Keats. We find this sense of disinheritance from pastoral conventions also in the Hardian *locus amoenus* and the larger landscape. One example is "A Spot," from the volume *Poems of the Past and the Present* of 1901:

> In years defaced and lost,
> Two sat here, transport-tossed,
> Lit by a living love
> The wilted world knew nothing of:
> Scared momently
> By gaingivings,
> Then hoping things
> That could not be. . . .
>
> Of love and us no trace
> Abides upon the place;

The sun and shadows wheel,
Season and season sereward steal;
    Foul days and fair
    Here, too, prevail,
    And gust and gale
    As everywhere.

    But lonely shepherd souls
    Who bask amid these knolls
    May catch a faery sound
On sleepy noontides from the ground:
    'O not again
    Till Earth outwears
    Shall love like theirs
    Suffuse this glen!'

Hardy's poems of pastoral flowers suggest the poet's melancholy exile through the "decomposition" of nature. The disharmony within nature and between man and nature also suggests this melancholy. In "A Spot," the melancholy of Hardy's *locus amoenus* is bound up with the death of lovers. In J. O. Bailey's commentary on the poem, he cites an observation from Ruth Firor's *Folkways in Thomas Hardy*. Bailey says, "Firor points out that the poem makes use of the folk-belief in the power of shepherds to perceive emanations from a place that was the scene of strong emotional disturbance."[31] But the folk context in Hardy is not simply contemporary; it is related to Hardy's use of pastoral. Such is the case in "A Spot." The Hardian *locus amoenus* involves a strong sense of the passing of time and the absence of people and things that existed in the past.

Hardy conveys this sense of passing time in "A Spot" through such words and phrases as "In years defaced and lost," "wilted world," "Season and season sereward steal." The quality of pathos in Hardy derives from Virgil. One thinks especially of the sense of elegiac ending in the final line of *Eclogue* I: "maioresque cadunt altis de montibus umbrae" (and longer shadows fall from the mountain heights). One thinks, also, of Aeneas's tears before the picture of Troy on the walls of Carthage. The pathos, finally, is not simply about the passing away of loved people and things; it is about the sense of lonely exile the poet feels toward tradition. Hardy suggests this idea in the final stanza: he invokes the image of the lonely shepherd resting during the noon peace (a traditional pastoral topos). The shepherd looks back on the dead lovers. He writes their epitaph:

> 'O not again
> Till Earth outwears
> Shall love like theirs
> Suffuse this glen!'

The melancholy in this epitaph is two-fold. First, the *locus amoenus* or pleasance no longer contains their affirmative love; the landscape serves as their memorial. Second, the shepherd's song is a love elegy that is also an elegy for the end of pastoral song.

"In Front of the Landscape" also involves Hardy's transformation and development of the *locus amoenus* topos; it is the opening poem in the volume *Satires of Circumstance* of 1914. The poem is central to the argument about the Hardian *locus amoenus* and deserves quotation in full.

> Plunging and labouring on in a tide of visions,
>   Dolorous and dear,
> Forward I pushed my way as amid waste waters
>   Stretching around,
> Through whose eddies there glimmered the customed landscape
>   Yonder and near
>
> Blotted to feeble mist. And the coombs and the upland
>   Coppice-crowned,
> Ancient chalk-pit, milestone, rills in the grass-flat
>   Stroked by the light,
> Seemed but a ghost-like gauze, and no substantial
>   Meadow or mound.
>
> What were the infinite spectacles featuring foremost
>   Under my sight,
> Hindering me to discern my paced advancement,
>   Lengthening to miles;
> What were the re-creations killing the daytime
>   As by the night?
>
> O they were speechful faces, gazing insistent,
>   Some as with smiles,
> Some as with slow-born tears that brinily trundled

Over the wrecked
Cheeks that were fair in their flush-time, and now with anguish
    Harrowed by wiles.

Yes, I could see them, feel them, hear them, address them—
    Halo-bedecked—
And, alas, onwards, shaken by fierce unreason,
    Rigid in hate,
Smitten by years-long wryness born of misprision,
    Dreaded, suspect.

Then there would breast me shining sights, sweet seasons
    Further in date;
Instruments of strings with the tenderest passion
    Vibrant, beside
Lamps long extinguished, robes, cheeks, eyes with the earth's crust
    Now corporate.

Also there rose a headland of hoary aspect
    Gnawed by the tide,
Frilled by the nimb of the morning as two friends stood there
    Guilelessly glad—
Wherefore they knew not—touched by the fringe of an ecstasy
    Scantly descried.

Later images too did the day unfurl me,
    Shadowed and sad,
Clay cadavers of those who had shared in the dramas,
    Laid now at ease,
Passions all spent, chiefest the one of the broad brow
    Sepulture-clad.

So did beset me scenes, miscalled of the bygone,
    Over the leaze,
Past the clump, and down to where lay the beheld ones;
    —Yea, as the rhyme
Sung by the sea-swell, so in their pleading dumbness
    Captured me these.

For, their lost revisiting manifestations
    In their live time
Much had I slighted, caring not for their purport,
    Seeing behind

Things more coveted, reckoned the better worth calling
    Sweet, sad, sublime.

Thus do they now show hourly before the intenser
    Stare of the mind
As they were ghosts avenging their slights by my bypast
    Body-borne eyes,
Show, too, with fuller translation than rested upon them
    As living kind.

Hence wag the tongues of the passing people, saying
    In their surmise,
'Ah—whose is this dull form that perambulates, seeing nought
    Round him that looms
Whithersoever his footsteps turn in his farings,
    Save a few tombs?'

J. O. Bailey says that "In Front of the Landscape" "presents the behaviour of Hardy's mind in reverie when the senses drowse, but the memory calls up a train of flashing and dissolving images. They seem to stand 'in front of the landscape' and to obscure it." Bailey points out that the imagery suggests a person walking through a fog. And he also tries to pinpoint the actual places around Dorsetshire that are described here.[32] The actual places are less important than the way Hardy situates these places within the pastoral conventions of the *locus amoenus*.

Donald Davie argues for the importance of Virgil in Hardy, especially in the "Poems of 1912–13" sequence in *Satires of Circumstance*. [33] Hardy's epigraph for that sequence is *Veteris vestigia flammae*. Dido speaks these words after having seen Aeneas. The phrase means "signs of the old flame"; it signifies the new love developing in Dido for Aeneas. The pathos in Hardy's poems about love owes much to Virgil and the Dido episode.

Hardy is indebted also to Virgil in his placing or situating of his landscapes. "In Front of the Landscape" is not simply about past places and loved ones; it is about the literary past, the conventions, here Virgilian, which form the poem. The key passage in Virgil in terms of the Hardian *locus amoenus* is the famous description of Elysium in Book VI:

    devenere locos laetos et amoena virecta
    Fortunatorum Nemorum sedesque beatas.

largior hic campos aether et lumine vestit
purpureo, solemque suum, sua sidera norunt.[34]

(VI, 638–641)

They came upon the lands of gladness, glades
of gentleness, the Groves of Blessedness—
a gracious place. The air is generous;
the plains wear dazzling light; they have their very
own sun and their own stars.[35]

But in "In Front of the Landscape," Hardy transforms Virgil's "delightful place." Hardy changes Virgil's "purple light" into a "feeble mist" that "blots" the "customed landscape." Hardy's landscape is not invested with the transforming light of love; it is invested with a light that connotes the insubstantiality of the landscape and of love. The various parts of the natural scene, when

Stroked by the light,
Seemed but a ghost-like gauze, and no substantial
Meadow or mound.

In "In Front of the Landscape," the speaker does not emphasize the blessed state in the Elysium fields; the speaker emphasizes the darker, unhappier aspects of the Virgilian underworld. As with much of the leaf-corpse imagery in Hardy, the imagery here suggests the sufferers in the underworld. It is appropriate that the *locus amoenus* becomes "ghost-like." Hardy's landscape is the place where the speaker sees and remembers people who suffer the pathos of death and exile:

O they were speechful faces, gazing insistent,
    Some as with smiles,
Some as with slow-born tears that brinily trundled
    Over the wrecked
Cheeks that were fair in their flush-time, ash now with anguish,
    Harrowed by wiles.

This passage looks back to Virgil's unburied dead hoping to be ferried across the river to their final home (*Aeneid*, VI, 295–330). Gittings tell us that Dante's *Comedy* was Hardy's mother's favorite work of literature.[36] The passage quoted above could be based on Dante. Virgil, however, provides a sufficient model.

Hardy envisions not the groves of blessedness, but the underworld as hell. The inhabitants of this landscape are "Harrowed by wiles" and

> shaken by fierce unreason,
> Rigid in hate,
> Smitten by years-long wryness born of misprision,
> Dreaded, suspect.

Death transforms the positive scenes in this landscape. In stanza six, the "shining sights, sweet seasons" close with death: "Lamps long extinguished, robes, cheeks, eyes with the earth's crust / Now corporate." Here Hardy provides a fine transition to stanza seven: He carries on the image of the buried dead in the earth in the image of the decay of the landscape itself:

> Also there rose a headland of hoary aspect
> Gnawed by the tide. . . .

The words "hoary" and "gnawed" express age and decay. The images of burial and death continue. In stanza eight the speaker describes "later images":

> Shadowed and sad,
> Clay cadavers. . . .

Stanza eight closes with the image of one of the dead "sepulture-clad."

In the last four stanzas, Hardy shifts from the landscape to the poet/speaker describing it. Here the speaker describes the pathos of exile. The speaker realizes he did not pay enough attention to these people when they were alive. They have come back to haunt him:

> Thus do they now show hourly before the intenser
> Stare of the mind
> As they were ghosts avenging their slights by my bypast
> Body-borne eyes,
> Show, too, with fuller translation than rested upon them
> As living kind.

The melancholy sense of exile here is not simply from the people who are dead; Hardy describes the exile of the poet. The poet feels that the landscape has become a place of death. Here is how the speaker's neighbors view the poet figure:

> "—whose is this dull form that perambulates, seeing nought
>   Round him that looms
> Whithersoever his footsteps turn in his farings,
>   Save a few tombs?"

They perceive the speaker as an outsider.

Because the landscape incorporates the *locus amoenus* topos, Hardy's transformation of it into a place of death is a sign of his sense of the poet as outsider; it is a sign of his disinheritance from tradition. The death landscape implies the death of poetry. As in Tennyson's "Demeter and Persephone," the *locus amoenus* in "In Front of the Landscape" is transformed by the emergence of death from the underworld. The pastoral pleasance is no longer a place of escape. Escape into the bower world of innocence is still a possibility in Keats, but the inchoate sense of poetic exile in Keats, and the more troubled sense of exile in Tennyson, is felt to an even greater degree in Hardy. The relation of the speaker to the landscape expresses this sense of exile: the speaker is "in front of" the landscape rather than within it. This configuration suggests also the poet's sense of poetic disinheritance: speaker and landscape do not exist in close relation. Since the landscape represents a traditional literary topos, there is the suggestion here that the speaker is apart from that tradition. This is similar to the distancing of voice and framing of scene in the classical pastoral idyll. Tennyson's framing and fragmented imagery carry the idyll toward symbolism. Hardy's fragmented landscape does not even achieve that kind of unity. The poet's discontinuity with tradition is more severe.

Not all of Hardy's "pleasances" are as somber as the one in "In Front of the Landscape." A more positive poem about remembered love and the pastoral landscape is "Under the Waterfall." The poem is a dramatic monologue spoken by a woman remembering a spot where she and her lover once had a picnic. She describes a particular incident that occurred there: while rinsing a wine glass in a pool beneath the waterfall, she let the glass slip into the pool. In the poem, the poet frames the incident in several ways. In the opening stanza, the speaker describes the feelings that arise whenever she puts her arm into a basin of water. She feels "The sweet sharp sense of a fugitive day / Fetched back from its thickening shroud of gray." Her listener asks her why this action produces these feelings. Here follows her answer:

> "Well, under the fall, in a crease of stone,
> Though where precisely none ever has known,
> Jammed darkly, nothing to show how prized,
> And by now with its smoothness opalized,
>   Is a drinking-glass:
>   For, down that pass
>   My lover and I
>   Walked under a sky
> Of blue with a leaf-wove awning of green,
> In the burn of August, to paint the scene,
> And we placed our basket of fruit and wine
> By the runlet's rim, where we sat to dine. . . ."

Then, as the speaker tells how the wine glass fell into the pool, she rapidly shifts from the remembered idyllic scene to the water basin with which she has been comparing it:

> "The basin seems the pool, and its edge
> The hard smooth face of the brook-side ledge,
> And the leafy pattern of china-ware
> The hanging plants that were bathing there."

"Under the Waterfall" is a pastoral idyll. It contains Hardy's modern use of the classical device of ecphrasis. At the beginning of the passage, the speaker describes a pastoral bower scene, with the blue sky and the "leaf-wove awning of green." One classical analogue could be the following from Virgil *Eclogue* VII; Meliboeus remembers the singing match between Corydon and Thyrsis:

> Ye mossy springs, and grass softer than sleep, and the green arbutus that shields you with its scant shade, ward the noontide heat from my flock. Now comes the summer's parching, now the buds swell on the gladsome tendril.[37]

But what is interesting about Hardy's treatment of the *locus amoenus* here is the way he then frames it through an imitated picture of the same scene. The framing occurs in the passage that begins "The basin seems the pool." The speaker describes the water basin as if it were the pool beneath the waterfall, and the leaf-pattern on the basin as if it were the plants around the water's edge. This is an example of the classical device of ecphrasis.

One example of ecphrasis from Theocritus is the description of the cup in *Idyll* I. The ivy-fringed cup in *Idyll* I is given to Thyrsis after he sings the elegy for Daphnis. The drinking glass and the ecphrastic imitation of the bower scene in the water basin are modern idyllic counterparts; they express the speaker's memory of her lover. The ecphrastic moments are the poetic figures for the "rhyme of love / Persistently sung by the fall." "Under the Waterfall" constitutes a positive type of idyll in which Hardy uses pastoral ecphrasis to maintain through art a remembered bower and the remembered loved person within it.

The poet uses the *locus amoenus* and ecphrasis in "Under the Waterfall" to create an affirmative type of pastoral that has strong roots in traditional pastoral conventions. The Hardian idyll and ecphrasis take on a more ambivalent nature in the poem "The Pedigree" (from the volume *Moments of Vision*). J. O. Bailey says, "'The Pedigree' expresses Hardy's absorbed interest in his ancestry. Consulting parish registers, he worked out several pedigrees, now in the Dorset County Museum. . . . He was interested in the natural laws governing heredity."[38]

This poem does not contain a landscape from nature. Nor does it contain any of the attributes associated with the traditional *locus amoenus*. But in a curious way, "The Pedigree" is an example of Hardy's modern idyll.

> I bent in the deep of the night
> Over a pedigree the chronicler gave
> As mine; and as I bent there, half-unrobed,
> The uncurtained panes of my window-square let in the watery
>   light
> Of the moon in its old age:
> And green-rheumed clouds were hurrying past where mute and cold
>   it globed
> Like a drifting dolphin's eye seen through a lapping wave.

This is a moment of pastoral ecphrasis that follows the line back through Tennyson, Keats, Spenser, Virgil, and Theocritus. In the pastoral convention, the speaker is looking at a picture of something; in this case the picture is the pedigree. The moment exemplifies Hardy's new pastoral *locus amoenus*, which tends to be a house rather than a bower. Finally, the stanza contains Hardy's use of figurative language to describe the natural world. The use of pathetic fallacy may also stem from pastoral conventions. The poet speaks of the "moon in its old age"; the moon is also "mute" and "cold." Hardy describes the moon with the clouds passing over it as "Like a drifting dolphin's eye seen through a lapping wave."

In the second stanza, the speaker represents the pedigree through figurative language.

> So, scanning my sire-sown tree,
> And the hieroglyphs of this spouse tied to that,
> With offspring mapped below in lineage,
>   Till the tangles troubled me,
> The branches seemed to twist into a seared and cynic face
> Which winked and tokened towards the window like a Mage
> Enchanting me to gaze again thereat.

As he looks at the pedigree and traces his ancestors, the tree of names turns into a "seared and cynic face." It is an example of a Hardian pathetic fallacy that is forced and ironical. Here the poet uses pathetic fallacy and anthropomorphism to create distance between the speaker and his surroundings. Hardy's rhetoric suggests that the world is deceptive: the pedigree that turns into the cynical face of the Mage is a type of false guide, like those found in some of Spenser's negative bowers. The words "winked," "tokened," and "enchanting" suggest that the window the Mage points to may contain false and deceptive images.

In stanza three, the speaker gazes at the window, "a mirror now." He sees the long line of his "begetters." "Generation and generation of my mien, and build, and brow." These images in the window-turned-mirror lead to pessimistic thoughts in stanza four.

> And then did I divine
> That every heave and coil and move I made
> Within my brain, and in my mood and speech,
>   Was in the glass portrayed
> As long forestalled by their so making it;

> The first of them, the primest fugleman of my line,
> Being fogged in far antiqueness past surmise and reason's reach.

The speaker believes the glass presents a picture of more than his ancestors: the glass presents a picture of himself, a picture that limits and defines him. J. O. Bailey says, "This reasoning leads to the conclusion that . . . he enjoys no freedom of will."[39]

In "The Pedigree," imitation and ecphrasis do not produce a moment of pastoral freedom; they are not ways of standing outside of and inside of tradition at the same time. We saw that pattern in Tennyson. We also saw pastoral ecphrasis as expressing positive memory in "Under the Waterfall." There the ecphrastic image produced by the water basin helped the speaker remember her lover. But in "The Pedigree," the ecphrastic image entangles the speaker in traditions of family (and secondarily of poetry) which he finds oppressive and limiting.

> Said I then, sunk in tone,
> "I am merest mimicker and counterfeit!—
>   Though thinking, *I am I,*
>   *And what I do I do myself alone.*"
> —The cynic twist of the page thereat unknit
> Back to its normal figure, having wrought its purport wry,
>   The Mage's mirror left the window-square,
>   And the stained moon and drift retook their places there.

Here the classical devices of framing and ecphrasis do not enable the speaker to distance himself from his subject matter; rather, the devices implicate the speaker in his subject matter's falseness and his own unoriginality: "I am merest mimicker and counterfeit."

But even at this moment, the speaker realizes that the idyll is not entirely negative. "*I am I, / And what I do I do myself alone.*" The poem is not simply about the speaker's interest in his ancestors and heredity; "The Pedigree" is about the poet/speaker's relation to poetic tradition. And the window-mirror and the pedigree are examples of a modern ecphrasis of extreme ambivalence. They are the frames through which the speaker realizes his relationship to tradition.

"The Photograph," also from the volume *Moments of Vision*, is another example of Hardy's modern idyll.

The flame crept up the portrait line by line
As it lay on the coals in the silence of night's profound,
      And over the arm's incline,
And along the marge of the silkwork superfine,
And gnawed at the delicate bosom's defenceless round.

Then I vented a cry of hurt, and averted my eyes;
The spectacle was one that I could not bear,
      To my deep and sad surprise;
But, compelled to heed, I again looked furtivewise
Till the flame had eaten her breasts, and mouth, and hair.

'Thank God, she is out of it now!' I said at last,
In a great relief of hurt when the thing was done
      That had set my soul aghast,
And nothing was left of the picture unsheathed from the past
But the ashen ghost of the card it had figured on.

She was a woman long hid amid packs of years,
She might have been living or dead; she was lost to my sight,
      And the deed that had nigh drawn tears
Was done in a casual clearance of life's arrears;
But I felt as if I had put her to death that night! . . .

                    . . .

—Well; she knew nothing thereof did she survive,
And suffered nothing if numbered among the dead;
      Yet—yet—if on earth alive
Did she feel a smart, and with vague strange anguish strive?
If in heaven, did she smile at me sadly and shake her head?

"The Photograph" has the typically Hardian elegiac tone about lost love. R. L. Purdy notes that Hardy said this story actually took place at Max Gate.[40] J. O. Bailey suggests the photograph may have been of Tryphena Sparks, the cousin Hardy was in love with before he married Emma Lavinia Gifford.[41] The biographical elements of "The Photograph" are important. But the poem has an aesthetic dimension also. Hardy uses the photograph as a modern equivalent of the framed world of artistic representation that goes back to Theocritus *Idyll* I and Homer's description of the shield of Achilles. Bailey's comments on this poem downplay the importance of literary tradition. The use of ecphrasis and the elegiac quality of feeling and thought in "The Photograph" stem from Virgil.

Two moments in *The Aeneid* are especially relevant to this argument. The first is a key moment of ecphrasis. In Book I Aeneas looks at the pictures of the Trojan War on the walls of Carthage:

> First in this grove did a strange sight appear to him and allay his fears; here first did Aeneas dare to hope for safety and put surer trust in his shattered fortunes. For while beneath the mighty temple, awaiting the queen, he scans each object, while he marvels at the city's fortune, the handicraft of the several artists and the work of their toil, he sees in due order the battles of Ilium, the warfare now known by fame throughout the world, the sons of Atreus, and Priam, and Achilles, fierce in his wrath against both. He stopped and weeping cried: "What land, Achates, what tract on earth is now not full of our sorrow? Lo, Priam! Here, too, there are tears for misfortune and mortal sorrows touch the heart. Dismiss thy fears; this fame will bring thee some salvation."
>
> So he speaks, and feasts his soul on the unsubstantial picture, sighing oft-times, and his face wet with the flood of tears.[42]

We saw this passage's bearing on "Tears, Idle Tears." The passage is relevant here because a Virgilian pathos characterizes many of Hardy's poems about the passing love. It is relevant, as well, because of Virgil's use of the imitated world or picture as a way of expressing Aeneas's state of exile. "The Photograph" is in part a poem about the poet's disinheritance, not simply from past love but from past poetry (such as Virgil's). The burning of the photograph is an image of the transience of art and the artist.

The second passage from the *Aeneid* that is important in this context is the description of Dido's suicide. By burning the photograph, the speaker betrays the woman. Dido's suicide is the result of what she perceives as the betrayal of Aeneas. Dido has a sacrificial pyre built and then:

> [She] bursts into the inner courts of the house, mounts in madness the high pyre and unsheathes the Dardan sword, a gift he sought for no such end! Then, as she saw the Trojan garb and the familiar bed, pausing awhile in tearful thought, she threw herself on the couch and spoke her latest words:
>
> "O relics once dear, while God and Fate allowed! take my spirit, and release me from my woes! I have lived, I have finished the

course that Fortune gave; and now in majesty, my shade shall pass beneath the earth. A noble city I have built; my own walls I have seen; avenging my husband. I have exacted punishment from my brother and foe – happy, ah! too happy, had but the Dardan keels never touched our shores!" She spoke, and burying her face in the couch, "I shall die unavenged," she cries, "but let me die! Thus, thus I go gladly into the dark!"[43]

The death of Dido is one of the most moving passages in the *Aeneid*. And it implicates the pious Aeneas in destruction and suffering, even as he heads forth to build the new community in Italy. Hardy's "The Photograph" is not about such heroic action and its consequences: it is a personal poem. But the artist-creator figure's implication in destruction and suffering is a part of Hardy's poem too. Finally, that destructiveness and the elegiac tone redound upon the speaker in "The Photograph." The ecphrastic picture mocks the speaker, as it did in "The Pedigree." The envisioned woman looks down on the helpless speaker. He is the one who is sorrowful here; he is in a state of permanent exile. She has found a home: "If in heaven, did she smile at me sadly and shake her head?"

In Tennyson, the ecphrastic frame makes the poet figure an exile but one whose distance gives him power over the scene. The sense of exile and disinheritance is only partial. In Hardy's "The Photograph," the ecphrastic frame places the poet figure in a position of total exile. The speaker's sense of guilt – "But I felt as if I had put her to death last night" – involves Hardy's sense of the way artistic work is implicated in types of destruction and violence. It involves also the theme found in Tennyson: the death of poetry. Hardy's use of the classical device of ecphrasis produces, then, similar effects to his transformation of the pastoral *locus amoenus*. Hardy emphasizes disharmony, violence, and death both in nature and in poetry.

Let us now look briefly at one more poem by Hardy in terms of a writer of pastoral in the century before Keats. We can read Hardy's poem "Afterwards" in terms of Gray's "Elegy." "Afterwards" is the final poem in *Moments of Vision*. It is one of Hardy's poems about nature and death; it is also an elegy for the poet. In each of the five stanzas, the speaker describes with precision and detail certain phenomena in the natural world. These moments occur in an envisioned future. At the close of each stanza, the speaker imagines what his neighbors will say about him. The implicit assumption here is that the speaker imagines himself as dead.

The speaker in "Afterwards" imagines his own pastoral elegy. It is important to note the tone of gentle self-acceptance. The neighbors are not ghostly visions nor are they mockers, as they are in, respectively, "Wessex Heights" and "In Front of the Landscape." And we get the sense that the speaker did lead a life in which he felt bonds with nature and the landscape. Here, for example, is the first stanza:

> When the Present has latched its postern behind my tremulous
>   stay,
>   And the May month flaps its glad green leaves like wings,
> Delicate-filmed as new-spun silk, will the neighbours say,
>   'He was a man who used to notice such things'?

This is a poem that builds a picture of the natural world and of a community of people within it.

There is a sense of melancholy in the poem, but this sense derives from the pastoral themes of the passing of time and the cycles of life. As J. O. Bailey says, "In structure the poem touches upon each of the seasons."[44] And another critic notes, "A sense of time runs through the poem."[45] The sense of melancholy is not the result of the poet's feelings of exile from nature or from poetry.

One of Hardy's models here is Gray's "Elegy." The "Elegy" is a poem that provides a melancholy sense of the cycles of natural and human life. It is also an elegy for the poet's self. Toward the poem's close, Gray imagines the pastoral elegy for his own death. The elegy begins like this:

> Haply some hoary-headed Swain may say,
>   "Oft have we seen him at the peep of dawn
> Brushing with hasty steps the dews away
>   To meet the sun upon the upland lawn."[46]

Gray goes even further: he writes his own epitaph. But reading the "Elegy" alongside of "Afterwards" gives us a good sense of the extent to which Hardy was indebted to pastoral tradition. The epitaph poem goes back to the classical pastoral tradition as found in Theocritus's *Epigrams* and the *Greek Anthology*. Here is *Epigram* XV from Theocritus:

> Now, wayfarer, I shall learn whether thou honourest good men and true, or whether one who is base has like measure too from thee. Thou wilt say, "A blessing on this tomb for light it lies over the hallowed head of Eurymedon."[47]

Gray's "Elegy" and Hardy's "Afterwards" look back to this tradition, but Hardy's poem is a modern elegy for the death of the poet and the death of poetry. In this regard, "Afterwards" has affinities also with Keats's "To Autumn." As does "To Autumn," Hardy's poem moves through the various senses and various aspects of the natural world; and again, as does "To Autumn," the poem achieves its closure with the fading of pastoral sound. This is the opposite structure from Gray's "Elegy," which *begins* with the fading of sounds and day.

> The Curfew tolls the knell of parting day,
>   The lowing herd wind slowly o'er the lea,
> The plouman homeward plods his weary way,
>   And leaves the world to darkness and to me.[48]

The "Elegy" opens with the fading of sound and sight; it closes with the emphasis on the visual scene. The speaker urges the reader to "look" at the epitaph. "To Autumn" moves from the tactile to the visual and then to the aural; the sequence of scenes is not identical in "Afterwards," but it is similar. The first stanza describes foliage with a kind of tactile precision: "glad green leaves like wings, / Delicate-filmed as new-spun silk." Stanzas two, three, and four emphasize sight: the speaker describes a hawk crossing the sky, a hedgehog traveling across a lawn, and his neighbors "Watching the full-starred heavens that winter sees." In stanza five, the poet emphasizes sound or its absence. The speaker describes the bell tolling his own death:

> And will any say when my bell of quittance is heard in the
>   gloom,
>   And a crossing breeze cuts a pause in its outrollings,
> Till they rise again, as they were a new bell's boom,
>   'He hears it not now, but used to notice such things'?

The close is in keeping with the tone of "Afterwards" as a whole. The poem's affirmations of bonds between the speaker and nature and the community are posed as questions or conditional states: "will thy neighbours say," "a gazer may think," "One may say," "Will this thought rise," "will any say." Despite the sense of community, textual and social, in the poem, the tentative voice and the fading sounds give a melancholy quality to that sense of affirmation. It is a fitting close to *Moments of Vision*. And it is a paradigmatic moment in Hardy's Victorian pastoral.

V

A Dwelling's Character:
From Pastoral to
the Country House in Hardy

THE RELATION BETWEEN THE COUNTRY-HOUSE
poem and pastoral is complex. Pastoral poems in Virgil and Theocritus sometimes contain houses or farms as places of retirement.
But the country-house poem takes as its special origin the contrast
between country and city in Horace. In English literary history,
the central tradition for the country-house ideal is Jonson, Marvell, Pope—all poets who had an interest in pastoral as well.[1] The
Romantic poets on the whole did not pursue the country-house
ideal. Nor do the major Victorians write country-house poems in
a strict sense. But what makes Hardy especially important is his renewal of earlier genres abandoned by Romanticism and its inheri-
tors, and at the same time his experimentation with these forms.

Hardy's experimentation with these forms involves what one
might call "subliminal allusion." Hardy writes poems that allude
to the country-house tradition, but in ways that disrupt the country-
house ideal. These disruptions involve issues of poetics and the
structure of representation in the poems. Hardy's house poems ignore or overturn boundaries of genre, so that his poems are also
pastoral and georgic simultaneously. If Hardian pastoral is about
the exile from poetic community, Hardy's house poems reveal,

from within the locus of community values, the breakdown of
those values. The breakdown of generic structure both imitates
and reflects the breakdown of the reciprocity between man and the
community, which had characterized the country-house ideal.

To see the way Hardy's house poems derive in part from the
country-house tradition, and to see the way he uses this tradition
in conjunction with pastoral and georgic motifs, we may turn to
one of Hardy's earliest poetic efforts, "Domicilium." Florence Emily
Hardy placed the poem at the front of *The Early Life of Thomas
Hardy.*[2] Even apart from this prominent position in the *Early Life,*
"Domicilium" is important. The poem shows in a somewhat rough
form some of the pastoral themes Hardy explores by way of the
idea of houses and the ideal of the country-house tradition. The
Latin title suggests a high value placed on traditions of origin and
language; those traditions are a central concern of the poem. But
Hardy also disrupts traditional concepts in "Domicilium." We see
one type of disruption in the opening stanza, with its foregrounding or exaggeration of pathetic fallacy:

> Wild honeysucks
> Climb on the walls, and seem to sprout a wish
> (If we may fancy wish of trees and plants)
> To overtop the apple-trees hard by.

Here the poet describes the exterior of the house where he was
born. The wild honeysucks struggle against the walls and against
the apple trees behind the house; Hardy begins this poem and essentially his poetic career with an image of struggle in nature. The
struggle defines a pastoral that is not simply about domicile, but
about the figure of the poet in exile from poetic community emblematized by the house. The speaker, in describing this pastoral
struggle among the vines, the apple trees, and the wall, uses a figurative language that calls attention to its own artifice: "seem to
sprout," "if we may fancy wish." This figural exaggeration is a technique and a way of thinking that Hardy uses often.[3] He uses pathetic fallacy, but openly acknowledges the figurative nature of his
description, thus disrupting the fiction of the poetic scene. The
figural disruption parallels the disruption of the pastoral scene
through violent struggle in nature as signalled by the word "overtop."

The major country-house poems, such as Jonson's "Penshurst," Marvell's "Upon Appleton House," and Pope's Horatian *Epistles*, emphasize order, an economy of householding, and peaceful retirement. What is interesting about Hardy's "Domicilium" is the tense balance between such peaceful economies and the pastoral energies that threaten to overwhelm, to "overtop," them. We see that balance in the second stanza, where, despite the flowers that flourish untrained, there is an orderly distribution of spatial flowers and fields. After the flowers, there are "herbs" and "esculents." And the poet follows these with phrases beginning with "and" or "then": "and farther still a field," "then cottages with trees," "and last / The distant hills and sky." Here we have an orderly project from near to far, from domestic flowers to the distant sky. It is also an orderly balance between the domesticated economy of the home on the one hand, and, on the other, the important labor found in the fields and the implied laborers in the surrounding cottages. This is the country-house ideal, with its abundance of natural growth signalling the prudent and comfortable life of the house's inhabitants.

But domestic economy gives way in an abrupt transition at the opening of the third stanza: "Behind, the scene is wilder." This stanza turns back from the prospect and, in part, undoes the ordered economy of the house in the first two stanzas. In stanza three, the speaker turns from pastoral order, the type of order we associate with Jonson or Pope, to a pastoral that emphasizes the wildness of nature. This "wildness," which in terms of poetics draws on Hardy's Romantic heritage, is signalled by such phrases as "uneven ground" and "stunted thorn." The scene pictures a house put in nature and put in a poetic history that is not a traditional economy but an energetic growth exceeding the bounds of convention. The poet represents this energy in the image of the oak emerging from the pit:

> and from a pit
> An oak uprises, springing from a seed
> Dropped by some bird a hundred years ago.

These lines develop the idea of "a wilder scene" set forth in the opening line of the stanza. Here the speaker explicitly joins together the idea of nature's wildness with an expansiveness of time that constitutes a sense of the poet and even of tradition. It is curious also that the poet echoes the figurative image of the sprouting wish here with the "springing from a seed." In the first stanza, the emphasis on falling created a disruptive sense of uncertainty about the natural imagery, while also calling into question the idea of poetic community through the exaggerated nature of the literary figure; this is one way that Hardy creates a feeling of poetic exile from the house of tradition in this poem and in many others also. In stanza three, the scene creates a similar disruption of the pastoral's reality through the sense of time itself: the vast expanse of time emphasizes the transience of the scene. In this stanza, Hardy hints at the way time itself disrupts the ordered pastoral economy of the country house.

Time's effect on the country house becomes the central theme in the fourth stanza. The speaker emphasizes the sense of time through such phrases as "days bygone," "long gone," and "at such a time." Hardy "undoes" the peaceful order and domesticity of this country house through his extreme insistence on the power of time itself. Just as the uprising oak images the passage of years, time becomes a way of demystifying the order and the superficial domestication of nature.[4] As the speaker in "Domicilium" walks with his grandmother, she describes the pastoral scene in its primitive state fifty years earlier:

> "Fifty years
> Have passed since then, my child, and change has marked
> The face of all things. Yonder garden-plots
> And orchards were uncultivated slopes
> O'ergrown with bramble bushes, furze and thorn:
> That road a narrow path shut in by ferns,
> Which, almost trees, obscured the passer-by."

If the vines on the walls of the house impinge on the order of the house in stanza one, here in stanza four, the past itself more severely disturbs that order. In the present, changes over time mark the objects of nature; in the past, the wildness of the scene blocks out the perception of human presence: the ferns "obscured the passer-by." It should be observed also that the second half of the poem mirrors, in terms of structure, the first half. In stanza two, the order of the country house unfolds through a progressive series of spaces: garden, flowers, field, cottages, hills, and sky. In stanza four, the layers of time—from "days bygone," "now," and "Fifty years have passed"—which recede into the past, parallel the layers of landscape receding into the past in stanza two. While stanza four mirrors stanza two in terms of receding landscape parallel to receding time, stanza four also undoes the order of the country house. The speaker's grandmother tells him that "Yonder garden-plots / And orchards were uncultivated slopes." The speaker replaces the reciprocity between home and surroundings, the peaceful economy of the pastoral retreat in temporal retrospect, with a house isolated in an uncultivated wilderness:

> "Our house stood quite alone, and those tall firs
> And beeches were not planted. Snakes and efts
> Swarmed in the summer days, and nightly bats
> Would fly about our bedrooms. Heathcroppers
> Lived on the hills, and were our only friends;
> So wild it was when first we settled here."

Hardy's houses are houses of poetic tradition, and when the poet reveals the tenuous hold on cultivated land and cultural life that his early home possessed, he is acknowledging also his own sense of exile from the pastoral poetry of retirement.

In Hardy's house poems, the ideal of retirement to the country retreat shifts toward retirement into the past. The country house becomes not an emblem of a reciprocal economy between people and the land, but a sign of the placelessness, the sense of exile, when the people who lived in the house have died. The country house becomes a memento mori. We see the elegiac quality in "Night in the Old Home." The "old home" brings back the past to the solitary man who still remains there.

> When the wasting embers redden the chimney-breast,
> And Life's bare pathway looms like a desert track to me,
> And from hall and parlour the living have gone to their rest,
> My perished people who housed them here come back to me.

One cannot claim that this is in a strict sense a country-house poem. But the house as an ideal draws upon that tradition. The speaker explores and also overturns the ideal in part through the

intense subjectivity of his voice. The country-house poem usually
involves a civic, public tone, but here the speaker, as usual in Hardy,
is deeply personal; nevertheless, this speaker does draw upon the
country-house ideal through types of negative allusion. Instead of
the welcoming hearth, the fireplace contains "wasting embers."
The speaker also plays on the idea of the host/guest relation typical
of the country-house ideal. But this relation interacts with the idea
of death and absence. The crucial line is the third in stanza one:
"And from hall and parlour the living have gone to their rest." The
speaker may be describing guests who, at the end of the evening,
retire to their rooms, but the line also suggests those who were living but are now dead. The poet heightens the sense of absence
through the images in the preceding line: "Life's bare pathway" and
the "desert track."

The speaker pursues the idea of host/guest in the country house
in the second stanza. The speaker becomes the host, and the guests
are the spirits of the past; thus, he transforms the celebration of
abundance and peace in the country retreat into a mournful elegy
on the house's past and the past of its inhabitants:

> They come and seat them around in their mouldy places,
> Now and then bending towards me a glance of wistfulness,
> A strange upbraiding smile upon all their faces,
> And in the bearing of each a passive tristfulness.

The speaker transforms and envisions the country house as a ghost
house.[5]

In "Night in the Old Home" the speaker not only alludes to
the country-house ideal of festive social relations between host and
guest, he changes the host/guest relation into a commentary on
the poet's attitude toward life. Implicit within that commentary
one observes Hardy's concern about his relation to poetic tradition
as well. A ghostly past inhabits the house, and the sole living being, the speaker, discovers himself to be a kind of ghost. The irony
of the poem lies in that the ghosts of the house are stronger than
the poet/speaker. Witness the speaker's address to the ghosts in
stanza three:

> "Do you uphold me, lingering and languishing here,
> A pale late plant of your once strong stock?" I say to them;

> "A thinker of crooked thoughts upon Life in the sere,
> And on That which consigns men to nights after showing the
>   day to them?"

While the ghosts have a "passive tristfulness," it is the speaker
who is the weak figure in the poem. Although he is alive, he por-
trays himself as spiritually and emotionally dead. He is "lingering"
and "languishing." He uses a telling metaphor here: "A pale late
plant of your once strong stock." The idea of being too late occurs
frequently in Hardy's poems. It usually refers to the poet's relation
to tradition, and refers, as well, to the melancholy separation that
the living feel for loved ones who are dead. The speaker in stanza
three describes the futility of his own "crooked thoughts." His
imaginative activity becomes associated with death, as if to think
about death were to summon it prematurely. As the poem progresses, the sense of the house as a place of retirement recedes. Yet
the relation between the speaker and the ghostly visitors continues
the allusion to the ideal of host and guest in the country-house
tradition. The reversal of values between the two, however, makes
"Night in the Old Home" an ironic turn on this ideal. It is the
dead who are the true celebrants of life. It is the poet/speaker, as
the ghosts indicate, who cultivates a kind of imaginative death,
alone in the house:

'–O let be the Wherefore! We fevered our years not thus:
Take of Life what it grants, without question!' they answer me seemingly.
'Enjoy, suffer, wait: spread the table here freely like us
And, satisfied, placid, unfretting, watch Time away beamingly!'

In a strange way, the ghosts' advice involves the country-house
ethos: "Take of Life what it grants," "spread the table here freely like
us." The ghosts, former inhabitants of the house, celebrate the
house's and life's festive abundance unquestioningly. Indeed the
ghosts' sadness stems from their perception that the poet/speaker's
brooding is a kind of imaginative death, one more destructive than
death itself. The poem shares with the country-house ethos the
concern with how life should be lived; it departs from that ethos
in its emphasis on the power of time and death to bring life to an
end. In terms of the latter, Hardy draws upon the elegiac strain

within the pastoral tradition. But Hardy disrupts both traditions by having the dead be the happy ones who try to cheer up the mournful poet. In Hardy's ironic transformation of the country-house poem, the dead celebrate the festive life in the country retreat, while the living, caught in the memories of the past, are emotionally dead.

Hardy's house poems usually contain spectral presences of the past. The house constitutes an emblem of the past: it contains signs of the people now dead who once lived there. In "The Ghost of the Past," the poet combines georgic and country-house elements to create the speaker's meditations on the fading power of memory. Behind this meditation lies a secondary one on the poet's relation to tradition, with the house standing for the latter. The poet's house constitutes a house of tradition in several senses of the term:

> We two kept house, the Past and I,
>   The Past and I;
> Through all my tasks it hovered nigh,
>   Leaving me never alone.
> It was a spectral housekeeping
>   Where fell no jarring tone,
> As strange, as still a housekeeping
>   As ever has been known.

The speaker describes the past of tradition as a "spectral housekeeping." It is as if the ghosts of the dead, familial and literary, provide the order that festive celebration provides in the traditional country-house poem. The past becomes a double, both a loved one and a poetic alter ego, and this doubling is also the characteristic structure of the poem: the poem explores the alterity of its own poetic structure. This temporal double hangs above the speaker: "it hovered nigh." And the double from the past bears qualities that comment on poetic sound. This "was a spectral housekeeping / Where fell no jarring tone."

The economy of this house of tradition is "strange" and "still," suggesting both the speaker's alienation from tradition and the tradition's silence for him now. The silence of tradition suggests the difficulty with which the speaker can respond to the poetic past, as well as the difficulty he has "hearing" the poetic past in the present. Again the imagery evokes the alterity, the radical otherness, of tradition for the poet/speaker. And yet this alterity implies gain as well as loss.

In stanza two, the speaker states that he "did not mind the Bygone there – / The Present once to me." Here we note the autobiographical element, as this passage becomes yet another chapter in Hardy's exploration of his marriage following Emma's death.[6] But the stanza tells us something else about the poet as well: it shows us much of the positive sense of reconciliation, not only with the woman from whom he became estranged, but within his estrangement from a poetic tradition that defines so much that is valuable in Hardy's poetics. His companionship with the absent beloved bears in it "Something of ecstasy." Again there is an implicit contrast with the country-house ethos. In the country-house poem, friendship is of central importance: friends gather to share in the fruitful abundance that the country-house economy produces. But in Hardy's reversal of country-house ideals, the friends are absent; the festivity is one of emptiness, absence, and silence. Out of this deprivation and solitude, however, arises a kind of creative impulse: the speaker cannot discuss this "Something of ecstasy." It is the pleasure of a poetics concerned with alterity itself, with the radical otherness of creation.

But Hardy's poetics demands such an ironic reading that even the "ecstasy" does not remain. This too constitutes an aspect of his poetic practice:

> And then its form began to fade,
>   Began to fade,
> Its gentle echoes faintlier played
>   At eves upon my ear
> Than when the autumn's look embrowned
>   The lonely chambers here,
> When autumn's settling shades embrowned
>   Nooks that it haunted near.

By "form," the speaker means the past and the woman who is now dead. But the speaker also means poetic form, and the sounds of poetry. We observe the poet's emphasis on sound: "Its gentle echoes faintlier played / At eves upon my ear." For Hardy, the love of the past and past loves intertwine with poetry as the form or body of traditional utterance. We have seen that Hardy often represents his relation to the poetic past and his estrangement from it through spectral figures in autumnal scenes. Stanza four of "The Ghost of the Past," with "chambers" and "woods" "embrowned" by autumn, rehearses once again this scene. The country house begins to decay, and the scenes of the poetic past begin to fade. As elsewhere, Hardy here invokes Keats's "To Autumn" as touchstone for the problematic of the poet's relation to tradition.

The final stanza of this poem contains the poet's conscious allusion to the poem's own underlying structure. The poem hangs on a country-house "skeleton," just as the speaker's memories of the beloved become a mnemonic skeleton.

> And so with time my vision less,
>   Yea, less and less
> Makes of that Past my housemistress,
>   It dwindles in my eye;
> It looms a far-off skeleton
>   And not a comrade nigh,
> A fitful far-off skeleton
> Dimming as days draw by.

Hardy describes here not simply the fading vision of the past or the woman of his past, he describes the poetic economy of the house of tradition as it informs, and gives shape to, the skeletal support for his poetic house in the present.[7] If there is an "ecstasy" in the companionship of the past, there is also sadness as the poet replaces the poetic past by his own poetry of the present, a poetry which he believes to involve a lessening of vision. The speaker emphasizes this poetic diminishment: "with time my vision less / Yea, less and less." The skeleton constitutes the ghost of the speaker's full poetic vision.

Hardy often employs the motif of the fading house as a metonymic image for fading memory and fading poetic vision. The fading or moribund house allows the poet to experiment not only with the country-house idea, but with pastoral and georgic ideas. The moribund, both literal and figurative, state of the country-house framework subverts generic boundaries. The country-house poem provides a skeletal substructure for many of Hardy's poems, but it does not prescribe generic or thematic limits. Thus, in "Where They Lived," Hardy explores the topoi of leaves within a pastoral scene, but combines it with the device of a type of country house. In the first stanza, the poet creates a picture of an autumn scene in which leaves of various hues cover a bank where two lovers once sat, one of them being the speaker of the poem. A special moment between the lovers occurred on this bank. In the second stanza, the speaker says there had been a summerhouse here. But time has changed that:

> The summerhouse is gone,
> Leaving a weedy space;
> The bushes that veiled it once have grown
> Gaunt trees that interlace,
> Through whose lank limbs I see too clearly
> The nakedness of the place.

As in other house poems in Hardy, the poet uses images of growth and decay to describe the creative imagination in its confrontation with the materials the imagination uses to produce art. The stanza explores absence and loss through the house image, and through the interrelation of spacial plenitude and poverty. Paradoxically, with the decay of the house comes the growth of flora to replace it. But this pastoral vegetative growth presents a curious perspective on both the space left vacated by the house and on the psychic space of the imagination that is the underlying concern of this speaker. This pastoral garden involves both growth and decay. With the house gone, all that is left is a "weedy space." Full green bushes once veiled the house, but they have "grown" into "gaunt trees" with "lank limbs." In other words, the "growth" that replaces the house increases the sense of desolation and absence. But as so often is the case in Hardy, this poverty stirs the imagination and clarifies vision. The bushes "veiled" the house, but now through the interlacing boughs the speaker sees "too clearly."

The speaker now realizes the deceptiveness of the summerhouse and of the moments lived out within its space. For Hardy, the country-house ideal of festive celebration and friendship deceives by attempting to evade time and its power to destroy everything. The speaker in "Where They Lived," and Hardy also, believe that the true vision of life demands looking clearly at the "nakedness of the place." This vision constitutes, in one sense, the exact opposite of the country-house ideal, which celebrates domestic festivity and friendship. But in another sense, what the poet describes is not the opposite of the country-house ideal, but the logical fulfillment of that vision, its temporal completion, in which the plenitude inevitably turns to emptiness, and the celebration of friendship turns to the mourning of its absence.

Hardy approaches the interrelation of house, lovers who dwell within it, and time which destroys both, from another perspective in the poem "Everything Comes." The poem involves a dialogue between a woman and her lover. In "Where They Lived," the landscape conveyed the desolation of the present in the light of the past; in "Everything Comes," it is the house's newness that is, surprisingly, desolating:

> "The house is bleak and cold
>   Built so new for me!
> All the winds upon the wold
>   Search it through for me;
> No screening trees abound,
> And the curious eyes around,
>   Keep on view for me."

Hardy plays on the idea of the badly built country house, one in which the inhabitants do not feel at ease. In many of his house poems, the house is in a state of decay, but here it is the house's newness that creates the sense of desolation. The house is "bleak" and "cold." It does not provide shelter. The winds "search" through it. In the light of Hardy's use of the house as an emblem for the economy of poetic creation and tradition, this poem explores the other side of this dialectic: not the way tradition impinges on creation, but the way creation must necessarily build on tradition. The house lacks "screening trees." In other words, without a type of pastoral garden the house affords neither emotional nor aesthetic shelter from the critical eyes of the neighboring audience. The screening trees become an emerging pastoral space, through which the poet combines the country-house problem (how one should build one's house) with the pastoral notion of retirement in nature:

> "My Love I am planting trees
>   As a screen for you
> Both from winds, and eyes that tease
>   And peer in for you.
> Only wait till they have grown,
> No such bower will be known
>   As I mean for you."

The speaker demonstrates his love and devotion to the woman by building the bower of trees. The imagery in this stanza relates to the idea of poetic creation: the act of "planting" is like the seeding of a page with words. The proleptic image of the trees after they are grown works along with the speaker's acknowledgement of intention: "as I mean for you." The work of building the bower becomes, analogously, the work of poetic making and meaning: the building through language of country-house and pastoral ideals.

But as so often in Hardy's exploration of the values and conventions of poetic tradition, in "Everything Comes," time destroys what tradition creates. The speaker builds tradition through the grove or bower, but its building requires years: "with years, there grew a grove." Through time the speaker builds up the country house, surrounding it with a pastoral grove. One should understand this movement to be bound up with the processes of poetic creation emerging out of the grounds of tradition. But at the very same time, in typica' Hardian irony, all that the speaker works for is being made meaningless. Through time he builds the grove for the house, but through that very same time the woman begins to die. She acknowledges his work, but also its futility. "Yes, I see! / But—I'm dying; and for me / 'Tis too late." We have observed the expression "too late" elsewhere in Hardy's work: in Hardy, this phrase always carries within it implications of the poet's disinheritance. The speaker mourns the death of his lover, but he also mourns his inability through work to stem time's destruction. His poetic work is also "too late."

Hardy's house poems insistently explore memory and love, as well as poetic memory. In "The Strange House," a visitor takes a

tour with a knowledgeable guide of a house whose past keeps re-
emerging in the present. Spectral presences besiege him. In the
first stanza, the speaker hears a piano "Just as a ghost might play."
The speaker concludes from this episode that this is a "strange
house." In the second stanza he hears sounds: "I catch some under-
tone here, / From some one out of sight." This house seems strange
to the speaker because a past which he does not entirely understand inhabits it; the house seems strange not only in the sense of
odd or unusual but in the sense of foreign. The house's strangeness
mirrors the speaker's estrangement from it. Here we have the country house as place of exile in which festivity and friendship exist,
but only as spectral hauntings from the past. Building the house
in "Everything Comes" signifies the poetic task. In "The Strange
House," the poetic task involves uncovering these spectral hauntings to figure out their significance. Indeed, the guide says the principal speaker possesses visionary and poetic power.

> –"Ah, maybe you've some vision
>   Of showings beyond our sphere;
> Some sight, sense, intuition
>   Of what once happened here?
> The house is old; they've hinted
>   It once held two love-thralls,
> And they may have imprinted
>   Their dreams on its walls."

We can see how the house incorporates memory. The creative
imagination of the two lovers who formerly lived here inscribes
this love on the house. The walls become a type of memento mori:
"they may have imprinted / Their dreams on its walls." In this
sense, Hardy's country house turns into a ruin, over and about
which the speaker creates an elegy. But the creative economy exists
not only in the house itself as a sign of the lovers who once lived
there; it gains force in the speaker's act of remembering and envisioning these lovers of the past. The speaker reads the writing the
lovers once wrote. And he hears the sounds which bespeak their
presence in the house now. The strange distance between speaker
and former inhabitants constitutes a telling reminder, as well, of
the distance between the poet and poetic tradition.

Hardy's house poems represent a psychic economy that is also a poetic economy. Hardy often divides this economic structure in two, and this division may be understood as a telling critique of the poet's relation to tradition. In "The Two Houses," the poet creates a dialogue between age and youth. The new house boasts of its immaculate condition, and at the same time this new house looks scornfully at the dilapidated state of the old house: "Your gear is gray, / Your face wears furrows untold." But the old house provides a response that draws upon the country-house ideal while also calling up themes from pastoral elegy: "'–Yours might,' mourned the other, 'if you held, brother, / The Presences from aforetime that I hold.'" The old house becomes an emblem of the poet that bears the full weight of tradition impressed on its structure. As elsewhere, the house functions as a spectral allegory of the poet's relation to tradition. Spectral figures constitute not simply people from the past haunting the present, but an analogous poetic process as well. The new house thus becomes a poetic ephebe who must learn the wisdom that the old house bears within it. The old house says:

> "You have not known
> Men's lives, deaths, toils, and teens;
> You are but a heap of stick and stone:
> A new house has no sense of the have-beens."

The old house goes on to provide a catalogue of the various types of inmates who have left their marks of presence on him: babes, corpses, dancers and singers, bridegroom and bride. These presences are mnemonic and poetic; they define the character of a country-house festivity that exists solely by virtue of the past and past inhabitants. They define as well the poetic character:

> "Where such inbe,
> A dwelling's character
> Takes theirs, and a vague semblancy
> To them in all its limbs, and light, and atmosphere."

The key to the analogue between house and poem lies here in the phrase "vague semblancy," a phrase that defines the poet's task as one involving representation and error or difference from that being represented. The turn away from pure representation constitutes the peculiarity of language as it defines poetry and the poetic character. The phrase "vague semblancy" also suggests the spectral or ghostly nature of the poet who feels his exile from the very subjects he wishes to represent. These subjects are always in the past, and they always achieve their presence in the poem through a kind of "haunting," what Stevens calls "ghostlier demarcations." When the new house achieves this poetic character, when it is no longer an ephebe, it too will bear the burden of this haunting:

> "Such shades will people thee,
>   Each in his misery, irk, or joy,
> And print on thee their presences as on me."

It is no accident that the poet chooses to represent the memories of the past as a type of writing, since the two houses suggest a new or inchoate poet, and a mature poet who has faced tradition and bears marks of the struggle. Here the country-house ideal is very subtly alluded to, but not as an external celebration of the retired life, rather as an internal struggle with the past in the creation of a poetic text.

Hardy's house poems insist on this connection between memory and the building and decay of houses. In "The Man Who Forgot," the speaker's memories about a house and its inhabitants deceive him. The speaker finds himself at a crossroads, recalling the house where a woman he once loved still, he thinks, resides. He asks a passer-by to find the house for him, convinced that it still exists:

> "A summer-house fair stands hidden where
>   You see the moonlight thrown;
> Go, tell me if within it there
>   A lady sits alone."

When the boy returns, the speaker's illusion is "laid bare" both literally and figuratively. The house's presence, so strong in the speaker's mind, clashes with the reality, as conveyed by the boy's words, of its absence.

> "I went just where you said, but found
>   No summer-house was there:
> Beyond the slope 'tis all bare ground;
>   Nothing stands anywhere."

The emptiness of the space overturns the possibility of the speaker's realizing a country-house ideal of friendship in retirement to the summer-house. In stanza six, the boy describes his encounter with a man who in turn describes the way the house "grew rotten." This decomposition reminds one very much of the many pastoral poems in Hardy's work which describe flowers and trees in a state of decay. Hardy modulates from country-house retirement to his recurrent motif of a negative pastoral space in the process of decomposition. This process of decomposition has bearing on his poetics. The speaker does not so much forget, despite the poem's title, as remember too well. His pictured pastoral scene from the past replaces the actual scene of the present. Thus, as in "The Two Houses," the poetic material or memories define the speaker's mind and shape his representation of the present. In fact, it is the past which gives him voice. Faced with present realities the speaker is silent:

> My right mind woke, and I stood dumb;
>   Forty years' frost and flower
> Had fleeted since I'd used to come
>   To meet her in that bower.

But Hardy's exploration of the interplay between country house and pastoral bower sometimes sounds a more positive and less elegiac note. Sometimes pastoral song endures in the present; the country house stands intact and the pastoral bower remains, not merely in memory, but in the day-to-day repetitions of reality. Hardy celebrates the pastoral moment and the poetry of the country domicile in "A Bird-Scene at a Rural Dwelling." In this poem, the speaker describes birds singing outside of a country house. As the human inhabitants wake up, the birds move further away from the house. But the birds never stop singing; near the house they "whistled sweetly." Further away:

> they seek the garden,
> And call from the lofty costard, as pleading pardon
>   For shouting so near before
>   In their joy at being alive. . . .

In Hardy's poems, bird song allies itself with pastoral song. And the poet here celebrates the power of poetry as a joyful force. Yet

even here, time's power qualifies this joy: "Meanwhile the hammer-
ing clock within goes five." In an uncharacteristically affirmative
reversal, Hardy transforms the power of time into a type of poetic
repetition that celebrates pastoral song in the rural dwelling:

> I know a domicile of brown and green,
> Where for a hundred summers there have been
> Just such enactments, just such daybreaks seen.

Here the house is not haunted by the past but exists in a joyful
present created by the repetition of its "enactments" and "day-
breaks."[8] For Hardy, it is an unusually positive vision of the retirement theme and its bearing on pastoral song.

The poem "Silences" is more characteristic of Hardy's transformation and turn from the country-house ideal and from the ideals
of pastoral song. Like "Afterwards," this is a poem about the end
of a tradition as well as the end of life. The economy of landscape
and house mirrors the dialectic between pastoral song and silence.

> There is the silence of a copse or croft
> When the wind sinks dumb,
> And of a belfry-loft
> When the tenor after tolling stops its hum.

We observe the powerful sense of resonance and echo which the
speaker creates through images of the after-sounds of types of
song: "the wind sinks dumb," "after tolling stops its hum." These
after-sounds continue in stanza two, where the speaker describes
a "lonely pond." But it is not simply a pond; it is a place where
a man drowned. Here the silence becomes a sign of death, an
auditory memento mori; the passage reminds us of how crucial a
role the pastoral elegy plays in Hardy's poetry. But the substructure, the skeletal spectral figure, of the country house lies here also.

> But the rapt silence of an empty house
> Where oneself was born,
> Dwelt, held carouse
> With friends, is of all silences most forlorn!

Here Hardy "undoes" the country-house ideal, not through
images of decay but through images of emptiness. The absence of

people, of life and festivity, produces silence, but paradoxically that silence constitutes eloquent testimony to the power of Hardy's poetic language. We see this power in such phrases as "rapt silence"; the word "rapt" connotes careful attention. There is an energy in this silence that, in a sense, emerges from the ruins of the poem's pastoral and country-house themes. Even the phrase "of all silences most forlorn" is a kind of poetic ruin. One thinks of Keats's "forlorn" and the demands of reality confronting those of the imagination.

But what is especially interesting in terms of Hardy's use of the house is the way that, in alluding to the absence of poetic song and country-house festivity, he brings them forward to mind in retrospect. The melancholy of pastoral elegy intertwines with country-house pleasure. In the poetic economy of Hardy's country house, the ideal of retirement remains, but it always turns to the past. Within this past it turns to themes of absence and loss.

Conclusion

IN TENNYSON'S VICTORIAN PASTORAL, THE poet explores emotional choices through types of figural language. But in exploring the rhetoric of tradition, Tennyson subverts conventional pastoral forms in ways both radical and new. Pastoral has always taken, as part of its subject, song and the play of language. But Tennyson foregrounds the play of language in pastoral to lay bare the irony in his relation to tradition. In Tennyson, the subversion of pastoral forms works as a commentary on his sense of exclusion from the rhetoric of tradition.

Each time we return to the pastoral poetics of Tennyson, we are struck by the way melancholia of voice works by means of the poet/speaker's exile from a textual community. We observe Tennyson using figural language that pastoral poetics informs but that also turns from these informing traditions. Melancholy becomes not simply the psychological stigmata of the human figure within the poem, but the poet's response to a sense of placelessness within the language of his text. Each poem constitutes a literary palimpsest within which the poet's voice cannot find itself, but rather is lost within the web of textual echoes which he has constructed.

Irony comes into play. Tennyson as pastoral shepherd may complicate our attitude toward the act of mourning in *In Memoriam*; the relation between pastoral strategies and the pastoral figure as poet undoubtedly does complicate our response to a poem such as "Mariana." The taxonomy of pastoral tropes Mariana employs in her love-lament makes a "straightforward," non-ironic reading highly problematic. We recognize Mariana's problem, the literal repetition of her search, as the poet's. And if Mariana's problem projects a broader and deeper awareness of the poet's relation to tradition, how must we read "Demeter and Persephone"? Tennyson's mythological forays implicate the poet within the turns of language's error. Persephone's journey through Milton's Enna bears witness to a disruption of poetic texts, a subversion of pastoral forms, as violent and transformative as her ravishment and descent to the underworld. "Demeter and Persephone" maps out the generic wanderings of the poet, while demonstrating Tennyson's transformation of the rhetoric of tradition through figurative error.

After Tennyson, Hardy's rhetorical wanderings seem to stay closer to home. Hardy's pastoral poetry appears more domestic, less mythically adventurous, than Tennyson's. But like Tennyson, Hardy explores the rhetoric of tradition as it imposes its constraints and inhibitions on his poetic work. And like Tennyson, Hardy enables these rhetorical constraints and inhibitions to emerge as figural error and thus, to subvert and renew pastoral forms. No less than Tennyson's "Demeter and Persephone," Hardy's "In Front of the Landscape" reveals an allegory of the poet's exile and exclusion from a rhetorical community constituted by the texts of pastoral tradition. The decomposition of Hardy's pastoral spaces works through the disfiguration of pastoral rhetoric. Both Tennyson and Hardy situate poet figures within a decomposing nature that functions as an analogue to the foregrounding of pastoral rhetoric as the means to its own dissolution.

In the last chapter, we saw similar types of exclusion and constraint within Hardy's house of tradition. Hardy's country house is itself a type of pastoral figure, and one that bears a strong relation to the pastoral retreat in Tennyson. Mariana's pastoral space sets forth the boundaries of poetic repetition as one of the inhibitions imposed on the poet by tradition. The pastoral space she inhabits functions as a metonymy for the rhetoric of tradition out of which she cannot escape. Hardy's country houses present an analogous structure of the inhibiting boundaries of pastoral rhetoric, figured forth by the houses themselves, and their potential subversion by the spectral poet figures who haunt them. In both Tennyson and Hardy, we observe poet figures burdened by a traditional rhetoric of repressive force, the duplicity of which they exploit to overturn the forms of their own literary confinement.

Notes

INTRODUCTION

1. Among the many books on pastoral, I have found the following especially valuable: Thomas G. Rosenmeyer, *The Green Cabinet: Theocritus and the European Pastoral Lyric* (Berkeley: University of California Press, 1969); Paul Alpers, *The Singer of the* Eclogues (Berkeley: University of California Press, 1979); Renato Poggioli, *The Oaten Flute* (Cambridge, Mass.: Harvard University Press, 1975).

2. Two very different approaches to this dialectic are found in Friedrich Schiller, *On the Naive and Sentimental in Literature*, trans. Helen Watanabe-O'Kelly (Manchester: Carcanet, 1981); and William Empson, *Some Versions of Pastoral* (1935; rpt. New York: New Directions, 1974).

3. For discussions of the retirement theme in Homer, Virgil, and Horace, see Michael O'Loughlin, *The Garlands of Repose* (Chicago: University of Chicago Press, 1978).

4. On voice and poetic response, see John Hollander, *The Figure of Echo* (Berkeley: University of California Press, 1981).

5. One of the best explorations of the country-house ideal in English poetry and its classical heritage is Maynard Mack's discussion of retirement in Pope in *The Garden and the City* (Toronto: University of Toronto Press, 1969).

6. See Raymond Williams, *The Country and the City* (New York: Oxford University Press, 1973).

7. For his distinction between genre and mode, see Alastair Fowler, *Kinds of Literature* (Cambridge, Mass.: Harvard University Press, 1982).

8. Critical work of high quality has been done on the English elegy recently in terms of figural language and the "psycho-poetics" of mourning. See Peter Sacks, *The English Elegy* (Baltimore: The Johns Hopkins University Press, 1985).

9. See Ernst Robert Curtius, *European Literature and the Latin Middle Ages,* trans. Willard Trask (Princeton, N.J.: Princeton University Press, 1973).

10. On "Melancholia Artificialis," see Erwin Panofsky, *Albrecht Dürer* (Princeton, N.J.: Princeton University Press, 1943). Apart from the work of Panofsky and his colleague Fritz Saxl, the most brilliant and acute analysis of melancholy in Western literature is found in Walter Benjamin, *The Origin of German Tragic Drama,* trans. John Osborne (London: Verso, 1977).

11. For a comprehensive discussion of melancholy in Elizabethan and Jacobean drama, see Lawrence Babb, *The Elizabethan Malady* (East Lansing: Michigan State University Press, 1951).

12. Two surveys of melancholy poetry in England during the seventeenth and eighteenth centuries are Amy Reed, *The Background of Gray's Elegy* (New York: Columbia University Press, 1924); and Eleanor Sickels, *The Gloomy Egoist* (New York: Columbia University Press, 1932). See also Bridget Gellert Lyons, *Voices of Melancholy* (London: Routledge & Kegan Paul, 1971).

13. On the Victorian crisis of faith, see Walter Houghton, *The Victorian Frame of Mind* (New Haven: Yale University Press, 1957); Jerome H. Buckley, *The Victorian Temper* (Cambridge, Mass.: Harvard University Press, 1951); and for an exploration of the attempts by several Victorian writers to come to terms with this crisis, see J. Hillis Miller, *The Disappearance of God* (Cambridge, Mass.: Harvard University Press, 1963).

14. For Tennyson's relation to the modern long poem, see M. L. Rosenthal and Sally M. Gall, *The Modern Poetic Sequence* (New York: Oxford University Press, 1983), pp. 19–24.

15. See Northrop Frye, *Anatomy of Criticism* (Princeton, N. J.: Princeton University Press, 1957); E. D. Hirsch, *Validity in Interpretation* (New Haven: Yale University Press, 1967); and for more flexible and transformative theories of genre, see Tzvetan Todorov, *The Fantastic,* trans. Richard Howard (Ithaca: Cornell University Press, 1975); Fowler, *Kinds of Literature*; and Adena Rosmarin, *The Power of Genre* (Minneapolis: University of Minnesota Press, 1985).

16. On "arbitrary metrical choice" in Hardy, see John Hollander, "The Metrical Frame" in *Vision and Resonance,* 2nd ed. (1975; rpt. New Haven: Yale University Press, 1985), p. 137.

CHAPTER I

1. T. S. Eliot, "In Memoriam," in *Critical Essays on the Poetry of Tennyson,* ed. John Killham (New York: Barnes and Noble, 1960), p. 214.

2. W. H. Auden, quoted by Arthur J. Carr, "Tennyson as a Modern Poet," in Killham, *Critical Essays,* p. 41.

3. See Christopher Ricks, *Tennyson* (New York: Collier Books, 1972); and Robert Bernard Martin, *Tennyson: The Unquiet Heart* (Oxford: Clarendon Press, 1980).

4. See Ann Colley, *Tennyson and Madness* (Athens: University of Georgia Press, 1983).

5. Killham places Nicolson within the context of modern Tennyson criticism in the Introduction to *Critical Essays*.

6. See E. D. H. Johnson, *The Alien Vision of Victorian Poetry* (Princeton: Princeton University Press, 1952).

7. Jerome Hamilton Buckley, *Tennyson: The Growth of a Poet* (Boston: Houghton Mifflin Company, 1960), p. 40.

8. John Stuart Mill, "Tennyson's Poems," in *Tennyson's Poetry,* ed. Robert W. Hill, Jr. (New York: W. W. Norton, 1971), p. 562.

9. W. David Shaw, *Tennyson's Style* (Ithaca and London: Cornell University Press, 1976), p. 79.

10. James R. Kincaid, *Tennyson's Major Poems: The Comic and Ironic Patterns* (New Haven and London: Yale University Press, 1975), p. 22.

11. See Ricks's notes to the poem in his edition of *The Poems of Tennyson* (London: Longman, Green and Co., 1969), p. 187; and Ricks, *Tennyson*, p. 50.

12. Robert Pattison, *Tennyson and Tradition* (Cambridge, Mass.: Harvard University Press, 1979), p. 13.

13. Paul Turner, *Tennyson* (London: Routledge & Kegan Paul, 1976), pp. 45–47.

14. Pattison, *Tennyson and Tradition*, p. 14.

15. Mill, "Tennyson's Poems," pp. 561–62.

16. Buckley, *Tennyson*, p. 40.

17. Martin, *Tennyson*, p. 109.

18. Alfred Tennyson, "Mariana," in *The Poems of Tennyson*, ed. Christopher Ricks (London: Longman, Green and Co., 1969), pp. 187–88. All further quotations from Tennyson's poems are from this edition.

19. Joseph Warton, "Ode to Fancy," in *The Works of the English Poets*, XVIII (1810; rpt. New York: Greenwood Press, 1969), 164.

20. Reed, *The Background of Gray's Elegy*, pp. 38–80.

21. See Reed, *The Background of Gray's Elegy*, pp. 77, 151, and 182; and Eleanor Sickels, *The Gloomy Egoist* (New York: Columbia University Press, 1932), pp. 53, 252, and 303.

22. Quoted in G. B. Harrison, introd. *Webster and Ford Selected Plays* (London: Dent, 1933), p. xi.

23. George H. Ford, *Keats and the Victorians* (New Haven: Yale University Press, 1944), pp. 22–48.

24. Quoted in Ricks, ed. *The Poems*, p. 188.

25. Martin, *Tennyson,* p. 109.

26. See Rosenmeyer, *The Green Cabinet,* pp. 65–97 and pp. 179–203; and Poggioli, *The Oaten Flute*, p. 9 and *passim.*

27. Ricks, *Tennyson*, p. 46.

28. W. J. Fox, quoted in Ricks, *Tennyson*, p. 46.

29. Martin Dodsworth, "Patterns of Morbidity: Repetition in Tennyson's Poetry," in *The Major Victorian Poets: Reconsiderations,* ed. Isobel Armstrong (Lincoln: University of Nebraska Press, 1969), pp. 10–11.

30. Turner, *Tennyson*, p. 47.

31. See W. K. Wimsatt, "'Prufrock' and 'Maud': From Plot to Symbol," in *Hateful Contraries* (Kentucky: University of Kentucky Press, 1965), pp. 211–12; and H. M. McLuhan, "Tennyson and Picturesque Poetry," in Killham, *Essays*, pp. 73–75.

32. See Ralph Rader, *Tennyson's "Maud": The Biographical Genesis* (Berkeley: University of California Press, 1963).

33. Edward Bulwer-Lytton, quoted in Killham, *Essays*, p. 110.

34. Ford, *Keats and the Victorians*, p. 37.

35. Paul Turner, "Some Ancient Light on Tennyson's 'Oenone,'" *Journal of English and Germanic Philology*, 51, (January, 1962), 57–72.

36. Turner, "Some Ancient Light," pp. 57–58.

37. Ovid, "Paris to Helen," in *Heroides and Amores*, trans. Grant Showerman (1921; rpt. London: William Heinemann, 1931), pp. 200–1.

38. Turner, "Some Ancient Light," p. 58.

39. Douglas Bush, *Mythology and the Romantic Tradition in English Poetry* (New York: Pageant Books, 1937), pp. 204–5.

40. Dodsworth, "Patterns of Morbidity," p. 33.

41. Thomas Warton, "The Pleasures of Melancholy," in *The Works of the English Poets*, XVIII (1810; rpt. New York: Greenwood Press, 1969), 97.

42. Sickels, *Gloomy Egoist,* pp. 36–37.

43. James Thomson, *The Seasons,* ed. James Sandbrook (Oxford at the Clarendon Press, 1981), pp. 84–85.

44. Shaw, *Tennyson's Style*, p. 83.

45. Turner, "Some Ancient Light," p. 59.

46. Dodsworth, "Patterns of Morbidity," p. 31.

47. Turner, "Some Ancient Light," p. 59.

48. Homer, *The Odyssey*, trans. Richmond Lattimore (New York: Harper and Row, 1968), p. 139.

49. Carr, "Tennyson as a Modern Poet," p. 52.

50. Bush, *Mythology,* p. 208.

51. Shaw, *Tennyson's Style,* p. 66.

52. Martin, *Tennyson*, pp. 163–64.

53. Alan Grob, "Tennyson's 'The Lotos-Eaters': Two Versions of Art," *Modern Philology*, 62 (1964), 118–29.

54. Poggioli, *Oaten Flute*, pp. 1 and 9.

55. Theocritus, *Idyll* VII, in *Theocritus: Idylls and Epigrams*, trans. Daryl Hine (New York: Atheneum, 1982), p. 31.

56. Rosenmeyer, *Green Cabinet*, pp. 190–91.

57. Rosenmeyer, *Green Cabinet*, pp. 55–59.

58. Kincaid, *Tennyson's Major Poems*, p. 38.

59. Rosenmeyer, *Green Cabinet*, p. 15.

60. Turner, *Tennyson*, pp. 67–68.

61. Erwin Panofsky, "*Et in Arcadia Ego*: Poussin and the Elegiac Tradition," in *Meaning in the Visual Arts* (Harmondsworth: Penguin Books, 1955), pp. 345–47 and *passim*.

62. See especially, Turner, *Tennyson*, p. 68.

63. Kincaid, *Tennyson's Major Poems*, p. 39.

64. Virgil, *Eclogue* III, in *Virgil: The Eclogues*, trans. Guy Lee, rev. ed. (Harmondsworth: Penguin Books, 1984), pp. 48–49.

65. A. Dwight Culler, *The Poetry of Tennyson* (New Haven: Yale University Press, 1977), p. 5.

66. Laurence Lerner, *The Uses of Nostalgia* (New York: Schocken Books, 1972), pp. 57–62.

CHAPTER II

1. Richard Jenkyns, *The Victorians and Ancient Greece* (Cambridge, Mass.: Harvard University Press, 1980), p. 30.

2. Jenkyns, *The Victorians and Ancient Greece*, pp. 31–32.

3. Bush, *Mythology*, p. 210.

4. Hartley Coleridge, quoted in Frank M. Turner, *The Greek Heritage in Victorian Britain* (New Haven: Yale University Press, 1981), p. 78.

5. Feldman and Richardson, *Rise of Modern Mythology*, quoted in Turner, *Greek Heritage*, p. 82.

6. A. C. Bradley, "Old Mythology in Modern Poetry" (1881), quoted in James Kissane, "Victorian Mythology," *Victorian Studies*, 6, (1962), 24.

7. See Kissane, "Victorian Mythology," p. 6 and *passim*.

8. George Grote, *History of Greece*, I (1875), quoted in Kissane, "Victorian Mythology," p. 8.

9. John Addington Symonds, quoted in Kissane, "Victorian Mythology," p. 14.

10. Kissane, "Victorian Mythology," p. 16.

11. Symonds, quoted in Kissane, "Victorian Mythology," p. 16.

12. Walter Pater, "Demeter and Persephone," in *Greek Studies* (London: Macmillan, 1901), p. 91.

13. Pater, "Demeter and Persephone," pp. 98–99.

14. Pater, "Demeter and Persephone," pp. 110–11.

15. A. C. Bradley, quoted in Kissane, "Victorian Mythology," p. 24.

16. A. Dwight Culler, "Monodrama and the Dramatic Monologue," *PMLA*, 90 (May, 1975), 368, 381, and *passim*.

17. Culler, *The Poetry of Tennyson*, pp. 90–93.

18. Jenkyns, *Victorians and Ancient Greece*, p. 33.

19. Tennyson, quoted in Culler, *The Poetry of Tennyson*, p. 90.

20. Culler, *The Poetry of Tennyson*, p. 90.

21. Culler, *The Poetry of Tennyson*, pp. 90–91.

22. Hallam Tennyson, *Alfred Lord Tennyson: A Memoir*, (London: Macmillan, 1897), I, 196.

23. Tennyson, quoted in James Knowles, "A Personal Reminiscence," *Nineteenth Century*, 33 (1893), 182.

24. W. W. Robson, "The Dilemma of Tennyson" in Killham, *Critical Essays*, p. 158.

25. E. J. Chiasson, "Tennyson's 'Ulysses'–A Re-Interpretation," in Killham, *Critical Essays*, pp. 165–66.

26. Johnson, *The Alien Vision of Victorian Poetry*, p. 41.

27. Bush, *Mythology*, p. 209.

28. Bush, *Mythology*, pp. 209–10.

29. Robert Langbaum, *The Poetry of Experience: The Dramatic Monologue in Modern Literary Tradition* (New York: W. W. Norton & Company, 1963), p. 90.

30. Langbaum, *Poetry of Experience*, p. 91.

31. Goldwin Smith, quoted in Ricks, *Tennyson*, p. 123.

32. Pater, "Demeter and Persephone," p. 99.

33. Pater, "Demeter and Persephone," p. 99.

34. Culler, *The Poetry of Tennyson*, p. 94.

35. Culler, *The Poetry of Tennyson*, p. 94.

36. Shaw, *Tennyson's Style*, p. 86.

37. Matthew Arnold, "On Translating Homer," Lecture III, in *Essays by Matthew Arnold* (1914; rpt. London: Oxford University Press, 1936), p. 293.

38. Jenkyns, *Victorians and Ancient Greece*, pp. 21–38.

39. Shaw, *Tennyson's Style*, p. 87.

40. Carlyle, quoted in Hallam Tennyson, *A Memoir*, I, 214.

41. Ricks, *Tennyson,* p. 127.

42. Tennyson, quoted in Ricks, ed., *The Poems of Tennyson*, p. 566.

43. See E. B. Mattes's discussion of the *Theodicaea Novissima* in *In Memoriam: The Way of the Soul* (New York: Exposition Press, 1951), pp. 12–23.

44. Benjamin Jowett, quoted in Ricks, *Tennyson,* p. 128.

45. Emily Tennyson, quoted in Hallam Tennyson, *A Memoir,* I, 135.

46. See Ricks's headnote to "Tithonus" in his edition of *The Poems of Tennyson.*

47. Bush, *Mythology,* pp. 211–12.

48. Bush, *Mythology,* p. 211.

49. Culler, *The Poetry of Tennyson*, p. 87.

50. W. J. Bate, *The Burden of the Past and the English Poet* (New York: Norton, 1970), p. 107.

51. Virgil, *Eclogue* VI, in *Virgil*, trans. H. Rushton Fairclough, rev. ed. (1935; rpt. Cambridge, Mass.: Harvard University Press, 1978), I, 44–45.

52. Ricks, *Tennyson,* p. 130.

53. Ricks, *Tennyson,* pp. 132–33.

54. See Langbaum, *The Poetry of Experience*, pp. 75–108.

55. See Culler, "Monodrama and Dramatic Monologue," *PMLA*, 90 (1975).

56. Jacob Korg, quoted in Kincaid, *Tennyson's Major Poems,* p. 46.

57. Pattison, *Tennyson and Tradition*, pp. 86–87.

58. Bush, *Mythology,* p. 220.

59. Hallam Tennyson, *A Memoir,* II, 364.

60. Hallam Tennyson, *A Memoir,* II, 364.

61. Buckley, *Tennyson,* p. 264.

62. Buckley, *Tennyson,* p. 247.

63. Bush, *Mythology,* p. 221.

64. Bush, *Mythology,* p. 221.

65. Johnson, *The Alien Vision,* p. 66.

66. G. Robert Stange, "Tennyson's Mythology: A Study of 'Demeter and Persephone,'" in Killham, *Critical Essays,* p. 140.

67. James Kissane, "Victorian Mythology," pp. 25–28.

68. Buckley, *Tennyson,* pp. 246–47.

69. Buckley, *Tennyson,* p. 245.

70. Stange, "Tennyson's Mythology," p. 145.

71. Stange, "Tennyson's Mythology," pp. 145–46.

72. On the relation of this passage from Milton to pastoral and melancholy, see Empson, *Some Versions of Pastoral*, pp. 173 and 187.

73. See Jenkyns, *Victorians and Ancient Greece,* pp. 21–38.

74. Shaw, *Tennyson's Style*, p. 252.
75. Stange, "Tennyson's Mythology," p. 144.
76. Sir James George Frazer, *The Golden Bough* (New York: Macmillan, 1922), p. 462.
77. Stange, "Tennyson's Mythology," pp. 143–44.
78. Stange, "Tennyson's Mythology," p. 144.
79. Bion, "Lament for Adonis," in *The Greek Bucolic Poets*, trans. A. S. F. Gow (Cambridge: Cambridge University Press, 1953), p. 145.
80. Moschus, "Lament for Bion," in *Greek Bucolic Poets*, trans. Gow, p. 133.
81. Walter Pater, "Winckelmann," in *The Renaissance* (1893), ed. Donald Hill (Berkeley: University of California Press, 1980), p. 162.

CHAPTER III

1. F. R. Leavis, quoted in Pattison, *Tennyson and Tradition*, p. 100.
2. Bush, *Mythology*, p. 227.
3. Bush, *Mythology*, p. 228.
4. Cleanth Brooks, "The Motivation of Tennyson's Weeper," in Killham, *Critical Essays*, p. 181.
5. Graham Hough, "Tears, Idle Tears," in Killham, *Critical Essays*, p. 186.
6. Leo Spitzer, "'Tears, Idle Tears' Again," in Killham, *Critical Essays*, p. 197.
7. J. W. Mackail, *Lectures on Greek Poetry* (London: Longmans, Green and Company, 1910), p. 222. I was alerted to this work by H. M. McLuhan's important article, "Tennyson and the Romantic Epic," in Killham, *Essays*, pp. 86–98.
8. On the Greek notion of *pothos* and Theocritus, see Jenkyns, *The Victorians and Ancient Greece*, p. 153, and Hine, introd., *Theocritus*, p. xix.
9. Tennyson, quoted in Hallam Tennyson, *A Memoir*, II, 253.
10. Hough, "Tears, Idle Tears," p. 190.
11. James Kissane, "The Passion of the Past and the Curse of Time," *ELH*, 32 (1965), 94.
12. Kissane, "The Passion of the Past," pp. 94–95.
13. Geoffrey Hartman, *Wordsworth's Poetry* (New Haven: Yale University Press, 1964), p. 7.
14. Shaw, *Tennyson's Style*, p. 122.
15. Thomson, *The Seasons*, ed. Sandbrook, pp. 184–186.

16. M. H. Abrams, "The Correspondent Breeze," in *English Romantic Poets*, ed. M. H. Abrams (New York: Oxford University Press, 1975).

17. Kissane, "The Passion of the Past," p. 95.

18. Kissane, "The Passion of the Past," p. 95.

19. Thomas J. Assad, "Tennyson's 'Tears, Idle Tears,'" *Tulane Studies in English*, 13, (1963), 80.

20. Shaw, *Tennyson's Style*, p. 123.

21. Brooks, "The Motivation," p. 181.

22. Assad, "Tennyson's *Tears, Idle Tears*," p. 7.

23. See Kincaid, *Tennyson's Major Poems*, especially pp. 1–14.

24. Tennyson to James Knowles, quoted in Ricks, ed. *The Poems of Tennyson*, p. 785.

25. Lerner, *The Uses of Nostalgia*, pp. 41–62.

26. Douglas Bush, *Mythology*, p. 228; and W. P. Mustard, *Classical Echoes in Tennyson* (New York: Macmillan, 1904), p. 103.

27. Virgil, *Aeneid*, trans. Allen Mandelbaum (New York: Bantam, 1972), Bk. I, p. 17.

28. Dodsworth, "Patterns of Morbidity," p. 21.

29. Valerie Pitt, *Tennyson Laureate* (London: Barrie and Rockliff, 1962), p. 143.

30. Pitt, *Tennyson Laureate*, p. 144.

31. Gerhard Joseph, *Tennysonian Love: The Strange Diagonal* (Minneapolis: University of Minnesota Press, 1969), p. 89.

32. Joseph, *Tennysonian Love*, p. 90.

33. Kincaid, *Tennyson's Major Poems*, p. 75.

34. Tennyson, quoted in *The Poems of Tennyson*, ed. Ricks, p. 835.

35. Pattison, *Tennyson and Tradition*, p. 7.

36. Mackail, *Lectures on Greek Poetry*, p. 222.

37. Turner, *Tennyson*, pp. 102–3.

38. James Kissane, *Alfred Tennyson* (New York: Twayne Publishers, 1970), p. 97.

39. See John Killham, *Tennyson and* The Princess: *Reflections of an Age* (London: Athlone Press, 1958), pp. 1–19, and 267–98.

40. John Ruskin, quoted in Ricks, *Tennyson*, p. 203.

41. Hallam Tennyson, quoted in *The Poems of Tennyson*, ed. Ricks, p. 835.

42. Kincaid, *Tennyson's Major Poems*, p. 75.

43. Rosenmeyer, *The Green Cabinet*, p. 63.

44. Shaw, *Tennyson's Style*, p. 127.

45. Kissane, *Alfred Tennyson*, p. 98.

46. Pitt, *Tennyson Laureate*, p. 146.

47. Culler, *The Poetry of Tennyson*, p. 148.

48. See Killham, *Tennyson and the Princess*, pp. 1–19, and *passim*.

49. Ricks, *Tennyson*, p. 202.

50. Ford, *Keats and the Victorians*, pp. 17–48.

51. See W. J. Bate, *John Keats* (Cambridge, Mass.: Harvard University Press, 1963), pp. 582–85; and David Perkins, *The Quest for Permanence* (Cambridge, Mass.: Harvard University Press, 1959), pp. 258–301.

52. Douglas Bush, ed. *Selected Poems and Letters by John Keats* (Boston: Houghton Mifflin Company, 1959), p. 359.

53. Theocritus, *Idyll* VII, in *Theocritus*, trans. Hine, p. 31.

54. Rosenmeyer, *The Green Cabinet*, p. 63.

55. Rosenmeyer, *The Green Cabinet*, p. 46.

56. Theocritus, *Idyll* VII, in *Theocritus*, trans. Hine, p. 32.

57. Theocritus, *Idyll* VII, in *Theocritus*, trans. Hine, p. 31.

58. See Frank Kermode, *The Romantic Image*, (London: Routledge & Kegan Paul, 1957), pp. 7–10; and Helen Vendler, *The Odes of John Keats* (Cambridge, Mass.: Harvard University Press, 1983), pp. 275, 285, and *passim*.

59. Bate, *John Keats*, p. 582.

60. Rosenmeyer, *The Green Cabinet*, p. 262.

61. Bate, *John Keats*, p. 582.

CHAPTER IV

1. Thomas Hardy, "In a Wood," from *The Complete Poems of Thomas Hardy*, ed. James Gibson (New York: Macmillan, 1976), p. 64–65. All further quotations from Hardy's poetry are from this edition.

2. J. O. Bailey, *The Poetry of Thomas Hardy: A Handbook and Commentary* (Chapel Hill: University of North Carolina Press, 1970), p. 98.

3. F. E. Hardy, *The Early Life of Thomas Hardy: 1840–91,* (New York: Macmillan, 1928), p. 62.

4. Robert Gittings, *Young Thomas Hardy* (Boston: Little Brown & Company, 1975), pp. 79 and 146.

5. Ovid, *Metamorphoses*, trans. Rolfe Humphries (Bloomington: Indiana University Press, 1955), p. 237.

6. Curtius, *European Literature and the Latin Middle Ages,* pp. 194–95.

7. Bailey, *Handbook*, p. 153.

8. F. E. Hardy, *Early Life*, p. 21.

9. Quoted in Michael Millgate, *Thomas Hardy* (New York: Oxford University Press, 1985), p. 34.

10. William Barnes, "Tweil," in *Select Poems of William Barnes*, ed. Thomas Hardy (London: Humphrey Milford, 1922), pp. 156–57. All further quotations from the poetry of Barnes are from this edition.

11. Hardy, Preface, *Select Poems*, pp. iii–iv.

12. Hardy, Preface, *Select Poems*, p. ix.

13. "Lament for Bion," in *The Greek Bucolic Poets*, trans. Gow, p. 133.

14. Bailey, *Handbook*, p. 165.

15. See Donald Davie, "Hardy's Virgilian Purples," in *The Poet in the Imaginary Museum* (New York: Persea Books, 1977), pp. 221–35.

16. *Virgil*, trans. Fairclough, I, 526–29.

17. *Virgil*, trans. Fairclough, I, 528–29.

18. William H. Pritchard, *Lives of the Modern Poets* (New York: Oxford University Press, 1980), p. 25.

19. See R. P. Blackmur, "The Shorter Poems of Thomas Hardy," in *Language as Gesture* (New York: Columbia University Press, 1980), pp. 51–79.

20. Bailey, *Handbook*, p. 375.

21. Ovid, *Metamorphoses*, trans. Humphries, p. 240.

22. Ovid, *Metamorphoses*, trans. Humphries, p. 240.

23. Bailey, *Handbook*, p. 396.

24. Barnes, "Leaves A Vallèn," in *Select Poems*, ed. Hardy, pp. 94–95.

25. Bailey, *Handbook*, p. 508.

26. Gittings, *Young Thomas Hardy*, p. 79.

27. Thomson, *The Seasons*, ed. Sandbrook, p. 184.

28. Thomson, *The Seasons*, ed. Sandbrook, p. 194.

29. *Virgil*, trans. Fairclough, I, 104–5.

30. *Virgil*, trans. Fairclough, I, 206–7.

31. Bailey, *Handbook*, p. 158.

32. Bailey, *Handbook*, p. 158.

33. See Davie, "Hardy's Virgilian Purples," pp. 223–26 and 231–32.

34. *Virgil*, trans. Fairclough, I, 550.

35. *The Aeneid*, trans. Mandelbaum, p. 153.

36. Gittings, *Young Thomas Hardy*, p. 9.

37. *Virgil*, trans. Fairclough, I, 52–53.

38. Bailey, *Handbook*, p. 366.

39. Bailey, *Handbook*, p. 366.

40. R. L. Purdy, *Thomas Hardy: A Bibliographical Study* (1954; rpt. London: Oxford University Press, 1968), p. 197.

41. Bailey, *Handbook*, p. 371.

42. *Virgil*, trans. Fairclough, I, 272–73.

43. *Virgil*, trans. Fairclough, I, 438–41.
44. Bailey, *Handbook*, p. 427.
45. Samuel Hynes, *The Pattern of Hardy's Poetry* (Chapel Hill: University of North Carolina Press, 1961), p. 126.
46. Thomas Gray, "Elegy Written in a Country Church-Yard," in *Selected Poems of Thomas Gray and William Collins* ed. Arthur Johnston (London: Edward Arnold, 1967), pp. 46–47.
47. Theocritus, *Epigram* XV in *The Greek Bucolic Poets*, trans. Gow, p. 121.
48. Gray, "Elegy," in *Selected Poems*, ed. Johnston, p. 40.

CHAPTER V

1. On retirement and the country house in Pope and Horace, see Mack, *The Garden and the City*.
2. In the *Early Life*, "Domicilium" is described as "Wordsworthian" and Hardy's "earliest discoverable poem." See F. E. Hardy, *Early Life*, p. 4.
3. Figural exaggeration is part of Thomas Hardy's larger aesthetic. In the *Early Life*, Hardy says, "Art is a disproportioning–(i.e., distorting, throwing out of proportion)–of realities, to show more clearly the features that matter in these realities" (p. 299).
4. Time's disruptive power is a theme throughout Hardy's work. In the fiction, one interesting example occurs in *A Pair of Blue Eyes*, when Henry Knight finds himself stranded on the side of a cliff. "Time closed up like a fan before him. He saw himself at one extremity of the years, face to face with the beginning and all the intermediate centuries simultaneously." Thomas Hardy, *A Pair of Blue Eyes* (London: Macmillan, 1975), p. 240.
5. There is a famous description of Hardy's theory of "spectral consciousness" in the *Early Life*: "For my part, if there is any way of getting a melancholy satisfaction out of life it lies in dying, so to speak, before one is out of the flesh; by which I mean putting on the manners of ghosts, wandering in their haunts, and taking their views of surrounding things. To think of life as passing away is a sadness; to think of it as past is at least tolerable. Hence even when I enter into a room to pay a simple morning call I have unconsciously the habit of regarding the scene as if I were a spectre." (F. E. Hardy, *Early Life*, p. 275).
6. I have not chosen to focus on the "Poems of 1912–13"; however, in terms of Virgilian melancholy, their importance is indisputable. For recent work on this group of poems, see William Morgan, "Form, Tradi-

tion, and Consolation in Hardy's *Poems of 1912–13*," *PMLA* 89, (May, 1974) 496–505; William Buckler, *The Victorian Imagination: Essays in Aesthetic Exploration* (New York: New York University Press, 1980), pp. 297–309; Rosenthal and Gall, *The Modern Poetic Sequence*, pp. 82–95; and Sacks, *The English Elegy*, pp. 234–59.

7. The point being made here is different from but related to the accounts, in the *Later Years*, of Hardy writing down "verse skeletons." See F. E. Hardy, *The Later Years of Thomas Hardy: 1892–1928* (New York: Macmillan, 1930), pp. 79–80.

8. On the function of repetition in Hardy's fiction, see J. Hillis Miller, *Fiction and Repetition* (Cambridge, Mass.: Harvard University Press, 1982), pp. 116–175.

Index

Abrams, M. H., 118
Allegory, 13, 15, 26, 28-31, 34, 41, 64, 66, 71, 122, 143, 146-47, 149-53, 173, 220
Alpers, Paul, 221n. 1
Ambiguity, 85, 102, 113, 129, 139, 161, 164, 176-77
Anaphora, 81, 133
Anthropomorphism, 31, 50, 52, 105, 163, 192
Apostrophe, 26-27, 129-30
Arnold, Matthew, 18-19, 75
Assad, Thomas, 119, 121
Auden, W. H., 21

Babb, Lawrence, 222n. 11
Bailey, J. O., 159, 166, 171, 174, 180, 183, 186, 191, 193, 194, 197
Baring, Rosa, 38
Barnes, William, 167-68, 179-80
Bate, W. J., 80, 142, 146, 151
Beattie, James: *The Minstrel*, 13-14, 18
Benjamin, Walter, 222n. 10
Bion, 45, 84, 104-5, 163, 169, 175
Blackmur, R. P., 173
Bloom, Harold, 80
Bradley, A. C., 62, 66
Brooks, Cleanth, 112-13, 117, 120
Buckler, William, 233n. 6
Buckley, Jerome Hamilton, 22, 92-93, 96
Bulwer-Lytton, Edward, 38-39
Burton, Robert: *Anatomy of Melancholy*, 12, 14, 15, 27, 38

Bush, Douglas, 41, 48, 61, 69, 79, 80, 90, 93, 112, 125, 142

Carlyle, Thomas, 77
Carr, Arthur J., 48
Chiasmus, 49, 140
Chiasson, E. J., 68-69
Closure, poetic, 76, 82, 87, 140-41, 144-45, 153-56, 164, 198-99
Coleridge, Hartley, 62
Coleridge, Samuel Taylor, 134, 154
Colley, Ann, 22
Collins, William, 168
Community, textual, 4-5, 7, 9, 23, 28-30, 34, 37, 54, 56, 89, 92, 97, 105, 144, 153, 165-66, 182, 197, 199, 200-203, 219-20
Culler, A. Dwight, 58, 66-67, 73, 80, 86, 138
Curtius, E. R., 163

Dante, Alighieri: *The Inferno*, 68, 75-77, 187
Darwin, Charles, 159, 161
Davie, Donald, 171, 186
Decomposition, 182-83, 216, 220
Dickens, Charles, 61
Dodsworth, Martin, 33, 42, 46, 125-26
Dryden, John, 167, 171
Dürer, Albrecht: *Melencolia* I, 11-12
Dyer, Edward, 26

Economies, poetic, 8, 22, 202-4, 207, 209, 211, 213-14, 218

Ecphrasis, 56, 89, 92, 125-26, 183, 190-96
Eliot, T. S., 21, 29, 37, 106
Empson, William, 221n. 2, 227n. 72
Error, figural, 214, 220
Exaggeration, figural, 158, 201, 203, 214-15

Figures, rhetorical. *See* individual listings
Firor, Ruth, 183
Fitzgerald, Edward: "The Rubáiyát of Omar Khayyám," 174
Ford, George H., 27, 39, 141
Ford, John, 27
Fowler, Alastair, 9
Fox, W. J., 32-33
Frazer, Sir James George, 102, 109
Frye, Northrop, 19

Gall, Sally M., 222n. 14, 233n. 6
Gifford, Emma Lavinia, 194
Giotto, 64, 71
Gittings, Robert, 159-60, 180, 187
Gray, Thomas, 16, 26, 155, 168, 196-98
Grob, Alan, 48-49
Grote, George, 63

Hallam, Arthur Henry, 18, 68, 69, 77-79, 90, 115; *Theodicaea Novissima*, 78
Hardy, Emma, 208. *See also* Gifford, Emma Lavinia
Hardy, Florence Emily, 159, 201
Hardy, Thomas, 1-2, 19-20, 37, 157-58, 219-20; "Afterwards," 196-99; "A Backward Spring," 177-79; "A Bird Song at a Rural Dwelling," 216-17; "Domicilium," 201-4; "Everything Comes," 211-12; "To Flowers from Italy in Winter," 166-70; "In Front of the Landscape," 184-89; "The Ghost of the Past," 207-9; "The Last

Chrysanthemum," 170-73; "The Later Autumn," 179-82; "The Man Who Forgot," 215-16; "Night in the Old Home," 204-6; *A Pair of Blue Eyes*, 232n. 4; "The Pedigree," 191-93; "The Photograph," 193-96; "A Spot," 182-84; "The Strange House," 212-13; ; "Transformations," 174-77; "The Two Houses," 214-15; "Under the Waterfall," 189-91; "Where They Lived," 210-12; "In a Wood," 158-56; *The Woodlanders*, 158
Hartman, Geoffrey, 116
Hine, Daryl, 225n. 55, 228n. 8
Hirsch, E. D., 19
Hollander, John, 20, 221n. 4
Homer: *Iliad*, 3, 10, 75; *Odyssey*, 3, 10, 47-48, 68
Horace, 3, 79, 200
Hough, Graham, 113, 115
Houghton, Walter, 222n. 13
Huxley, T. H., 174
"Hymn to Aphrodite," 78
"Hymn to Demeter," 90, 104
Hynes, Samuel, 232n. 45

Internalization, 29, 146, 149, 153-55

Jebb, R.C., 90-92
Jenkyns, Richard, 60-61, 66-67, 75, 98
Johnson, E. D. H., 22, 69, 93
Jonson, Ben, 200, 202
Joseph, Gerhard, 127-28
Jowett, Benjamin, 79

Keats, John, 27-32, 38-39, 41, 42-43, 124, 134, 161, 182, 189; "To Autumn," 110, 117, 122, 141-56, 179-80, 198, 209; "To George Felton Mathew," 160; "Hyperion," 88; "Isabella," 22-23; "Ode on Melancholy," 17; "Ode to a Nightingale," 120-21; "Sleep and

Poetry," 160; "To Solitude," 160
Kermode, Frank, 145–46
Killham, John, 130, 138–39
Kincaid, James, 23, 52, 55, 122, 128, 135–36
Kissane, James, 63, 93, 115–16, 118–19, 130, 138
Knowles, James, 226n. 23
Korg, Jacob, 87

Langbaum, Robert, 69, 86
Leavis, F. R., 112
Lerner, Laurence, 123
Locus amoenus, 9–11, 32, 101, 106, 161, 163–65, 175, 182–92, 196
Lucretius, 52–53
Lyons, Bridget Gellert, 222n. 12

Mack, Maynard, 221n. 5, 232n. 1
Mackail, J. W., 114, 129
Mallarmé, Stephane, 29
Martin, Robert Bernard, 21, 25, 28, 32, 48
Marvell, Andrew, 200, 202
Mattes, E. B., 227n. 43
McLuhan, H. M., 224n. 31, 228n. 7
Metaphor, 52, 132, 137
Metonymy, 85, 99, 103, 132, 134, 220
Mill, John Stuart, 22, 24–25
Miller, J. Hillis, 222n. 13, 233n. 8
Milton, John, 43; "L'Allegro," 12–14, 106, 155; *Paradise Lost,* 96–99; "Il Penseroso," 12–14, 100, 106, 155
Modernity, 1, 61–62, 92, 95, 98
Morgan, William, 232–33n. 6
Moschus, 84, 104–5, 163, 169, 175

O'Loughlin, Michael, 221n. 3
Ovid, 129; *Fasti,* 90; *Heroides,* 24, 39–42, 45, 86; *Metamorphoses,* 90, 104, 162–65, 176–77
Oxymoron, 113, 117, 120, 121, 122, 123

Panofsky, Erwin, 53
Pater, Walter: "Demeter and Persephone," 63–65, 67, 70–71; "Winckelmann," 107
Pathetic fallacy, 31, 40–41, 50–52, 104–5, 163, 169–70, 173, 175, 178, 192, 201
Pattison, Robert, 23, 24, 87
Periphrasis, 118
Perkins, David, 142
Personification, 13–16, 26–27, 31, 34, 133, 143, 145–52, 155–56
Pitt, Valerie, 127, 138
Poggioli, Renato, 32, 50
Pope, Alexander, 200, 202
Pritchard, William, 231n. 18
Prolepsis, 37, 146, 212
Prosopopoeia, 66
Purdy, R. L., 194

Rader, Ralph, 224n. 32
Reed, Amy, 26
Repetition, 33–35, 46, 52, 56–59, 81, 130, 216–17, 219, 224n. 29, 233n. 8
Ricks, Christopher, 21, 23, 32, 77, 129, 139
Robson, W. W., 68
Rosenmeyer, Thomas, 32, 51, 52, 138, 143, 148
Rosenthal, M. L., 222n. 14, 233n. 6
Rosmarin, Adena, 222n. 15
Ruskin, John, 63, 134

Sacks, Peter, 9
Schiller, Friedrich, 221n. 2
Shaftesbury, third earl of, 181
Shakespeare, William, 10, 12
Shaw, W. David, 22–23, 48, 74, 76, 98–99, 120, 138
Shelley, Percy Bysshe: "Mont Blanc," 134
Sickels, Eleanor, 26, 43
Simile, 50, 52, 94, 120, 124, 132
Smith, Goldwin, 69
Sparks, Tryphena, 160, 194

Spenser, Edmund, 159-60, 162-65
Spitzer, Leo, 113
Stange, G. Robert, 93, 97, 99, 102-3
Symonds, John Addington, 63

Tennyson, Alfred, 1-2, 18-20, 157-58, 166, 168-70, 175, 178, 189, 219-20; "The Ancient Sage," 58; "Check Every Outflash," 154; "Come Down, O Maid," 126-42, 147-56; "Demeter and Persephone," 90-110, 168-69; "Far far away," 57; "The Gardener's Daughter," 87-89, 125; "The Grasshopper," 78; "Locksley Hall," 38; "The Lotos-Eaters," 47-59; "Mariana," 22-38; *Maud*, 38; *In Memoriam*, 18, 21, 115; "Morte d'Arthur," 61, 125; "Now Sleeps the Crimson Petal," 126-27; "Œnone," 38-47; "To Professor Jebb," 90-92, 168, 170; "Rosalind," 135; "Tears, Idle Tears," 111-26; "Tithon," 78; "Tithonus," 78-90; "Ulysses," 66-78
Theocritus, 3, 6, 36, 66, 138, 167; *Idylls*, 4, 7, 24, 33, 38-39, 46, 50-51, 114, 125-26, 128-29, 142-45, 148, 191
Thomson, James: *The Seasons*, 14-15, 43-44, 117-19, 155, 180-81
Todorov, Tzvetan: *The Fantastic*, 222n. 15
Turner, Frank, 62
Turner, Paul, 23-24, 33, 39-40, 45-46, 52-53, 129

Vendler, Helen, 145-46
Virgil, 7, 9, 52, 79-81, 93, 112, 160, 191; *Aeneid*, 3, 45, 56, 123-24, 171-73, 175, 183, 186-87, 194-96; *Eclogues*, 2, 4, 10, 32-33, 38-39, 46, 53-56, 82-83, 86, 107-9, 145, 152-53, 183, 190; *Georgics*, 3, 181-82

Warton, Joseph, 14-15, 25-27, 29, 34, 144, 155
Warton, Thomas, 14-15, 42-44, 155
Williams, Raymond, 221n. 6
Wimsatt, W. K., 224n. 31
Wordsworth, William, 18, 31; *The Prelude*, 134; "Tintern Abbey," 114-19